PRINCIPAL NEWSPAPER OFFICES IN LONDON.

Aberdeen Free Press—149 Fleet Street, E.C.
Academy—63 Lincoln's Inn Fields, W.C.
Adelaide Advertiser—160 Fleet Street, E.C.
Adelaide Observer—80 Fleet Street, E.C.
Advocate of India—Basinghall Street, E.C.
Agricultural Gazette—8 Bream's Buildings, E.C.
Amateur Gardening—148 Aldersgate Street, E.C.
Architect—Imperial Buildings, Ludgate Circus, E.C.
Army & Navy Gazette—22 Essex Street, W.C.
Athenæum—11 Bream's Buildings, E.C.
Australasian—80 Fleet Street, E.C.
Autocar—20 Tudor Street, E.C.
Baptist Times and Freeman—4 Southampton Row, W.C.
Bazaar, Exchange and Mart—Drury Lane, W.C.
Belfast News Letter—167, Fleet Street, E.C.
B'ham. Daily Mail—88 Fleet Street, E.C.
B'ham. Gaz. & Expr.—17 Bouverie St., E.C.
Birmingham Post—88 Fleet Street, E.C.
Bloemfontein Post—82 Fleet Street, E.C.
Board of Trade Journal—Fetter Lane, E.C.
Bombay Gazette—66 Fenchurch Street.
Bookseller—12 Warwick Lane, E.C.
Bradford Telegraph—62 Ludgate Hill, E.C.
Bristol Evening News—59 Fleet Street, E.C.
Bristol Observer—59 Fleet Street, E.C.
Bristol Times and Mirror—185 Fleet Street, E.C.
Bristol Western Daily Press—59 Fleet Street, E.C.
British Congregationalist—16 Pilgrim Street, E.C.
British Journal of Nursing—431 Oxford Street, W.
British Medical Journal—429 Strand, W.C.
British Weekly—St. Paul's House, Warwick Sq., E.C.
Broad Arrow—Temple Avenue, E.C.
Builder—4 Catherine Street, Strand, W.C.
Building News—Effingham House, Arundel Street,W.C.
Bystander—Tallis House, Tallis Street, E.C.
Canada—Kingsway House, W.C.
Cape Times—14 St. Mary Axe, E.C.
Capitalist—11-12 Clements Lane, E.C.
Carlisle Journal—5 New Bridge Street, E.C.
Catholic Times—8 Bouverie Street, E.C.
Ceylon Times—27 Mincing Lane, E.C.
Chemical News—16 Newcastle Street, E.C.
Christian Globe—185 Fleet Street, E.C.
Christian World—13 Fleet Street, E.C.
Church Family News—17 Tavistock Street, W.C.
Church Times—7 Portugal Street, W.C.
Citizen—2 Copthall Buildings, E.C.
City Press—148 and 149 Aldersgate Street, E.C.
City Review—12 Basinghall Street, E.C.
Civil Service Gazette—12 Fetter Lane, E.C.
Civilian—76 and 78 Clerkenwell Road, E.C.
Coal Merchant, &c.—165 Strand, W.C.
Colliery Guardian—30 and 31 Furnival Street, E.C.
Commercial Motor—7-15 Rosebery Avenue, E.C.
Country Life—8 Southampton Street, W.C.
County Gentleman & Land & Water—36 Southampton Street, W.C.
Court Journal—34 Norfolk Street, W.C.
Critic—4 Moorfields, E.C.
Cycling—7-15 Rosebery Avenue, E.C.
Daily Chronicle—80 Fleet Street, E.C.
Daily Citizen—92 Fleet Street, E.C.
Daily Express—St. Bride Street, E.C.
Daily Graphic—Tallis Street, E.C.
Daily Mail—Carmelite Street, E.C.
Daily Mirror—23 Bouverie Street, E.C.
Daily News and Leader—67 Fleet Street, E.C.
Daily Telegraph—135 Fleet Street, E.C.
Draper—46 Aldersgate Street, E.C.
Draper's Record—155 Cheapside, E.C.
Dublin Evening Mail—151 Fleet Street, E.C.
Dublin Irish Times—59 Fleet Street, E.C.
East Anglian Daily Times—149 Fleet Street, E.C.
Eastern Daily Press—151 Fleet Street, E.C.
Economist—3 Arundel Street, W.C.
Edinburgh Evening Dispatch—45 Fleet Street, E.C.
Educational Times—89 Farringdon Street, E.C.
Egyptian Gazette—Egypt House, New Broad Street, E.C.
Electrical Review—4 Ludgate Hill, E.C.
Electrical Times—Sardinia House, Kingsway, W.C.
Electrician—1, 2 & 3 Salisbury Court, E.C.
Electricity—36 Maiden Lane, Strand, W.C.

Engineer—33 Norfolk St., Strand, W.C.
Engineering—35 and 36 Bedford Street, W.C.
English Churchman—74 Strand, W.C.
English Mechanic—Effingham House, Arundel St., W.C.
Era (The)—5 Tavistock Street, Strand, W.C.
Evening News—Carmelite Street, E.C.
Evening Standard & St. James's Gazette—134 Fleet St.
Family Doctor—358 Strand, W.C.
Farm and Garden—148 Aldersgate Street, E.C.
Farm, Field & Fireside—3 Wellington St., Strand, W.C.
Farmer and Stockbreeder—6 Essex Street, W.C.
Field—Bream's Buildings, E.C.
Finance—Broad Street House, E.C.
Financial News—111 Queen Victoria Street, E.C.
Financial Standard—Broad Street House, E.C.
Financial Times—72 Coleman Street, E.C.
Financier and Bullionist—54 Wool Exchange, E.C.
Fishing Gazette—19 Adam Street, W.C.
Freeman's Journal—211 Strand, W.C.
Freemason—5 Whitefriars Street, E.C.
Gardeners' Chronicle—41 Wellington Street, Covent Garden, W.C.
Gardeners' Magazine—148 Aldersgate Street, E.C.
Gardening Illustrated—17 Furnival Street, E.C.
General Weekly Shipping List—13 St, Mary Axe, E.C.
Gentlewoman, The—70 Long Acre, W.C.
Glasgow Daily Record—65 Fleet Street, E.C.
Glasgow Herald—112 Fleet Street, E.C.
Glasgow Weekly Mail—173 Fleet Street, E.C.
Globe—367 Strand, W.C.
Graphic—Tallis Street, E.C.
Guardian—29 King Street, W.C.
Health—358 Strand, W.C.
Hearth & Home—26 Henrietta Street, W.C.
Homœopathic World—12 Warwick Lane, E.C.
Homeward Mail—65 Cornhill, E.C.
Hongkong Daily Press—131 Fleet Street, E.C.
Hospital—28 Southampton Street, W.C.
Hull Daily Mail—74 Fleet Street, E.C.
Hull Eastern Morning News—159 Fleet Street, E.C.
Illustrated London News—195 Strand, W.C.
Illustrated Sporting & Dramatic News—172 Strand, W.C.
Indian Daily News—Temple Chambers, Temple Avenue, E.C.
Insurance, Banking and Financial Review—4 Newman Street, W.
Iron and Coal Trades Review—165 Strand, W.C.
Jewish Chronicle—2 Finsbury Square, E.C.
Johannesburg Star—85 Fleet Street, E.C.
John Bull—93 Long Acre, W.C.
Journal of Education—3 Broadway, Ludgate Hill, E.C.
Knowledge and Illustration Scientific News—42 Bloomsbury Square, W.C.
Labour News—10 Farringdon Avenue, E.C
Ladies' Field—7 Southampton Street, W.C.
Lady—39 & 40 Bedford Street, Strand, W.C,
Lady's Pictorial—172 Strand, W.C.
Lancet—423 Strand, W.C.
Law Journal—37 & 39 Essex Street, W.C.
Law Times—Bream's Buildings, E.C.
Leeds Mercury—65 Fleet Street, E.C.
Le Journal—190 Fleet Street, E.C.
Le Matin—160 Queen Victoria Street, E.C.
Literary World—13 Fleet Street, E.C.
Live Stock Journal—8 Bream's Buildings, E.C.
Liverpool Courier—81 Fleet Street, E.C.
Liverpool Daily Post and Mercury—Liverpool Echo—Liverpool Weekly Mercury—and Liverpool Weekly Post—138 Fleet Street, E.C.
Lloyd's Weekly News—12 Salisbury Sq., Fleet St., E.C.
London Gazette—Fetter Lane, E.C.
London Opinion—15 York Buildings, Adelphi, W.C.
Manchester Courier—69 Fleet Street, E.C.
Manchester Daily Dispatch—Sunday Chronicle—Daily Sketch—Evening Chronicle—Umpire—Sporting Chronicle—Athletic
Manchester Evening
Manchester Weekly
Manchester Guardian
Mark Lane Express—
Mary Bull—93 Long

Medical Press & Circular—8 Henrietta Street, Covent Garden, W.C.
Medical Times—Basinghall Street, E.C.
Melbourne Age—160 Fleet Street, E.C.
Melbourne Argus—80 Fleet Street, E.C.
Melbourne Leader—160 Fleet Street, E.C.
Methodist Recorder—161 Fleet Street, E.C.
Methodist Times—125 Fleet Street, E.C.
Midland Daily Telegraph—173-5 Fleet Street, E.C.
Mining Journal—15 George Street, Mansion House, E.C.
Mining World—Gresham House, E.C.
Money—35 Mansion House Chambers.
Money Market Review—2 Nicholas Passage, E.C.
Morning Advertiser—127 Fleet St., E.C.
Morning Post—346 Strand, W.C.
Motor—7-15 Rosebery Avenue, E.C.
Motor Boat—7-15 Rosebery Avenue, E.C.
Municipal Journal—Sardinia House, Kingsway, W.C.
Musical Times—160 Wardour Street, W.
Nation—10 Adelphi Terrace, W.C.
National Temperance Quarterly—34 Paternoster Row.
Nature—St. Martin's Street, W.C.
Naval & Military Record—47 Fleet Street, E.C.
Newcastle Chronicle—84 Fleet Street, E.C.
Newcastle North Mail and Northern Weekly Leader—53 Fleet Street, E.C.
News of the World—30 Bouverie Street, E.C., and 176 Fleet Street, E.C.
New York Herald—130 Fleet Street, E.C.
Notes and Queries—11 Bream's Buildings, E.C.
Nursing Mirror—28 Southampton Street, Strand, W.C.
Nursing Times—St. Martin's Street, W.C.
Observer—12 Newton St., High Holborn.
Onlooker—20-1 Essex Street, W.C.
Outlook—167 Strand, W.C.
Overland Mail—65 Cornhill, E.C.
Pall Mall Gazette—Newton St., High Holborn, W.C.
People—Milford Lane, Strand, W.C.
Photography—20 Tudor Street, E.C.
Poultry World—154 Fleet Street, E.C.
Primitive Methodist Leader—73 Farringdon Street, E.C.
Progress (Braille type)—206 Great Portland Street, W.
Public Opinion—125 Fleet Street, E.C.
Publishers' Circular—19 Adam Street, W.C.
Punch—10 Bouverie Street, E.C.
Quarry—30 & 31 Furnival Street, E.C.
Queen—Bream's Buildings, E.C.
Railway News—91 Temple Chambers, E C.
Railway Times—12 Norfolk Street, W.C.
Record—2 Red Lion Court, Fleet Street, E.C.
Referee—Victoria House, Tudor Street, E.C.
Regiment—7-15 Rosebery Avenue, E.C.
Reynolds's Newspaper—8 Temple Avenue, E.C.

Saturday Review—10 King Street, Covent Garden, W.C.
School Government Chronicle—21 New Bridge St., E.C.
Scotsman—45 Fleet Street, E.C.
Sheffield Daily Telegraph—Sheffield Weekly News—The Week—Weekly Telegraph—Yorkshire Telegraph and Star—181 Fleet Street, E.C.
Shipping Gazette and Lloyd's List—5 New St. Sq., E.C.
Sketch—172 Strand, W.C.
South Africa—6 Wormwood Street, E.C.
South Australian Register—80 Fleet Street, E.C.
South Wales Argus—88 Fleet Street, E.C.
South Wales Daily Post—74 Fleet Street, E.C.
South Wales Daily News—190 Fleet Street, E.C.
Spectator—1 Wellington Street, W.C.
Sphere—6 Great New Street, E.C.
Sport—211 Strand, W.C.
Sporting Life—27 St. Bride Street, E.C.
Sporting Times—97 Fleet Street, E.C.
Sports Argus—17 Bouverie Street, E.C.
Sportsman—139 and 140 Fleet St., E.C.
Stage—16 York Street, W.C.
Standard—104 Shoe Lane, E.C.
Star—Bouverie Street, E.C.
Stationery Trades Journal—12 Warwick Lane, E.C.
Statist—51 Cannon Street, E.C.
Sunday School Chronicle and Christian Outlook—57 Ludgate Hill, E.C.
Sunday Times—7 Essex Street, Strand, W.C.
Surveyor—24 Bride Lane, Fleet Street, E.C.
Sydney Mail—40 King St., Cheapside, E.C.
Sydney Bulletin—15 St. Bride Street, E.C.
Sydney Morning Herald—40 King St., Cheapside, E.C.
Sydney Telegraph—160 Fleet Street, E.C.
Tablet—19 Henrietta Street, W.C.
Tatler—6 Great New Street, E.C.
Territorial Service Gazette—99 Shoe Lane, E.C.
Times (& Times Weekly Edition)—Printing House Square, E.C.
Times of Ceylon—27 Mincing Lane, E.C.
Times of India—99 Shoe Lane, E.C.
Truth—10 Bolt Court, E.C
Vanity Fair—Portsmouth Street, Lincoln's Inn, W.C.
War Cry—Judd Street. King's Cross, W.C.
Weekly Dispatch—3 Tallis Street, E.C.
Western Mail—176 Fleet Street, E.C.
Western Morning News—47 Fleet Street, E.C
Westminster Gazette—10 Salisbury Sq., Fleet St., E.C.
Whitehall Review—163 St. Stephen's House, Victoria Embankment, S.W.
World—1 York Street, Covent Garden.
Yorkshire Daily Observer—172 Fleet Street, E.C.
Yorkshire Post—Yorkshire Evening Post — Yorkshire Weekly Post—170 Fleet Street, E.C.

TRANSFER AND DIVIDEND DAYS.

STOCK.	DIVIDENDS PAYABLE.	STOCK.	DIVIDENDS PAYABLE.
Bank Stock... ... ...Apl. 5 and Oct. 5.		India 3½ per Cent. Stock, Jan.5, Apl.5, July 5, Oct.5.	
2½ per Cent. Consols ..Jan. 5, Apl. 5, July 5, Oct. 5.		India 3 ,, ,, Jan.5, Apl.5, July 5.Oct.5.	
2½ per Cent. Consols...Jan. 5, Apl. 5, July 5, Oct. 5.		India 2½ ,, ,, Jan.5, Apl.5, July 5.Oct.5.	

TRANSFER DAYS.

Transfer Days are Monday, Tuesday, Wednesday, Thursday, and Friday. Instructions for Transfers are received between 9.30 and 1, and between 1 and 3 p.m. on payment of a fee of 2s. 6d. Transfers must be executed between 11 and 3, but can be accepted between 9.30 and 4 (9.30 and 2 on Saturday); they can be made on Saturday between 11 and 1 upon payment of a fee of 2s. 6d. Transfers of Bank Stock are charged 9s. for sums of £25 and under, and 12s. for sums over £25. Bank Stock Transfer Books are closed for about three weeks before the payment of each dividend.

LONDON CAB FARES.

BY DISTANCE.	s.	d.
For any distance not exceeding two miles	1	0
For any distance exceeding two miles, for each mile of the whole distance	0	6
For any fraction of a mile over and above the number of miles completed	0	6

The above fares are for two persons; if more are carried, a charge of 6d. each for the whole distance can be demanded. Two children under 10 years of age count as one adult. If one child under ten years of age be carried with two other persons, the extra charge is 3d. for the whole distance.

BY TIME.	4 Whls.		2 Whls.	
	s.	d.	s.	d.
For any time not exceeding one hour	2	0	2	6
If more than one hour, for each quarter of an hour of of the whole time ...	0	6	0	8
For any period of less than fifteen minutes beyond any completed quarter of an hour	0	6	0	8

Luggage inside cab, free; outside, 2d. each package any distance.

MOTOR CABS.

	s.	d.
For any distance not exceeding one mile or for a period of time, or a journey not exceeding ten minutes	0	8
Exceeding one mile, or ten minutes, for each quarter of a mile or for a period of time, or a journey not exceeding two and a half minutes	0	2
For any less period or distance	0	2
For each additional person carried beyond two 6d. extra the whole distance.		

SCRIMGEOUR'S

SMALL
SCRIBBLING
DIARY

SCRIMGEOUR'S
SMALL
SCRIBBLING
DIARY

1914-1916

THE TRULY ASTONISHING

WARTIME DIARY
AND LETTERS

OF AN EDWARDIAN GENTLEMAN,
NAVAL OFFICER, BOY AND SON

Compiled by Richard Hallam and Mark Beynon

CONWAY

For the men who lost their lives on board HMS *Invincible*,
and for Caroline Hallam.

A Conway Maritime Book

© Richard Hallam, 2008
'Rule Britannia': The Royal Navy in 1914 © Andrew Lambert, 2008

First published in Great Britain in 2008 by
Conway
An imprint of Anova Books Ltd
10 Southcombe Street
London W14 0RA
www.anovabooks.com

British Library Cataloguing in Publication Data
A record of this title is available on request from the British Library.

ISBN 9781844860753

Printed in the UK by CPI William Clowes Beccles NR34 7TL

To receive regular email updates on forthcoming Conway titles,
email conway@anovabooks.com with Conway Update in the subject field.

CONTENTS

LIST OF CHARTS AND ILLUSTRATIONS

ACKNOWLEDGEMENTS

It has been our good fortune to work alongside several people who have shared our enthusiasm for Alexander Scrimgeour's writing, and without whom this compelling collection would never have seen the light of day. First, Sonia Land, whose belief in the diaries was paramount; secondly our editor, Alison Moss, whose tireless hard work and guidance were integral; and finally our publisher, John Lee, whose vision and passion for the project have been nothing less than overwhelming.

We are indebted to Andrew Lambert for his commentary; Nick Swan at Aldro School for supplying us with Alexander's school photographs, and to Rick Beynon for slaving over a scanning machine for the best part of a day. On a more personal note, we would both like to thank our partners, Jodie and Vicky, for their patience and understanding.

Toby Hallam, who was born during the editing of the diaries, inherits the moniker of the Scrimgeour gentlemen, ensuring their legacy lives on.

Richard Hallam and Mark Beynon

FOREWORD

I have known of, and lived with, Alexander Scrimgeour's diaries since I was a child. As a young boy I grew up in Thorncombe House, near Godalming, Surrey, with my mother, grandmother and step-grandfather, Toby Scrimgeour. Toby, who I regarded as my surrogate father and patriarch, would often regale fascinating accounts from his wealth of family history, including the tale of Alexander Scrimgeour, his brave uncle who had lost his life at sea during the First World War. When he told me that he had been handed down Alexander's war diaries and letters by his father (Alexander's younger brother, Jim) and that they were safely concealed in his grand chest of drawers, I couldn't wait to cast my eager young eyes over them. I have many fond memories of Thorncombe, which to an inquisitive child was a real den of antiquity, rich in a historic and secretive past, but Alexander's diaries, and his portrait hanging on the wall, are what I remember most vividly.

Toby would often reiterate his desire to see the diaries published, and left the responsibility to my mother. When he passed away, my mother and I felt it would be a fitting tribute to both Toby and Alexander to publish the diaries he cherished, so we set about fulfilling his wish.

It was during the editing process that my mother was diagnosed with cancer, and after a brave battle, she sadly succumbed to her illness. Having been handed the baton, so to speak, I feel proud and privileged to have been part of bringing this humbling collection to a wider audience. I sincerely hope it inspires you as much as it did me.

Richard Hallam

INTRODUCTION

Born on 5 March 1897, Alexander Scrimgeour grew up in the picturesque Kentish village of Wickhambreaux, five miles outside Canterbury. At the time of his birth, the name Scrimgeour was synonymous with London stock broking – the family would later go on to achieve greater success under his younger brother, Jim. Alexander enjoyed a privileged upbringing as the eldest of four children, reaping the benefits of his father's (Alexander Caron Scrimgeour) wealth and status, both educationally and socially. As well as Jim, Alexander had a much young brother called Billy and a sister, Peggy.

To best understand his aspirations (or perhaps his father's aspirations for him) as a boy born at the turn of the century, it is important to consider Edwardian society, which, although brief, was undeniably fascinating in its attitudes. Most historians agree that the Edwardian era covers the period from the turn of the twentieth century to the outbreak of the First World War. The ambitions of a young upper-middle-class gentleman would have been dictated by a stringent list of professions. Many young Edwardians would follow in their father's footsteps, but Alexander joined the Royal Navy, a profession chosen for him by his father when Alexander was still a child, and this would have been deemed suitable by his family and their peers at a time when Britain was at the height of her imperial power.

Edwardian Britain afforded the affluent every chance in life. While the rich seemed to get richer and richer, the poor descended further into poverty. The dissent arising from this fanned a turbulent political climate. Britain was slowly coming to terms with the idea of the suffrage movement and the role of working women in its society – this would, of course, become commonplace in the munitions factories throughout the First World War. The theatre, which was enjoying a renaissance of its own, was suddenly inundated with strong and dominant female characters and an upturn in plays that shocked contemporary audiences with their frank portrayals of everyday life and sexuality. Similar female characters would make their mark on literature too. At a time when an enormous number of novels and short stories were being written and consumed, many would reflect the issues of the day. The emergence of Socialism, the age of the self-educated man, and a middle-class society that refused to support the flamboyant and gaudy trends of Edward VII and the upper class, would also be represented by a new era of fiction, which evolved from its Victorian predecessor.

Seemingly inspired by the many great writers of his era, Alexander decided to keep a day-to-day diary, which displayed his own adroit ability with prose. The diaries that have survived start in 1910, and cover his formative years from cadet training right through to his active service in war, and his cherished time spent at home with family and friends. Indeed, it is important to emphasize that this collection is not just a war diary. Alexander was efficient in writing his accounts and recording events as they happened, displaying a self-discipline that has left us with a sharp insight into the era, untouched by the vagaries of memory and post-war analysis.

The Scrimgeour family owned two properties: the first was Quaives Farm in Wickhambreaux; and the second was a flat at Cumberland Terrace near Regent's Park. Designed by John Nash, and still considered to be one of the more desirable postcodes in London, Cumberland Terrace has seen many illustrious dignitaries reside there over the years, such as the composer Bernard Herrman. At the front of his 1913 diary, Alexander lists the properties to which it should be sent if lost. As well as his home addresses, Alexander lists Hatton Court, Threadneedle Street, London, and Dudhope Castle in Dundee. It is fair to assume that Hatton Court was his father's place of work as it was situated right in the heart of London's banking district, and Dudhope Castle was, and still is, the seat of Clan Scrimgeour in Scotland.

Alexander received a first-class education, initially at Aldro School in Eastbourne, East Sussex. Having been groomed for a career in the armed forces, in 1910, at the age of 13, he joined the Royal Navy as a cadet. Together with his contemporaries, Thomas Cobb, Leopold Johnstone, Alexander Richardson, Richard Henderson, Desmond Tottenham, William Hutchinson (W.S.H. was Alexander's 'best friend') and 'Fober' Robinson, Alexander went through four years of rigorous tuition, two at Osborne Naval College at Cowes, Isle of Wight, and two at Dartmouth Royal Naval College, before being approved to train onboard the cadet-training ship HMS *Cornwall* at the beginning of 1914. (The *Cornwall*, a 9,800-ton *Monmouth* class armoured cruiser, would later go on to sink the German light cruiser *Leipzig* in the Battle of the Falklands and support the Dardanelles campaign.)

The group of cadets flourished and excelled in the demanding training conditions onboard the *Cornwall*. They were fortunate to find themselves frequently harboured in glamorous locations with ample free time on their hands. Unsurprisingly, they would make the most of their leave, often resulting in tales of high jinks. In the first half of 1914, the *Cornwall* was permanently away from Britain, including a three-month stay in the Mediterranean during which she visited Monte Carlo, Malta, Gibraltar, the Algarve, Tenerife, Nice, Cannes, Genoa and Algiers. Many evenings were spent at dances in the company of women of various nationalities – although the language barrier would often pose problems: 'However pretty a girl is and however well she dances, it is rather boring after a bit if you can't understand one another's language'.

Yet on a stopover on their return to Britain, there seemed to be little difficulty in communicating with the women of Norway. The cadets enjoyed a succession of whirlwind romances in Trondheim, and as they left, Alexander wrote: 'The 70 odd intact hearts which came here have been sadly injured'.

Arriving home the cadets continued their hedonistic lifestyles. Indeed, the events preceding the outbreak of the First World War highlight their priorities at the time. 'Findlay invited us all to a huge ball at the Legation. At the last minute it had to be cancelled due to the news of the assassination of Grand Duke Francis [sic], heir to the Empire of Austria. We were terribly disappointed. We went to a quiet reception there instead, but it only enhanced our sorrow for there was a gorgeous ball room and the most exquisite garden for sitting out.'

In July 1914, Alexander returned to Portsmouth, and on Saturday, the 18th, Winston Churchill, the First Lord of the Admiralty, came aboard the *Cornwall* to visit the crew, perhaps to herald what was to come. 'Winston Churchill, with the Sea Lords and Colonel Seeley [sic], came onboard at 10am'.

Just two weeks later and after less than a week of leave, Alexander was summoned to the naval barracks at Portsmouth where he and the other cadets were assigned to HMS *Crescent* (a first class cruiser of the *Edgar* class) as midshipmen. The First World War had begun, prompting Alexander to remark: 'I have been looking forward to war ever since I was a baby'.

The build-up to war had been gradual and inevitable. Germany looked to emulate Britain's empire and relations between the two countries became increasingly strained in the early 1900s following the 'scramble for Africa' and the alarming escalation of the arms race after the introduction of HMS *Dreadnought* in 1906. Alexander commented on the deteriorating situation in early July 1914: 'The continual diplomatic situation is very bad; Austria is bullying Serbia and Russia protests. I think it is all a German plot to test the Triple Entente'.

Under Rear-Admiral Dudley de Chair, who was in command of the Tenth Cruiser Squadron, and who was assigned the *Crescent* as his flagship, Alexander and company were given the task of maintaining a blockade in the North Sea to intercept all German commerce. Following severe damage to the *Crescent* during a storm, de Chair and the cadets were transferred to the Armed Merchant Cruiser *Alsatian* in December 1914. The strict blockade was continued during 1915, the ships negotiating the perils of mines and the ever-present threat of U-boats. In recognition of the work of the Tenth Cruiser Squadron, Rear-Admiral de Chair would receive the K.C.B.

On the infrequent occasions that Alexander was entitled leave his diary entries offer a tantalizing glimpse into how a footloose young Edwardian gentleman spent his time. Visiting many of the hotspots of London, Liverpool and Edinburgh, Alexander recorded the details of his social life, which, despite the war, was not short of frivolity. Indeed, before the outbreak of hostilities, London had a reputation for being the most glamorous city in the world, and although the reality of war had an effect on its glitz (in particular, the infrequent Zeppelin air raids), it merely dimmed the city's many lights, but never extinguished them. The most fashionable district was Piccadilly and Regent Street, in particular the Trocadero, Criterion, Monico and Café Royal restaurants. They were all grand affairs, afforded by only the middle and upper classes. Nearby, The Strand was equally chic: the Savoy, Simpson's, the Drury Lane and Covent Garden theatre district, and the new hotels in and around Aldwych and Holborn (including the Strand Palace and the Waldorf) provided the main sources of entertainment. It is unsurprising that Alexander would visit them all during his leave in London. Similarly, in Liverpool Alexander enjoyed visiting the Olympia Theatre and Adelphi Hotel. After he was transferred to HMS *Invincible* in July 1915 and joined the Battle Cruiser Fleet based at Rosyth in the Firth of Forth, as an officer he was able to make the most of all the delights of Scotland's capital city, frequenting the Waverley on Princes Street and the Haymarket Ice Rink in particular.

In August 1914, the House of Commons passed the Defence of the Realm Act (DORA) without debate. Fearing that the war effort was becoming hampered by drunkenness, the legislation allowed the government to control civilian behaviour, including the consumption of alcohol. David Lloyd George, the Chancellor of the Exchequer, famously claimed that Britain was 'fighting the Germans, Austrians and drink, and as far as I can see the greatest of these foes is drink'. Pub drinkers were the hardest hit by the new legislation, which limited opening times. But perhaps the most shocking change of all was the introduction of watered down beer. However, restaurants and hotels experienced an influx of young party-goers keen to avoid watered down beer in favour of wine, spirits and cocktails which, although heavily taxed, were still affordable. Following the Licensing (Consolidation) Act of 1910, those who were 16 and over were able to purchase alcoholic beverages, and Alexander as a 17-year-old in 1914 certainly made the most of his fortuitous position.

It was during his home leave that Alexander fell in love with 'Joko' Robertson, a family friend from the neighbouring village of Westenhanger, and an aspiring actress. However, their brief relationship was cut short when he was assigned to HMS *Invincible*. It was to be the first and last battle cruiser Alexander would serve in. Upon hearing of Alexander's death at the Battle of Jutland in May 1916, his heart-broken father, flexing his financial muscle, used his society status to investigate his son's last moments. Much like Rudyard Kipling did when his son Jack died at the Battle of Loos, Alexander Caron Scrimgeour interviewed the two highest-ranking officers of the six survivors from HMS *Invincible*. Not every family of the 1,026 dead would have been able to persuade Commander Dannreuther and Lieutenant Sandford to make a house call. But Alexander's father did.

When we examine and contextualize the diaries of Alexander Scrimgeour we are immediately struck by just how articulate and intelligent he was. Juxtaposing the rigours of life at sea during the war and the glamour of Edwardian society in London and Kent, Alexander seamlessly goes from love-struck teenage squire to proud midshipman. His love for his family is very much evident throughout, particularly in his letters to his mother, Helen, which although displaying a golden sarcastic wit, are always touching and heartfelt. Alexander signs his letters off as 'Toby', which was a long-standing moniker for the Scrimgeour men named Alexander – of which there have been many. His ability to poke fun at his own expense is charming, especially when he has an off day at the country shoot. Perhaps the most significant feature of the diaries is Alexander's willingness to record highly confidential information, including government 'cover-ups' and the movement of a German spy. This would have resulted in his court martial and expulsion from the Navy should his diaries have been discovered. On numerous occasions, one has the feeling that he was writing his diary, not just for his own personal record and gratification, but for something far grander.

The shift in tone from 1914 to 1915 is also worth noting. December 1914 saw Alexander spend his first Christmas away from his family, and the poignancy of the occasion is marked in his diary entries. The following year he barely acknowledges the holiday season at all. Indeed, his style of writing changes, too, as do his opinions of the war. Initially Alexander comes across as an eager patriot, and this is reflected in his prose. By 1915, however, a matter-of-fact bluntness replaces his initial enthusiasm. Bearing in mind the vast majority of those serving in the Royal Navy believed it would all be over by Christmas 1914, it seems evident that a year at sea during wartime sapped Alexander's spirits.

As part of their training, midshipmen were required to keep a detailed journal of their daily duties at sea (without personal opinion or conjecture). Supplied by the Admiralty, their purpose was to hone and improve the midshipman's knowledge and understanding of all things nautical. It was by chance that we discovered Alexander's Midshipmen's Journal covering his time on board *Crescent* and *Alsatian* during the editing of the diaries. We have seen fit to incorporate some of his hand-drawn charts and illustrations as well as supplement his journal entries when, for whatever reason, he hadn't recorded an entry in his personal diary. During 1915 Alexander left his diary at home for weeks at a time. We can only speculate as to why he did this, although it is fair to assume that he had become aware of the consequences of his diary falling into the wrong hands as the war dragged on. This is supported by the fact that his more controversial diary entries were written as amendments on scrap pieces of paper, and included loose.

In editing the diaries, we have kept Alexander's spellings, particularly of places names, which may differ from modern usage, but have corrected his punctuation where necessary.

Alexander made extra notes regarding the characters of the officers of the *Crescent* and *Alsatian* at the end of his 1914 diary, which are included at the back of this book as Appendix I. Additional appendices provide extra historical context to the naval blockade and the sinking of *Invincible*, and are introduced and discussed on pages 263–4.

As stated, Alexander's surviving diaries begin in 1910 and continue until 1915 (we are left to assume that his 1916 diary went down with him at Jutland). Although there is much of interest in his earlier diaries, we decided to begin from the outbreak of war. Both sides of Alexander's life are vividly brought to life in his writing. At once we get an idea of what the drab conditions were like in the ships of the British Fleet in the First World War, and yet the thrill of Edwardian society is so often brilliantly described. One wonders what might have become of Alexander had he survived Jutland and the war. Alexander's friend at Osborne, John Tovey, was Admiral of the Fleet during the Second World War and sank the *Bismarck*. As it is, we have a treasured record of a talented young life suddenly cut short – a tragedy of war.

Mark Beynon

'RULE BRITANNIA'
The Royal Navy in 1914

Alexander Scrimgeour served in the world's most successful fighting service, heir to Nelson, Trafalgar, and an almost unbroken run of success that stretched back even further still. The Royal Navy was responsible for the security, prosperity and power of the British State, the overseas empire and the trade that connected it. For a century it had provided the visible proof of British power that backed up the financial services, in which the elder Srimgeour made his money; and deterred war. Unrivalled in size, reputation and reach, the Edwardian Navy formed the armoured centre of British power, and the core of its culture, from sailor suits to Navy Days and Trafalgar Square. Britain was a maritime nation with a global empire and no one doubted the sea was the natural element of her people. The effortless superiority that Scrimgeour and his contemporaries assumed reflected an unchallenged reality – this was *the* Navy. Such organisations do not promote doubt or introspection. Furthermore, the culture of Edwardian Britain was dominated by values that amplified key elements of officer-like behaviour: 'self-restraint, perseverance, strenuous effort, courage in the face of adversity' and 'an abiding sense of duty'*.

Officer Education
At the turn of the twentieth century British naval education underwent a radical transformation. Cadets joined the service at 12 or 13 at the new Osborne College on the Isle of Wight, built amid the stable blocks of Queen Victoria's favourite home, where they would spend the first two years. Then they moved to Dartmouth, where the old *Britannia* stationary training ship for officer cadets, a wooden wall left over from the 1850s, had been replaced by a massive new shore-side college. In addition, the curriculum was brought up to date to include engineering and modern languages – in which Scrimgeour demonstrated considerable ability – English, history and seamanship. Under Alfred Ewing, Director of Naval Education and wartime code-breaker, the curriculum was strikingly modern, lacking the ancient languages and other mental exercises that continued to dominate in the public schools. Ewing recruited a high-

---

* Collini, S. *Public Moralists: Political Thought and Intellectual Life in Britain 1850-1930*, Oxford, 1991, p.100.

quality staff. The object was to produce commissioned officers ready for active duty in a highly technical profession by the age of 20. The architect of these reforms, Admiral John Fisher, wanted all cadets to be educated together, to a common curriculum, whether they were destined for engineering, the marines, or paymaster duty. This modern educational system was administered by naval officers who imbued the pupils with a rigid code of honour, one that led to a major *cause célèbre* in the Archer-Shee case of 1908, the basis for the drama *The Winslow Boy*. Young Archer-Shee was accused of stealing a Postal Order, and dismissed from the service without a hearing. It transpired the boy was entirely innocent, but the imputation of dishonesty was enough to end an Edwardian naval career. After a high profile court case, the Admiralty acknowledged their error, but they did not alter the strict moral code. This was the structure in place in 1910 and 13-year-old Alexander Scrimgeour joined Osborne under the shadow of the Archer-Shee case[*].

After four years at College cadets of Scrimgeour's generation went to sea in a training ship before being rated as midshipmen and joining the regular service. They would be 16 or 17. They were well equipped for the task. In August 1914 newly minted midshipman Scrimgeour was about to be posted to his first ship. By contrast the term below his were rushed into service at the outbreak of war, and many were lost in the armoured cruisers *Aboukir*, *Cressy* and *Hogue* in September.

The benefits of Fisher's new education system are obvious to any reader of Scrimgeour's diary. He was soon employed as an interpreter when seizing German trawlers, and made a useful effort at working on Norwegian radio messages. Furthermore, he was comfortable working with the latest fire control instruments, gun-sights and engines. As a well-connected young man from a prosperous upper-middle-class background it would be expected that Scrimgeour was destined for a career in the regular service, but by 1915 his obvious mechanical aptitude led him to consider shifting to engineering.

The diaries and letters that survive are those of a well-educated, technically sophisticated young man. The speed with which he adjusted to the demands of war, and the key role he and others like him played in providing up-to-date expertise for older reserve officers indicates the success of the system. His work on the *Crescent*, rebuilding gun sights, adding fire control gear, handling range finding and gunnery direction

---

[*] Partridge, M. *The Royal Naval College Osborne 1903-1921*, Stroud, 1999. Davies, E.L. & Grove. E. J., *The Royal Naval College Dartmouth*, Portsmouth, 1980.

demonstrate the success of the Osborne/Dartmouth system in generating the necessary young officers ready for service.

However, midshipmen at sea were still, in effect, under training. They did not qualify for a commission, as sub-lieutenants, until they had been examined in a wide range of specialist aspects of the profession: seamanship, gunnery, navigation, torpedoes and electricity. Throughout the diaries Scrimgeour expresses his anxiety to get first-class marks in his five examinations, which would accelerate his promotion to Lieutenant, and the limits of his instruction and instructors while serving with the Tenth Cruiser Squadron and on *Invincible*. Without quality instruction from the Naval Instructor, and experienced officers on the ships he could not produce the necessary journals and exercises, or master the subjects to the requisite standard. It may be surmised that Rear-Admiral de Chair was motivated to send him to the Grand Fleet to ensure a fine young officer was ready for the examinations. By May 1916 Scrimgeour was an acting sub-lieutenant, recognition of his experience, and his ability pending the examination. He had spent much of his time on *Invincible* working through the different departments of the ship, gunnery, engineering, etc., making the necessary drawings and journals.

Grand Strategy

In August 1914 Britain went to war with well-prepared plans for global war. The government defence co-ordinating body, the Committee of Imperial Defence, had developed a plan to harness the power of the empire and protect the commercial shipping that linked the various dominions and colonies with the home islands, while crushing German overseas trade and colonies through a tough economic blockade. This maritime war would complement the military efforts of Britain's Entente partners, France and Russia, who were expected to defeat the German and Austro-Hungarian armies in Europe. The small British Expeditionary Force would contribute to the defence of France and Belgium, but the government had no intention of raising or using mass armies on the continental model. They preferred to rely on the Royal Navy, while maintaining British trade and industry.

The lynchpin of British strategy was the Grand Fleet at Scapa Flow, which controlled access to the North Sea. By placing a superior fleet across Germany's international trade routes Britain ensured the destruction of her commerce and her empire, while protecting her own trade. This situation would only change if the Grand Fleet was defeated. The rest of the naval effort operated behind the strategic cover provided by Vice-Admiral Sir John Jellicoe's dreadnought battleships. There was no need for the British to seek out the German High Seas Fleet, because they expected the economic blockade to win the war and that when the Germans recognised this they would be obliged to take the initiative – to attack the British in the waters between Scotland and Norway.

The Blockade: HMS Crescent and the Tenth Cruiser Squadron

On the eve of war the Royal Navy quickly and efficiently mobilised its officers and men. Scrimgeour was ordered to HMS *Crescent*, a 7,700-ton protected cruiser of the *Edgar* class*. By 1914 these ships were twenty years old and woefully out dated; their obsolescent guns, fire control and engines denied them a place in the main fleet. However, they remained effective seaworthy vessels and gave good service through the war. The *Crescent* was flagship of the Tenth Cruiser Squadron, with her seven sister-ships, ordered to the seas off the north of Scotland for blockade service under Rear-Admiral Sir Dudley de Chair. Unfortunately they soon encountered threats they were ill-equipped to resist. U-boat torpedoes sank HMS *Hawke* while mountainous seas sent many back to base for extended repairs. Scrimgeour's striking description of one particular storm adds power and resonance to the usual laconic official report: boats were smashed, forty men injured and many compartments simply washed out.

The Tenth Cruiser Squadron occupied the front line of the economic war effort, the main British contribution to the defeat of Germany before mid-1916. The operation of the blockade depended on the interpretation of International Law dealing with the rights of belligerent states and neutrals. German merchant ships were fair game, and a few were taken trying to get home, but the real problem lay in the shipment of goods to Germany in neutral ships, and via neutral third parties. Britain asserted the right to stop neutral merchant ships on the high seas, and inspect their cargo for contraband; that is goods defined as likely to aid the enemy war effort – anything from guns and fuel to army reservists and food. On 4 August 1914 the British listed obvious war materials destined for Germany as absolute contraband, while food and other items as conditional contraband, liable to seizure if destined for enemy armed forces. On the

---

* HMS *Crescent* built Portsmouth Dockyard 1890-94, 360 feet long, 60-foot beam, 20 knots when built, no more than 18 by 1914. One 9.2-inch gun, twelve 6-inch guns and twelve 6-pounder guns.

20th the application of this regime was widened to include cargoes destined for contiguous neutrals, Denmark, Holland and Sweden. Six days later rumours that the army had taken control of all German food stocks saw food added to the list of absolute contraband, a serious change in the nature of the blockade, now clearly aimed at the entire population. The list was widened yet further as the year went on and the USA showed itself favourable to the Anglo-French alliance. With the North Sea defined as a war zone, all neutral merchant ships were obliged to stop for inspection in the Straits of Dover. An exception was made for the Scandinavians who were permitted to sail around the north of Great Britain, through the patrol lines of the Tenth Cruiser Squadron. On 11 March 1915 an Order in Council established a complete blockade of Germany, and began to limit the imports of the Scandinavian powers to stop them exporting any surplus to Germany. This was based on two coercive instruments, British naval power and control of the world's steam coal supply. While most ships were prepared to accept British demands, the Tenth Cruiser Squadron still had to patrol a vast area of rough and dangerous sea to intercept potential blockade breakers, facing the perils of U-boat attack, mines and a surface sortie by heavy German forces.

As might be expected the Scandinavian states and the Netherlands saw neutrality as an opportunity for profit, quickly generating large agricultural industries to supply Germany with processed animal fats, from butter to bacon. Swedish iron and copper, industrial products and horses all helped to sustain the German war effort while her manpower was detained in uniform. The British Government, unlike the Navy which simply assumed all would bend before the will of Britannia, was anxious to keep on good terms with these powers. This would ensure their merchant ships carried goods for the Allies, and prevent them from joining Germany. The German response – unrestricted submarine warfare – proved to be a diplomatic disaster. With a little help from British propaganda – the same machine that fed Scrimgeour and his friends with 'Hun' atrocity stories – the U-boats persuaded neutrals that Germany was more dangerous than Britain. As a result the blockade was never perfect, and took time to reach a level at which it began to seriously weaken the German war effort. But it was an effective instrument, well handled at all levels[*].

[*] Grainger, J. (ed.), *The Maritime Blockade of Germany in the Great War: The Northern Patrol 1914-1918*, Aldershot Navy Records Society, 2003, provides an extensive documentary collection on the work of the 10th Cruiser Squadron. Bell, A. C., *A History of the Blockade of Germany and the Central Powers*, London, 1937, is the official history.

Scrimgeour's first-hand account of the business of blockade and patrol reveals the combination of boredom and excitement (bad weather, poor food, discomfort and coaling ship) as they boarded ships and countered German efforts to break blockade with munitions, food, and reservists from the USA and elsewhere. Throughout the war naval officers constantly complained that the Foreign Office was weakening to blockade, kow-towing to the Americans and allowing neutral powers to act as conduits for German imports. This was a particular concern for the Tenth Cruiser Squadron, whose harsh and demanding regime must have been softened by the expectation of a rich haul of prize money. In the event the naval prize fund was homogenised and paid out *pro rata* to every man in the service. The complaints of naval officers were serious, but missed the bigger picture. The British Government was highly successful in persuading, or coercing neutrals into self-regulation; while the compliance of the US administration and covert intelligence operations predicted most suspect sailings and positioned ships to intercept. As cypher officer on the *Alsatian* Scrimgeour was ideally placed to see how these intelligence-led operations worked, and clearly understood how intelligence was used. Admiral de Chair understood the wider ramifications of the blockade, and remained involved in the economic war when he went ashore.

HMS Alsatian

Before the war the Admiralty had recognised the need to supplement the Navy's cruiser fleet with Armed Merchant Cruisers. Initially they looked at big Atlantic liners, such as the *Lusitania*, but by 1914 the choice had fallen on smaller, more economic ships that combined long endurance with good seaworthiness. Within months the first of these ships joined the Tenth Cruiser Squadron, replacing the elderly *Crescent* and her sisters over the winter of 1914–15. Scrimgeour moved to HMS *Alsatian*, a nearly new 18,000-ton Allan Line steamer built for the Liverpool–Canada trade. Armed with eight 6-inch guns she became the flagship. In 1915 she spent 262 days at sea, covering 71,500 miles and burning 40,287 tons of coal[*]. This was the grim reality of the economic blockade: hard sea service, for extended periods, stopping and searching merchant ships. Scrimgeour notes that between 8 March and 19 April 1915 367 ships were intercepted,

---

[*] Osborne, R., Spong, H., & Gover, T., *Armed Merchant Cruisers 1873-1945*, Windsor, World Ship Society, 2007, is the essential guide to these ships and their operations. *Alsatian* 600 feet by 72.4 feet, 18 knots, eight 6-inch guns. See p.93.

and 129 sent in for inspection with a prize crew on board. Every detail of the work was hard, not least the business of lowering a boat, rowing across to the suspect vessel and getting on board. Scrimgeour only went once or twice, but he got very wet. More significantly he was involved with *Alsatian*'s modern guns and fire control equipment. These ships were ideally suited to the task, and well equipped.

While Scrimgeour was apt to be dismissive of his Admiral (an opinion that others have repeated), de Chair knew that his young officers were the future of the Navy. He did not keep the best midshipmen in his squadron, where their education would suffer, and once the Armed Merchant Cruisers were up to standard he was content to get by with reserve officers and volunteers. If old 'Duds' had a soft spot for Scrimgeour, it was because the young officer had shown great promise in all aspects of his work. Clearly he had good links and impressed the men who mattered.

The dramatic, crushing British victory off the Falklands Islands in December 1914 ended the oceanic phase of the war at sea. This allowed the British to concentrate their naval effort in the main theatres, especially the North Sea where all modern capital ships were assembled. It also simplified the work of the Tenth Cruiser Squadron, which no longer needed to look over its shoulder in case German warships came in from the west.

HMS Invincible

In July 1915 Scrimgeour exchanged the hard graft of the blockade for the most glamorous posting in the Navy, the battle cruiser HMS *Invincible*, flagship of Rear-Admiral Sir Horace Hood's Third Battle Cruiser Squadron. The Battle Cruiser Fleet was based at Rosyth in the Firth of Forth. Completed in 1908, the 18,000-ton, 26-knot *Invincible* was the first of her type, a dreadnought armed with eight 12-inch guns, and powerful turbine engines[*]. Conceived by Admiral Fisher to combine the speed and firepower needed to deal with threats to ocean shipping the battle cruisers quickly became iconic. With three mighty funnels belching smoke to set off the high freeboard hulls and a powerful bow wave they looked every inch the ideal warship, and after action at the Heligoland Bight in August 1914, and the battle of the Falkland Islands in December, *Invincible* had a high profile. Under the dynamic leadership of Vice-Admiral Sir David Beatty the Battle

---

[*] Built at Newcastle, 567 feet long, 78 feet 6 inches broad, *Invincible* weighted 17,330 tons. Her engines produced 41,000 horse power.

Cruiser Fleet saw themselves as the elite of the service, and played hard living up to the image: the new boy soon discovered this was an expensive posting. Nevertheless, coaling ship remained a monumental task for the entire ship's company.

However, the battle cruiser type bought their speed, 6 or 7 knots faster than contemporary battleships, at the expense of reduced armour protection. After Jutland it was argued that this caused the loss of three of the type, and their glittering reputation suffered a sudden reverse[*].

Hood, the third son of the Fourth Lord Hood, was a direct descendant of Nelson's mentor, Admiral Samuel, Lord Hood. While Scrimgeour manages to confuse a little of the family tree in one of his letters home, he was well aware of the powerful dynastic connections between his Admiral and the greatest names in naval history. He also noted that Hood, like Beatty, had married an American lady, and picked up some of the speech and mannerisms of his in-laws. Hood was also a familiar figure; he had been Captain of the Osborne College during Scrimgeour's time.

In one vital respect the Battle Cruiser Fleet mirrored the Tenth Cruiser Squadron: both operated on intelligence leads provided by the Admiralty's code-breaking unit, Room 40. Poor German radio discipline gave the British precious insights into their plans, opportunities to intercept their infrequent sorties, and the luxury of waiting in harbour rather than patrol. In late November/early December 1915 a fleet exercise tested one scenario, a German battle cruiser sortie into the Atlantic. Scrimgeour and several of his contemporaries sat their examinations for sub-lieutenant early in 1916, and he passed. This brought him into the Navy as an officer holding the King's commission, and increased his responsibilities.

In March and April 1916 the Fleet went to sea, first to support a seaplane raid, and then to intercept a German sortie, and only missed contact by 50 or 60 miles. Returning from the second cruise *Invincible* collided with an armed yacht, and suffered considerable damage. The enforced docking gave Scrimgeour his last shore leave.

The Battle of Jutland
After the ship returned to sea the Third Battle Cruiser Squadron was detached to Scapa Flow for long overdue gunnery exercises: they could not conduct full-calibre shoots at Rosyth without breaking all the windows

---

[*] Tarrent, V.E., *Battle Cruiser Invincible: The History of the First Battle Cruiser, 1909-1916*, London, 1986, provides a full-length biography of the ship.

in Kircaldy. In their absence the Battle Cruiser Fleet was supplemented by the Fifth Battle Squadron. The exercises at Scapa were 'highly satisfactory'. Before they could return to Rosyth the Fleet sortied, and the Third formed up with Jellicoe's Grand Fleet, while the fifth Battle Squadron took their place in the Battle Cruiser Fleet. This time they would meet the Germans; the long-awaited day had come. Contemporary accounts, both those sent to Scrimgeour's parents, and others, make it clear the Fleet set out with high hopes of battle, and victory, having the chance to do their bit.

Acting ahead of Jellicoe's Grand Fleet, Hood's force missed the opening exchanges of the Run to the South between Beatty's battle cruisers and the German First Scouting Group. On a day when most British flag officers proved too cautious, and a few, Beatty (HMS *Lion*) and Robert Arbuthnot (HMS *Defence*), overly aggressive, Hood stands out. Listening to incomplete and confusing hints from the radio he used his initiative to bring his squadron into battle, and achieved decisive effect, smashing the German scouting forces that were looking for Jellicoe's main fleet, and crippling the enemy battle cruiser *Lutzow*, flagship, in a high-speed medium-range engagement, between 9,000 and 10,000 yards. The last words that Scrimgeour, as the officer of X turret, would a have heard were Hood's ringing endorsement of the ship's gunnery: 'Your firing is very good, keep at it as quickly as you can, every shot is telling'.

Then the smoke of battle parted and a second German battle cruiser, the *Derfflinger*, also opened fire. At 6.34 p.m. a German salvo, two 12-inch shells, hit *Invincible* amidships, smashing through the 7-inch-thick frontal armour of Q turret, exploding in the loading chamber. The explosion set off the loose cordite charges, blowing the roof off the turret, and instantaneously passed down through the ammunition hoists to the main amidships magazine, which exploded with catastrophic force. A vast crimson flame, followed by a hellish pall of cordite and coal smoke, covered a gaping void which, only seconds before, had been occupied by the centre of the ship. When the smoke cleared *Invincible*'s bow and stern were left pointing up to heaven like twin tombstones. Only six officers and men survived, most of them from the fire control top high on the foremast: 1,026 had died in an instant, among them Hood, Scrimgeour and every man in X turret. It was, as David Beatty observed 'a glorious death', but it was also entirely unnecessary.

Invincible was the third British battle cruiser to blow up that day. *Indefatigable* and *Queen Mary* had preceded her into eternity, in exactly the same way, with the same terrible human cost. At the loss of *Queen Mary* Beatty laconically observed; 'there seems to be something wrong with our bloody ships today'. After the battle an expert investigation concluded that the explosions were caused by human error, not design weakness. Following the action on the Dogger Bank in January 1915 Beatty had concluded that the answer to his tactical problems was to increase the rate of fire: his ships removed the air-tight safety interlocks in the ammunition hoists and allowed cordite charges to be stowed in exposed areas to achieve this. There is a hint of this ammunition production in the diary. As a result any hit on a heavy gun turret risked the fire reaching the magazines. Only one ship in Beatty's force had replaced the interlocks, and re-introduced proper ammunition handling practice – his flagship HMS *Lion*. As a result *Lion* survived the destruction of her Q turret during the heavy fighting in the Run to the South. Rather than admit the real cause of the triple catastrophe lay in human error, his own human error, Beatty had the report suppressed, blamed the disaster on inadequate armour and had unnecessary and largely useless additional armour put on the ships. The reputation of the battle cruiser type never recovered. Had the designed safety systems been in place on 31 May 1916 it is highly unlikely that *Invincible* would have exploded. Q turret would have been wrecked, and the gun crews killed, but the ship would have survived[*]. What tales Alexander Scrimgeour would have had to tell, like another Jutland turret officer, the future King George VI.

Invincible's sacrifice was not in vain. Hood had crushed the German reconnaissance force, and denied Admiral Reinhard Scheer the opportunity to locate Jellicoe's overwhelmingly superior Grand Fleet. Jellicoe, forewarned by Beatty and Hood, deployed his battleships just as Scheer's fleet came into range, still in line ahead. The British ships opened fired at medium range with devastating effect. Twice Scheer was forced to turn away into the mist and smoke. At nightfall the British Grand Fleet lay between the High Seas Fleet and the shelter of its home ports. Scheer managed to push through the tail of Jellicoe's fleet in a series of confused night actions, while the Admiralty failed to inform Jellicoe that a Zeppelin had been ordered up for first light to spot for Scheer. When dawn broke the Germans were well on their way home, leaving Jellicoe to rue lost opportunities.

---

[*] Roberts, J., *Battle Cruisers*, London, 1997, pp. 118-20. The final word on the subject of British battle cruiser design.

Jutland was an inconclusive battle, the Germans sank more ships than they lost, but they ran home, leaving the British in control of the North Sea. As a contemporary American journalist put it: 'the High Seas Fleet had assaulted its gaoler, but it was still in gaol'. A sense of unfinished business pervaded the British response to Jutland, leading many to focus on the human cost. Alexander Scrimgeour was one of 6,000 British officers and men who lost their lives that day.

Conclusion

These diaries offer another priceless insight into the mental world of the Edwardian Navy. While we usually see the First World War as the play of vast numbers of faceless men in a mechanised war across the globe, the men who went to sea in Fisher's dreadnoughts were all too human. Scrimgeour is so obviously an 18-year-old boy with all the cultural baggage of Edwardian England, from his effortless assumption of innate superiority, his contempt for the beastly Huns and distrust of foreigners more generally, to the mores of dating and courtship among his social class. Class differences are accepted, and are reason enough to exclude men from the officer class. He and his generation went to war willingly, laid down their lives to do their duty, and accepted the human cost. While much of this might seem a very long way from the modern world, Scrimgeour's emotions, his delight in the company of pretty girls and readiness to party hard are enduring aspects of the human condition.

That his parents were consoled by the thought that he met his end happy and glorious, tells us much about the age. A young life full of promise, snuffed out in an instant by a single catastrophic explosion, Alexander Scrimgeour would join a long list of Edwardian boys whose names will live in the memory for as long as the memorials of the Great War remain in place, bearing witness to the sacrifice of a generation. Unlike his army contemporaries, who lie in a neatly tended foreign field under a simple gravestone, his remains are entombed in the wreck of the *Invincible*, along with the last volume of his diary. There they rest, as part of a massive war grave in a shallow, dark North Sea, strewn with fishing nets and surrounded by empty cordite cases.

Professor Andrew Lambert

LIST OF ABBREVIATIONS AND TERMS
USED BY MIDSHIPMAN A. SCRIMGEOUR

A.B. .... Able Seaman

A.P. .... Assistant Paymaster

A.S.C. .... Army Service Corps

C.G. .... Coast Guard

C.-in-C. .... Commander-in-Chief

C.P.O. .... Chief Petty Officer

"Dogs". .... Dog-watches

E.R.A. .... Engine Room Artificer

"Flags" .... Flag-Lieutenant

Fx. .... Forecastle (Foc'sle)

G.Q.s. .... General Quarters

G.R. .... Gun Room

"Guns" .... Gunnery-Lieutenant (G.L.)

M.A.A. .... Master-at-Arms

No. 1. .... First Lieutenant

N.O. .... Naval Officer

O.O.D. .... Officer on Duty

O.O.W. .... Officer of the Watch

P.O. .... Petty Officer

Q.M. .... Quarter Master

Q.D. .... Quarter Deck

R.A. .... Rear-Admiral

R.F.R. .... Royal Fleet Reserve

R.M.L.I. .... Royal Marine Light Infantry

R.N.R. .... Royal Naval Reserve

R.N.V.R. .... Royal Naval Volunteer Reserve

"Snotties" .... Midshipmen

S.N.O. .... Senior Naval Officer

"Tanky" .... Assistant Navigator (T.T)

T.B.D. .... Torpedo Boat Destroyer

"Torps" .... Torpedo-Lieutenant

W.O. .... Warrant Officer

W.R. .... Ward Room

W.T. .... Wireless Telegraphy

"Wonks" .... "Useless" naval cadets or midshipmen

1914

JULY

Thursday 30

Went up by the boat-train from Canterbury and down to the Surrey-Kent match at Blackheath. Surrey had bad luck in losing the toss, and did well to get Kent out for 349. I travelled up with Mr. Furley, the hon. treasurer of the Kent County C.C. We ran over a soldier at Rochester Bridge. All the Reserves are mobilised. I intended to spend the night at Arthur Russell's flat, but daddy rang me up on the telephone, to say the Admiralty had wired for me to join R.N. Barracks, Portsmouth. So I met daddy at the Automobile Club and said goodbye, and then left Waterloo for Portsmouth. Met W.S.H. and O'Leary at the station by chance. After a visit to Gieves, we joined the R.N. Barracks at 10 p.m. Everybody in a state of suppressed excitement.

The mobilisation of the Naval Reserve, Fleet Reserve and Naval Volunteer Reserve has already commenced. Found lots of other officers, summoned to the barracks. I am very annoyed at having my leave stopped, but pleased at the thought of the excitement of war.

Friday 31

Hard work drilling with the Reserves, etc., all day at the barracks; but they do us very well at the mess, which is a boon. My uniform arrived by train.

Several of the Osborne officers arrived for the mobilisation today. I am afraid we shall have damned little leave, and I shall miss Canterbury, Dover, and Orkney, which I have been looking forward to for months. Still, it is all for the sake of the country. International situation worse in France, Germany, and Russia, but the peace party in England seems extremely strong at present.

July 1914
NAVAL BARRACKS, PORTSMOUTH
Friday (morning)

Dear Daddy,

Please thank mother for her letter. My clothes have not arrived yet (10 a.m.), but suppose they will get here some time today.

Gieves may be able to fit me out by midday. At present the lack of uniform is a boon, as all the others are with the Reservists at gun and signal drill, while I am doing nothing. I am afraid I can give you no information, and even if I could I should not, as all movements of ships and men, known to officers or men, are to be considered as strictly confidential.

We are all quartered at the barracks until further orders, and are doing duty in lieu of midshipmen with the Reservists. We are frightfully cramped for sleeping room, but they do us very well at the officers' mess, which is something. The whole town is in a hubbub of excitement, as the "terriers" are out, and everything seems alive.

We travelled down last night with a Stock Exchange man named Thurston; he seemed quite a good sort, and consumed large quantities of W. and S.

Give my best love to all at Wickhambreaux.

Hope to be home again before the end of August; damned nuisance missing cricket week!

Yours,
Toby
P.S.—I will let you know what ship I go to as soon as I know, but we shan't go for two or three days.
Please send my diary by post.

AUGUST

Saturday 1

Usual dull barrack drill all the morning, with Lieut.-Commanders Fenn, Robinson, and Leach. Saw Sergeant O'Dwyer and C.P.O. Woodcock. A party of us got a box in the theatre in the afternoon to see the "Clever Ones." In the middle there was a general recall to all naval and military officers and men in Portsmouth, and we had to leave (amidst the cheers of the crowd), which was a damned nuisance. Made the acquaintance of several nice girls in Portsmouth.

War rumours rife all day, some true, some untrue. I had a very wet evening. Learnt we are to leave the barracks and join a ship tomorrow.

Sunday 2

Germany has attacked France, and even our peace party cannot prevent war without dishonour. Left the R.N. Barracks at 8 a.m. and bade farewell to the mate, Mr. Macdonald, and other friends. Joined H.M.S. *Crescent*, a fairly old cruiser, flagship of the Tenth Cruiser Squadron, under command of Rear-Admiral de Chair. I found myself senior acting midshipman, and consequently president of the gun-room mess. Found our old friend P.O. Croxford was Chief Gunner's Mate. I was put in charge of picket-boat. We shall have lots of hard work, but it will be very interesting. Hope war will be declared soon.

Monday 3

Assistant-Clerk Glanville joined the gun-room from H.M.S. *Lion*. The other acting "snotties" are Johnstone, Cobb, Robinson, Richardson, Henderson, Hutchinson, and Tottenham. It is the irony of fate that I should be senior to them all. Weighed and left Portsmouth Harbour at 11 a.m., proceeded down the Solent, and made for the Lizard under sealed orders. G.Q.s fire stations and collision stations in the evening. The Captain gave us a harangue on the war. We have an extraordinary mixed assortment of men—C.G.s., R.N.R., R.N.V.R., R.F.R. men and boys under training, with a smattering of active service ratings. Not much of a crew, I am afraid, but we will get them into shape. The guns are inclined to be obsolete, and the control and ammunition supply systems hopelessly crude. Oh, to be in a First Fleet battleship! I attempted to repair the rate clock with the aid of the Gunner, Mr. Croughan. I had the early morning watch and the first night watch, and turned in at 12.15, absolutely dead with fatigue. The Captain's name is Trewby, and he is an excellent officer, but the R.A. is a bit of an old woman.

Tuesday 4

Passed Land's End and steered north at 6 a.m. *Edgar* joined Flag at 8 a.m.; G.Q.s after divisions. Lieutenant G.A. Wilson, Johnstone, and I tried to arrange an efficient fire control system. *Grafton* joined Flag at 11 a.m. Working control all the afternoon. I had the middle, and I am afraid the constant racket will begin to tell soon. Great Britain declared war on Germany at midnight. We are without any news except wireless. Sir John Jellicoe appointed Commander-in-Chief of Home Fleet in succession to Admiral Sir G. Callaghan, and Earl Kitchener made Secretary of State for War. Our course is due north, up the Irish Sea; we passed Isle of Man during the night. Some of our Service officers are Commander Wardle, Fleet Paymaster Lawford, Staff Paymaster Weston, Lieut.-Commanders Popham and Beasley, and Lieut.-Commander (Ret.) Kiddle.

Wednesday 5

Passed out of the Irish Sea; off Cantyre and Islay. War began in earnest; sighted a German steamer off Jura, and the R.A. sent the *Grafton* to capture her and take her into Belfast. Our small squadron is thus reduced to two ships, although at full strength it should consist of eight. Shaped a course up the west coast of Scotland, to make the Orkneys eventually, as for the present they are to be our base. We had G.Q.s all the morning and got the fire control system as perfect as possible. Rough weather all day. The gun-room atmosphere is very bad, due to poor ventilation. There are rumours of a great battle in the North Sea, but do not believe them. Wrote a line home in the "dogs." The other executive officers are Lieutenant (G.) Kenyon, Lieutenant (N.) Clark, Lieutenant (T.) Attwood, and Lieutenant Wilson. Do not know them yet.

August 5th
H.M.S. CRESCENT, AT SEA

Dear Daddy,

We joined this ship on Sunday and left a few hours later. It is flagship of the Tenth Cruiser Squadron, which is supposed to consist of eight ships, but at present only three are with the Flag. Being a nucleus crew ship, we have completed our complement with Reservists, coastguards, volunteers, and untrained boys; a pretty motley collection, I can tell you. But they are gradually shaking down, and I dare say we shall be able to make something of them. There are eight acting midshipmen in the ship and a few other clerks and people in the gun-room. I am senior gun-room officer. Things are none

too comfortable, but no one minds that. It is a great strain, as
we have a watch on the bridge (four hours) once every twenty-
four hours, and also a gun watch in the battery (four hours),
making eight hours' watch-keeping a day; we have general
quarters for action about three times in twenty-four hours,
each time taking roughly an hour; divisions and quarters take
about an hour a day, and the general work of the ship getting
everything ready and efficient about four hours a day; so that,
allowing two hours for meals—pretty scratch ones at that (as
we have run out of bread and all drinks)—we only get about
eight hours a day off duty.

I was very sorry to miss the cricket week, as I had been looking
forward to it for months, but am perfectly contented, as I have
been looking forward to war ever since I was a baby, and
considering there has been no naval warfare proper for over one
hundred years, we ought to think ourselves very lucky that we
have come in for it. We have no news at all, so I hope you will
keep all the daily papers, so that I can follow the course of events
if I get home soon. I wonder how long the war will last; it was
declared at midnight last night, and we did not have to wait long,
for we captured a German merchantman early this morning and
sent her into a British port with a prize crew. We hear rumours of
a big naval engagement in the North Sea, but can obtain no
definite details, as all the wireless messages are in different codes.
I am not allowed to give any information of our whereabouts, but
if you received my last telegram some days ago, just before I left
the Portsmouth barracks, you will, I dare say, make a rough
guess of our approximate station, where we are protecting British
vessels and intercepting all foreign or hostile shipping.

Rear-Admiral de Chair is our flag officer and Captain Trewby
the captain. Many of the officers are very antiquated
specimens, called up after years of retirement, and
consequently a large amount of responsibility rests with us
midshipmen, who are well up, of course, in all the modern
methods of gunfire control, etc. It is very rough at present and
damned unpleasant into the bargain.

Let's hope that the British Empire will give these Germans hell.

Good luck to all at Wickhambreaux.

Best love from
Toby
P.S.—If by any chance we, or I, get "scuttled," you may find
my diaries of interest; they are in different drawers of my
writing-desk. Please see they are not interfered with otherwise.

Thursday 6

I had the morning watch. We ran through the Minches and round Cape
Wrath along through the Pentland Firth and into Scapa Flow, passing the
First Battle Cruiser Squadron coming out. We anchored off Scapa and
coaled ship, taking in 350 tons. R.N.R. Lieutenant Oxlade joined the ship
from the *Edgar*. We left most of our boats behind to avoid splintering in
action, and I was in charge of mooring them off the pier – quite a tricky job.
I then went on shore in the picket-boat and just missed Uncle John from
Swanbister by five minutes; he had been seeing somebody off in the *St.
Ola*. Very sorry to miss him. Sent a note to Auntie Connie by the Harbour
Master. After coaling we proceeded with the rest of the squadron (three
ships) round west of Orkneys, intercepting all ships we met. We took in a
big supply of stores and ammunition from the Scapa base, which is strongly
protected by destroyers; also heard many vague war rumours. The First
Fleet are due to arrive at Scapa on the 7th.

Friday 7

Proceeded round to Fair Island, stopping and examining several ships, all
British or neutral, thus gaining little information and no prizes. Exercised
control at G.Q.s. A long job getting Dumaresq and rate clock into the top.
Cruised about on our patrol to the eastward of the Orkneys and
Shetlands. Arrived at a rendezvous 4 p.m. *Theseus, Endymion, Gibraltar*
joined the Flag, bringing strength of squadron up to six ships. *Royal Arthur*
and *Hawke* still adrift. There is a rumour of the capture of the German
battle cruiser *Goeben* in the Mediterranean. I had the middle gun watch
with Mr. Oxlade; he is an awful good sort. The engineer officers of the
ship are Eng.-Lieut.-Commander Fletcher and Eng.-Lieutenant Sims.
Rough night.

Saturday 8

Sighted and captured two German trawlers from Kegesack at 6 a.m. They seemed quite harmless, but had some incriminating papers. I went on board both as interpreter. I began fully to realise the horrors of war when I saw the misery of the crews (whom we took on board) at leaving their ship, their only means of sustenance. It was most touching to all of us. G.Q.s 8 a.m. The squadron exercised battle practice, using the empty trawlers as targets, both being sunk. Firing very satisfactory. My services as German interpreter much in need with regard to the prisoners. I also got something out of sonic Norwegian messages we intercepted by wireless. My opinion of Mr. Oxlade is still higher; he is a fine chap, keen on all sports, and has knocked about the world a bit. At 4 p.m. squadron divided, four ships going north-east to patrol the Norwegian coast. Bad news of a submarine attack on Dreadnought *Monarch*. I had first gun watch. A very dirty night.

Sunday 9

No G.Q.s, otherwise usual routine. Captain's rounds. War routine; short service on Q.D. Stopped and searched several neutral ships. The *Grafton* parted company to the eastward at 3 p.m., chasing a strange sail. Several Norwegian messages obtained. Bad news of the loss of the *Amphion* off the Thames*, but the *Birmingham* destroyed a German submarine off Fair Island. First Fleet left Scapa after coaling. Our squadron off east of Shetlands all day. We met the *Dryad* at a rendezvous; she gave us some stores, extra ratings and a few mails, and a new R.N.R., Lieutenant Bacon. She took our mails and the prisoners, to whom I bade farewell, and then proceeded to Scapa, the chief northern base.

Monday 10

We were patrolling to the north-east of the Shetlands all day.

The *Hawke* joined the Flag at 10 a.m. G.Q.s after divisions. News of German aircraft over the Shetlands. Personally I believe they have a secret base in the Danish Faroe Isles to the north-west. The *Royal Arthur* joined Flag at 4 p.m., bringing squadron up to full strength, counting the three ships off Norway. At 0.30 p.m. we detached the *Endymion* to Busta Voe, Swarbacks Minn, a deserted, out-of-the-way harbour in west of Shetlands,

---

** HMS *Amphion* was sunk on 6 August 1914 after hitting a mine off the Thames Estuary. 151 lives were lost plus 19 German sailors who had been rescued from the *Konigin Luise*, sunk by the *Amphion* a day earlier.

which is to be used as our new base (Tenth Cruiser Squadron only). Gunroom life is getting unbearable owing to bad atmosphere and food. A new cowl slightly improves the former. I wonder whether Lieutenant Tovey*, an old Osborne friend, was saved from the *Amphion*, of which he was first lieutenant.

Tuesday 11

Very rough all day, with a high gale. G.Q.s not a success in the morning. The Captain made a great joke at my expense on watch, but the R.A. turned it on to the back of Lieut. Commander Robinson, the Flag-Lieutenant. Very little news except of more German submarines and aeroplanes. The German battleships proper are all bottled up in Kiel, and I am afraid the mines will prevent their outward progress, even if they wanted to come out, so the chances of a big naval battle are small. This shows the unwillingness of the Germans to challenge our mastery of the seas. On watch Mr. Kiddle was very loquacious on the charms of gay Paris. Joined the three ships from Norway during the night, but each division returned to its original station after an exchange of signals.

Wednesday 12

The weather greatly improved. G.Q.s as usual. I was made Deputy or Assistant Gunnery Lieutenant and excused watch-keeping, so I shall never have a minute to myself now. The stores are giving out, and none of the luxuries of life are left. We boarded a Norwegian vessel in the afternoon and obtained some Norwegian newspapers full of war news. I spent three hours translating twenty-six pages of it, and the R.A. congratulated me on my work. W.T. messages say our submarines have volunteered to attack the Germans in Kiel, but Admiral Jellicoe will not allow them to, stating it to be a useless risk to valuable British lives at this early juncture. The *Drake* has been ordered to the Faeroes to investigate them. The other ward-room officers in the ship are Staff Surgeon W.P. Walker, Acting Surgeon Maxwell, A.P. Cockrem, and A.P. Egleton, R.N.R.; A.P. Gallichan, R.N.R.; Chaplain, Rev. Shell.

Thursday 13

Usual war routine all day. Hard at work with Gunnery-Lieutenant at our ammunition supply arrangements. Revolver shooting, drill, and practice

---

* Lieutenant John Tovey, later 1st Baron Tovey, would go on to become Admiral of the Fleet in 1943 during the Second World War.

Rough Plan of the disposition of Grand Fleet before
commencing sweep of the North Sea   (Aug 15ᵗʰ 1914)

○
○   4ᵗʰ battle
○   squadron
○⊞ Dreadnought

○   ○   ○
○   ○   ○
○   ○   ○
○⊞   ○⊞   ○⊞
○   ○   ○
○ 3ʳᵈ battle ○ 1ˢᵗ battle ○ 2ⁿᵈ battle
○   squadron ○   squadron ○   squadron

+ scout   King Edward   ○⊞   Marlboro ○⊞   ○ King George V   + scout
           VII   (Warrender)

          Iron Duke ○⊞ C. in C.
          (Jellicoe)

| | | | |

Destroyer Flotillas of the
     1ˢᵗ   Fleet

+ + + + +

        ○   ○
        ○ 10ᵗʰ ○
        ○ cruiser ○
        ○ squadron ·
        ○   ○⊞ Crescent
              (de Chair)

          1ˢᵗ lt cruiser   squadron
+   +   +   +   +
  (Goodenough)

+ scout   + scout

+ scout   + scout

          ○
          ○   1ˢᵗ battle cruiser
          ○   squadron
          ○   (12' ahead of main fleet)
  Lion ○⊞
 (Beatty)

on the Q.D. for two hours in the morning. I shot very well, so did Tottenham and Cobb. Rigged the coaling Asiatic stay in the dog-watches. Heavy firing was heard to the south-east at 4 p.m., and we proceeded on that bearing at full speed, but found it was only the *Theseus* gun firing on a deserted derelict. W.T. rumours that a secret German air base is in the Shetlands.

Friday 14

Usual war routine in the forenoon. Made Bussay Isle and anchored off Lerwick at 2 p.m. Obtained some very welcome newspapers, mails, and stores, which cheered us up very much. A friend of old Shearer's at Kirkwall came on board. A collier came alongside at 3 p.m., and we commenced to coal, intending to take in 400 tons, and looking forward to twenty-four hours in harbour afterwards, but the C.-in-C. sent us a special W.T. message, and we had to sweat like niggers till 7.30, when we had 287 tons, then unrig collier and proceed to sea by 9.30 to join C.-in-C. at a rendezvous with rest of our squadron. Our hold, the Fx, under the able guidance of Lieutenant Oxlade, Gunner Croughan, Robinson, and myself, did exceedingly well, being well ahead in spite of disadvantages. I had second gun watch with Lieutenant Bacon, R.N.R., a most interesting fellow, who seems to have shot in every part of the world.

Saturday 15

Joined First Fleet at 7 a.m., 200 miles due north of Wick. I don't quite realise what he intended to use our Tenth Cruiser Squadron for. The First Fleet look a very grim sight, and inspire the utmost confidence. We all proceeded over towards the Norwegian coast, the battle cruisers leading, with the battleships four miles behind in three imposing lines, and light cruisers and destroyer flotillas scouring the seas all round on every quarter. There are no submarines, aircraft, minelayers, or sweepers with us, however. W.T. messages say that aircraft bases have been found at Scapa and Thurso. We intercepted several insolent messages from German stations, obviously trying to induce us to appear off the German coast and probably entice us into a mine-field. In spite of their taunts, the Germans remain securely mined in Wilhelmshaven and Kiel, although I believe they have defeated the Russians in the Baltic.

Sunday 16

Swept down off the Norwegian coast past the Skager Rack, down the Danish coast to within forty miles of Heligoland, but could approach no further owing to the German mine-fields. The Germans refused to come out. Glorious day. We left the First Fleet 4 p.m., they steering south-west and we back to the Shetlands.

Monday 17

Joined *Dryad* at noon and obtained and despatched mails. I heard from Auntie Connie, answering by return and cadging for grouse, with which Uncle John seems to be supplying the Fleet. We arrived Lerwick at 5 p.m. with the remainder of the Tenth Cruiser Squadron, prepared ship for coaling tomorrow. Harbour mouth patrolled by picket-boats to insure against destroyers. I had charge of defence of southern entrance from midnight till four—a great responsibility—but nothing untoward occurred. We landed several field-guns for harbour defence, and armed our steamboats.

Tuesday 18

Coaled ship in the morning and took in 275 tons; the Fx did not do so well as last time, owing to bad rigging of whip, but did well when once started. We all went on shore, after coaling, for a few hours, and did some shopping and had tea, also examined the local territorial foot. Fleet Paymaster Lawford stood Glanville and myself tea, the Captain also turning up. I like both these officers very much. Weighed and proceeded to sea on our patrol at 7.30 p.m., joining rest of squadron. Wrote to Auntie Connie.

Wednesday 19

On the usual patrol all day. Very little doing of any interest. But Mr. Kenyon, myself, and remainder of gunnery department were hard at work nearly all the day. Sighted Norwegian coast at 2 p.m., and ran up coast for a few hours. The Allan liner *Alsatian*, the first of a batch of four requisitioned for naval purposes in the squadron, joined the Flag at 6 p.m.; her high speed will be of great use to us. A very dirty night, thick weather, Mr. Bacon on with me. He was in great form.

Thursday 20

Usual war routine. Gunnery department had a very busy morning. First of all, group control practice for night defence, then loader drill and gun drill.

The Commander and "Guns" do not get on well together. The former was a Gunnery-Lieutenant and thinks he still knows a lot about it, although he doesn't, and this annoys "Guns" intensely. Received a big mail by the *Dryad*, including thirteen brace of grouse from Swanbister. Boarded S.S. *Bergensfjord*, Norge-Amerika Line, and found papers correct, but captured two German reservists; the Norwegians were most hospitable, as they always are.

Friday 21

Boarded another Norwegian ship without result. Independent squadron G.Q.s. Target practice with 1-inch aiming tube and 303. Did seven runs, four starboard side and three port side, most of which were exceedingly successful, and the Captain was quite satisfied. Stopped engines for some time while a chief stoker of the *Gibraltar* was buried, having died of pneumonia. The Admiral thanked me for the Swanbister grouse, of which I gave him and the ward-room some.

Saturday 22

A partial eclipse of the sun. Independent squadron target practice again with 1-inch aiming tube and 303. We practised night defence stations instead of G.Q.s, with very pleasing results. The Gunnery-Lieutenant had several small targets made representing T.B.D.s, and we cruised round about them, exercising first, middle, and morning watch night-gun defence stations. I had another exceedingly busy afternoon with the gunnery department, making out five arc plans. Received a mail and some more grouse in the *Dryad* at 7 p.m. All my cousins seem to be joining the army and most of my friends as well. Rather bad news from the Front.

Sunday 23

Stopped engines at ten, and the Captains of several of the other ships of the squadron came on board to see the Admiral. Saw O'Kell, Dickson, and Macfarlane, who came on board in their various sea-boats. Heard that Japan had declared war on Germany. A very rough night. Rumours of the escape of some German ships.

Monday 24

A foggy morning. German submarines reported from Stromsay, Orkneys. Entered Lerwick Harbour at 11 a.m. and anchored there with the *Theseus*. Most people got on shore in the afternoon, and they brought off a goodly store of delicacies and stores. Personally I spent the afternoon in the store-ship *Alcinous*, superintending the transference of stores to our boats, which was a long and dreary job as it rained all the time. The *Forward* left at 2 p.m. for Scapa. Two destroyers and the armed liner *Mantua* came in at 7 p.m. All our battle squadrons are off the west of Scotland now; only the cruisers are in the North Sea.

Tuesday 25

Left Lerwick and proceeded back on to our patrol. Stopped and boarded two ships during the day, one French and one Swedish, but gleaned but little information. All sorts of rumours of German naval activity, but the fact remains that the bulk of the German Navy remains skulking in harbour, their plan being to destroy our numerical superiority by submarine attacks, several foreign submarines having been seen in the Orkneys and Shetlands, and attempts to destroy them are at present unavailing. I had a hard day's work with the First Lieutenant, Mr. Popham, taking down and rearranging his 92-inch voice pipe fire control connections.

Wednesday 26

The Rear-Admiral invited me to breakfast, and I quite enjoyed it. He is an extremely nice, quiet man, a perfect gentleman, but is, in my opinion, rather oppressed and nervy, due to the responsibility of his command, and relies very largely on Captain Trewby for his initiative. The Secretary Fleet Paymaster Lawford is a very good sort and reminds me of Denniston; he has very little to do, as there is a most extensive Paymaster's staff on board. I had another hard day with Mr. Popham, and in spite of much ridicule our efforts were crowned with some success. Received a signal from C.-in-C. to proceed to Scapa at full speed, but fog seriously retarded us. I was in very bad form in the evening. Wireless messages assure us that Namur has fallen. Bad news from the seat of war in Belgium. Heard that the *Highflyer* had sunk the German armed liner *Friedrich der Grosse**. Rumours of an action off Cape Wrath between two armed liners unsubstantiated, though the *Blonde* left Scapa in that direction with sealed orders. British aeroplanes in evidence all round the Orkneys.

Thursday 27

Entered Scapa Flow at 5 a.m., and at six we anchored with remainder of the Tenth Cruiser Squadron off Warkmill Bay. Found the majority of the First Fleet in harbour, with several depot-ships, store-ships, and supply-ships, and a whole legion of colliers and oilers. Coaled ship and took in 450 tons, not going nearly so fast as usual. I wanted to get on leave to Swanbister, but in the absence of the Rear-Admiral on a visit to the C.-in-C. the Captain would not let me go. It was very sickening seeing the house and the tennis court and the pier and yachts, and knowing that although they were only two miles off they might as well have been two hundred. Went to Scapa Pier in charge of the beef party in the duty steam-boat of

---

* HMS *Highflyer* sank the SS *Kaiser Wilhelm der Grosse* not the armed liner, *Friedrich der Grosse*.

the *Endymion*, as we had not lowered any boats. Made the acquaintance of Captain Hyde-Parker of the *Endymion*. All the Captains of our squadron came on board to a conference with the Admiral. First Fleet and destroyer flotillas put to sea at 7 p.m. The *Agincourt* arrived. Saw F.F. Turner and G.A.V. Harrison during the course of the day.

Friday 28

Weighed at 7 a.m. after losing our port bower anchor through cathead block carrying away. Five ships of the squadron—*Crescent* (flag), *Grafton*, *Royal Arthur*, *Hawke*, and *Theseus*—put to sea and proceeded to our new patrol between Duncansby Head in Caithness to Buchan Ness in Aberdeen, thus protecting the entrance to the Moray Firth and the shores of E. Caithness, E. Sutherland, E. Ross and Cromarty, E. Inverness, Elgin, Nairn, Banff, and North Aberdeenshire. We are to be based on Cromarty. We left the *Edgar* and *Endymion* in Scapa and despatched the *Gibraltar* to Rosyth for refit. Our old patrol off the Shetlands across to Norway is to be taken over by the armed merchantmen *Alsatian*, *Mantua*, and *Oceanic*.

Saturday 29

Despatched the *Theseus* to the White Sea to harass German trade there. There are no Russian warships there. Changed our patrol again to the east coast of Aberdeenshire and stretching about 120 miles out into the North Sea. Overhauled and examined several tramps during the course of the day. G.Q.s at 10 a.m. The Commander sent Henderson during a watch to the masthead as a punishment. The Yeoman of Signals, P.O. Todhunter, also in the soup. Sighted the *Achilles* and the remainder of Second Cruiser Squadron in the afternoon proceeding from Cromarty to a patrol off Heligoland. Good news of a successful British naval action between two of our cruiser squadrons and some German cruisers attempting to leave the Ems River. Two German cruisers sunk by gunfire and one torpedoed. The *Arethusa* and *Laertes* received injuries on our side[*]. A large number of prisoners sent into Rosyth in the *Gloucester*.

Sunday 30

On our beat all day. Intercepted and searched several ships without result. Met the *Drake* at 6 p.m. She is now flagship of Sixth Cruiser Squadron. The *Latona* sighted two German destroyers off Kinnaird Head, and we went full speed to intercept them, but they were too fast for us. I hope the *Hawke* will intercept them. Two of our submarines which have entered Wilhelmshaven report that the harbour is devoid of German warships.

Monday 31

On our patrol all day. Another German submarine reported from Linga Sound between Stromsay and Sanday in the Orkneys. Three-pounder shell firing practice in the morning; the first run a dismal failure, but things

---

[*] The Battle of Heligoland Bight was a welcome victory for the Royal Navy against the Germans. The first naval battle of the war saw Beatty's squadron of cruisers attack German patrols off the north-west German coast.

improved considerably later on; the Captain rather cantankerous, and I got in a furious temper with Mr. Coughan, who was in charge of the cable deck guns, and he effectually smothered any spark of intelligence he ever possessed by stolidly refusing to open fire, and consequently I had to take the blame of his shortcomings. Boarded several Norwegian ships; the amount of Norwegian shipping in these seas is phenomenal. An urgent wireless message from C.-in-C. saying an attempt will be made tonight to lay mines between Pentland Firth and Rathsay Head by a German mine-laying squadron supported by cruisers; consequently we are to co-operate with the First Battle Cruiser Squadron and Second and Third Cruiser Squadrons to sweep the threatened area and destroy the Germans. Midshipman Cobb went sick with tonsillitis.

SEPTEMBER

Tuesday 1

After an exciting night's watching, at about 4 a.m. we sighted three strange vessels showing dimly in a cloud-bank; we suspected them to be the enemy in question, and everything was prepared for action, but at the last moment they answered our challenge and eventually proved to be three pre-Dreadnought battleships of the Second Fleet belonging to the Fifth Battle Squadron, and were supported in a reconnaissance to be conducted along the Dutch coast by the eight First Fleet pre-Dreadnought battleships of the Third Battle Squadron and also a light cruiser squadron. Nevertheless, two hours later we sighted two German destroyers steering east-south-east at full speed in the horizon. They had eluded our blockade in the night and were being chased back to Cuxhaven or Emden by the *Boadicea*; we joined in the chase for one and a half hours, but they were too fast for us, so we left them to the *Boadicea*, who, however, so we heard later, was unable to catch them. We had G.Q.s at 10.30 a.m., a very busy and productive morning for the gunnery department; loader drill, mantles put up, hand clock constructed, arcs painted, and shell-bag reversed system trials. Thick fog prevented us from meeting *Dryad* and so exchanging mails, which was rather disappointing.

September 1st 1914
H.M.S. CRESCENT, AT SEA

Dear Mother,

Many thanks for your letters, and please thank Peggy very much
indeed for hers. Still all alive and kicking, but we are having a very
trying time, as I have only been on shore for two hours since we left
Portsmouth over a month ago, and we only get about five or six
hours' rest in twenty-four hours. Also all the luxuries of life such as
sugar and butter and bread are things of the past, except sometimes
when we manage to obtain stores during coaling. The Swanbister
grouse were a great boon after days of canned beef and salt fish;
I divided them between the Admiral, the ward-room, and the
gun-room, and they were very much appreciated. I had breakfast
with the Admiral a few days ago; he is quite a nice old chap, and
very like Norman Forbes-Robertson to look at.

We are having a certain amount of excitement, but all wish that
the "Grosse Deutsche Hoch-See Flotte" could be induced to come
out and fight, instead of indulging in the glorious pursuit of
sinking harmless neutral merchant and fishing vessels by mines.

I should be very pleased if you would start sending some weekly
papers again. The Referee, the People, and every Monday's
Sportsman would be very welcome; and, by the way, a pair or two
of these socks you are all knitting would also be very welcome.
Much as I enjoy getting news from home, stupid sentimental
twaddle from Mrs. Handfield Jones is not in great demand.

Has that renegade Canadian relative of yours decided to do anything? His Christian name savours of a better man.

If you do not burn this letter, see that it does not leave your
possession and is kept absolutely confidential. Please give my love
to Aunties Ethel, Ruth, and Maud, when you write.

Best love to all at home from
TOBY.

Wednesday 2

Met the *Dryad* and exchanged mails at 8 a.m. Very foggy all day again. Reports of a submarine attack on Scapa, but no details. Received some grouse again from Swanbister. Met the Second and Third Cruiser Squadrons with two destroyer flotillas at 4 p.m., and we swept with them across to the Norwegian coast, and, although we overhauled several neutrals, picked up no news. Chased and sank a small German armed tramp just before midnight, all the crew lost. Disquieting news from the French frontier, and also the Russians have received a check in Eastern Prussia. Wireless messages tell us that Kitchener is bringing home Ghurkhas and Sikhs to fight, and also 40,000 Russians have been taken round Norway and landed in France. The Germans are trying to turn our flank and are threatening Calais and Boulogne. No further Russian advance in Prussia, but they have defeated the Austrians in Galicia, and the Serbians have thrown back the Austrians in Bosnia.

Thursday 3

Thick fog all day necessitates extra gun watches. I had a very hard day's work, moving the loader, directing the construction of control instruments, examining night-sight switches, and was tired out. Had a long yarn with Lieutenant Bacon, Gunner Croughan, and P.O. Short. It is reported that four German cruisers and a bevy of submarines have eluded our blockade and are at large in the North Sea. Consequently we are making a big combined sweep to try and find them. I wish we could make more use of our sea-planes, as they would be very useful indeed as scouts. Deputy-Surgeon Buddle joined the ship temporary from an H.M.T.B.

Friday 4

On our patrol and in the North Sea all day. G.Q.s in the morning again a dismal failure. Mr. Beasley and Mr. Kiddle suggested sweeping changes in the control system, and after the usual wordy combat between the Commander and "Guns" it was decided to refer the matter to the Captain. Heavy firing heard during the forenoon caused a sensation, but proved eventually to be the *Drake* and *Leviathan* of the Sixth Cruiser Squadron doing battle practice. The four German cruisers, reported to be in the North Sea, seem to have made themselves very scarce, as, in spite of extensive searching sweeps, nobody has seen anything of them. The First Lieutenant has proposed that a mess committee should supersede the mess caterer, as the state of our messing is very poor under the present regime. Wireless messages report that the Germans are within forty miles of Paris, which is bad news. The French capital has been removed to Bordeaux for safety. Pray God the Allies may have the courage to continue this struggle to the bitter end.

Saturday 5

A German cruiser reported 200 miles due east of Pentland Firth by the *Thetis*. Four hours' chase at full speed proved her to be H.M. destroyer *Swift*, much to our chagrin, as we are all spoiling for a scrap. I hope we are not going to get nervy with this constant waiting, as German ships of mythical origin are continually being chased. Those lucky devils in the army are having all they want. The dastardly crimes of the Germans will commit them to everlasting damnation in the blackest depths of the nethermost hell. We met the *Dryad* at 4 p.m. and obtained some welcome news. I got in a shindy with "Guns" for not overhauling the foc'sle 6-inch gun night-sights correctly.

Sunday 6

Wireless news report the loss of H.M. ships *Pathfinder* and *Speedy*, blown up by German mines. This mine menace is becoming very serious indeed. I have devised a scheme for overcoming it, and shall lay it before the Admiral. The British marines, with whom L.L.G. went as surgeon, have been withdrawn from Ostend, and replaced by Russian troops which have been brought round from Archangel. The German advance on Paris is at last checked temporarily. A gorgeous day followed a still better night. Very busy with "Guns" all day. Worked out some rather complicated deflection problems, and perfected the fire control system. Very bucked as "Guns" complimented me on my work. Overhauled two ships without result.

September 6th 1914
H.M.S. CRESCENT, AT SEA

Dear Mother,

Many thanks for your letters. You have got to try to be a little less impatient and not draw so many odious comparisons with Captain Baird. A Captain can take the time to write a letter whenever he pleases, even in war-time, while a junior officer

has no time to spare. With luck I get from about four to six hours' sleep a night, and, with intervals for meals, am busy all day; I enjoy it, it is interesting, and it is in a good cause, but it is rather disheartening to be hauled over the coals by an exacting parent, for not wasting time writing continual letters when I am not allowed to give you any news. I have written three times to you and once or more to daddy; perhaps you have not received the letters. Another small point: Battleships, like that of which Captain Baird is in command, are often in harbour and consequently have frequent chances of sending mails; cruisers are almost continually at sea, and on an average mails leave us for home about once a week, although local communications are more frequent. Anyhow, I will write whenever it is reasonably possible. Please thank Aunties Ethel and Ruth for their letters, and say I will write after the war.

By the way, who is young Anderson, whom you say is killed? I don't remember the name.

So glad to hear that all my friends are enlisting; splendid of Burberry. It is good that Malcolm and Gertrude's fiancé are going. Well done, Canon "Stinkbreath"! He has lost a son in an excellent cause, and, I hope, is a proud man.

It is not so easy as it looks, this quashing Germany, as the Russians are deadly slow. I wish they would stop wasting time with the Austrians in Galicia and make a more determined advance in Prussia. There is a story being circulated that General Grierson, who is supposed to have died a natural death, was murdered by a German because of his extensive knowledge of the German Army and its methods*.

They seem to have no idea of the meaning of the words honour and chivalry. The Hunnish strain, which must have become ingrained in the German blood during the raids of the Huns a thousand years ago, is vindicating itself after ages of latency.

---

* It is generally believed that Lieutenant-General James Grierson died of an aneurism of the heart on a train near Amiens.

I wish these skulking brutes would come out of their damned
harbours, and we will soon increase the number of the
permanent German submarine fleet quartered on the sand at
the bottom of the North Sea. This minelaying game is typical of
the nation. I knew a man who was saved from the Amphion
very well; he was First Lieutenant.

A lot of frothy vapouring is being published in the Press about
the Heligoland action. It was certainly a most successful
venture, as it is hoped all our ventures will be. But to describe it
as a great naval victory is ridiculous, for there were only three
German small cruisers and a few torpedo-boats present, and
they were easily outnumbered. There will be only one great
naval victory, and that will be accomplished as soon as public
opinion forces the Germans to put to sea. Sinking unarmed
trawlers and laying mines may be a most amusing game, but it
won't avail much in the long run.

An interesting story is told of the Heligoland affair. When the
Mainz sank, a German officer was seen to be struggling at his
last gasp in the ditch. One of our officers immediately jumped
overboard and saved him. When they were both standing on
the deck once more, the chivalrous (?) German showed his
gratitude by spitting in the face of the chap who had saved him.
A splendid nation of gentlemen! This story is absolutely true, as
I have it from an eyewitness. The bottom of the sea is the best
place for people like this. Their outrages on the Belgians make
one livid with rage; I should have considerable pleasure in
gouging their eyes out, I feel so angry when I read of them.

Tootsie no doubt thinks she is remarkably smart, but it is very
dangerous to mention the movements of any ships even in
private correspondence or conversation, as things get round in
an extraordinary fashion, and there are plenty of friends to the
Germans about. As a matter of fact, although the King George
V. has been there several times, it is quite incorrect to say she
has been there all the time.

Some of us would be rather pleased if this ship was disabled or sunk by a mine, as in that case the survivors would be transferred to one of the latest ships, and would have a better chance of being in at the death when the Germans put to sea.

What do Uncle Jack and Aunt Do think of the war?

There is one of the most gorgeous sunsets tonight I have ever seen; I feel I must mention it; it is so striking, the cloud effects being particularly fine.

No time for more now as I am very sleepy.

Best love to all from
TOBY.
P.S.—Don't forget these socks you are knitting are just as useful to me as to the soldiers, for all mine are rags.

Monday 7

Left our patrol at midnight and shaped a course for Cromarty. Entered Moray Firth about 4 a.m. and made a landfall near Lybster, and then steamed down the coast and entered Cromarty Firth at 8 a.m., anchoring between Cromarty and Invergordon at 8.45. Found the Second and Third Cruiser Squadrons in harbour coaling, and also the *Edgar*, which leaves tonight. Pearson came on board in picket-boat from *Edgar*, and I sent them some grouse, as I have just received some more from Swanbister. This is first time we have anchored for eleven days, and we got some very welcome fresh provisions from Inverness and Cromarty. Coaled ship and took in 500 tons, a very tedious coaling. I hear some benevolent old gent has presented shoals of gramophones to the Fleet; I hope we get one. Two German cruisers and some destroyers are at large in the North Sea and have sunk fifteen trawlers. Unluckily all our ships are coaling, or we would give them blue hell. A Wilson liner blown up by another damned mine off Hull.

Tuesday 8

Went on shore at 6 a.m. to superintend stores and ammunition being brought off from Invergordon Quay. Superintended the racers being painted in the forenoon. Landed in the afternoon and hired a motor with a warrant, in order to take despatches from the Admiral to the naval victualling agent at Dingwall, and then had to go on through the Muir of Ord to Beauly to arrange about a trainload of new gun-fittings for our squadron to be sent on immediately to Invergordon. Got a square meal on my return to Dingwall. On the way home an aeroplane was seen to alight up in the deer forests above Alness. A sergeant of the Gordons stopped me and requested that I should lend him the motor to take his patrol up to investigate immediately, which I did. Unluckily I could not spare the time to go myself, so was obliged to charter a goods engine at Alness Station to take me back to Invergordon by rail at once. Heard on my return that the armed liner *Oceanic* had gone ashore in the Shetlands. A damned nuisance!

Wednesday 9

Oceanic became a total wreck. Good news from the Front in France. We weighed and left Cromarty at 10 a.m., proceeding eastward out into the North Sea on to our own patrol. C.-in-C. forbids use of wireless between ten and three tonight. The whole of the First Fleet, battleships, cruisers, and destroyers, are to go over to the German coast and try to force an action. Unluckily we and the rest of the Tenth (or Ragtime) Cruiser Squadron are to remain behind to sweep for minelayers. All very sick at it. *Royal Arthur* rammed and sank a Swedish ship in a fog. Government will have to apologise. I was superintending painter on "bearing races" and very busy indeed all day long.

Thursday 10

No news of the First Fleet; they are lying in wait off Heligoland. The German advance on Paris has still been thoroughly checked, and our troops seem to be taking the offensive on the banks of the Marne. We continued on our patrol all day. I had a very busy day again, reconstructing 6-inch sights, in this case the gunlayer's range dials of A1. The present state of affairs leaves me no time to get bored, which is a jolly good thing, and I am constantly employed. Mr. Kiddle is setting up an agitation to reconstruct the control system, but at present he hasn't met with much success in any direction.

Friday 11

On our patrol all day. The Commander sprang a surprise G.Q.s on us in the forenoon, much to the chagrin of "Guns," and this was followed by group exercise and drill. Very dirty weather all the day. We had extraordinary luck in the evening, just missing a mine by a few yards, and if it hadn't been for the rough weather we should have been almost certain to have struck it. We stopped, and exploded it with rifle fire; it made a terrific din and sent up a huge column of water. Later we sighted another farther off and exploded it as before. No news from the Front or of the First Fleet.

Saturday 12

Destroyed two more mines by rifle fire. The *King Alfred* of the Sixth Cruiser Squadron joined us for two days at 4 p.m., while her flagship, the *Drake*, is in harbour. Usual routine all day. Good news from the Front, where the Germans have commenced to retreat. The report that the *Pathfinder* was sunk by a submarine, and not a mine, is completely untrue and a fabrication*. At 6 p.m. the squadron captured a German sailing vessel, bound for Hamburg with beef and hide. We sent her into Scapa with a prize crew. Very rough all day, and the consequence was we could not carry any gun-room scuttles.

Sunday 13

First Fleet returned, having made a complete sweep of North Sea and Heligoland Bight, and seen nothing at all of German Fleet. Usual routine all day. Boarded two Danish steamers and got some Copenhagen news, but nothing that was of much interest. Still rough.

Monday 14

On our patrol all day. Heard that the *Vindictive* has made a valuable capture in the Atlantic. We sighted another mine at 7 a.m., and sent away the sea-boat to examine it. They took it on board, and we are to land it when next we go into port, in order that the authorities may attempt to glean some information from it. Six-inch aiming tube firing at a target in the forenoon: three runs either side, and quite good results on the whole. A very dull, dreary, wet, "North Sea" day. Had a very jovial evening in the gun-room, and the Commander sent down to request us not to make such a bloody din!

---

* HMS *Pathfinder* was sunk on Saturday, 5 September 1914 by the German U-21. The magazine exploded causing the ship to sink within minutes with the loss of 259 men. There were 11 survivors.

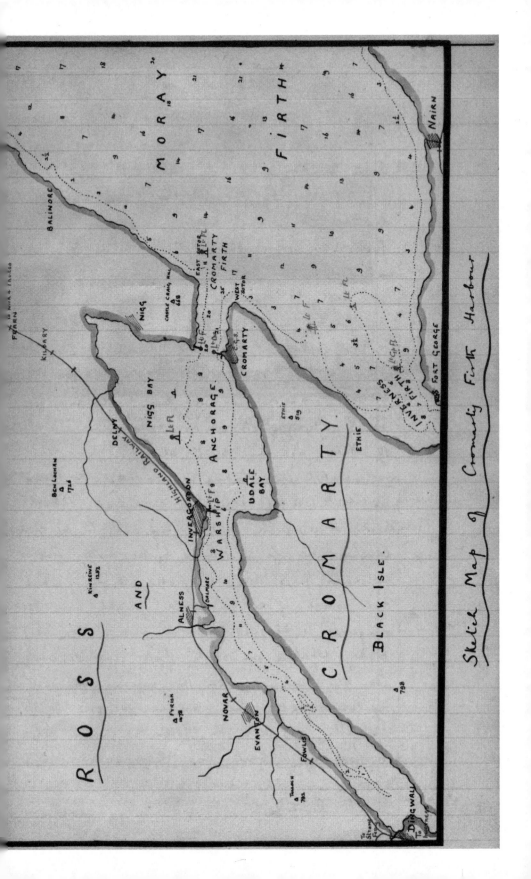

Sketch Map of Cromarty Firth Harbour

Tuesday 15

A big gale all day made things very uncomfortable. Those of us who sleep on after shelter deck had to go below at 2 a.m. The squadron at full strength with the exception of the *Theseus* and *Edgar*. Considerable difficulty in getting Poldhu* through owing to the unfavourable weather conditions. Although when we eventually did get it through it was very satisfactory. Today our seniority as midshipmen commences, as we are dated from September 15th. The Captain told me we shall now have to start keeping midshipmen's journals, and the Staff Paymaster will demand them.

Wednesday 16

We communicated at 7 a.m. with rest of squadron and then left them for Cromarty. Passed the *Roxburgh* at 10 a.m. Divisional gunnery drills and lectures in the forenoon. I got the old Dumaresq out of the top, passed down the range dial, and got the painter on with his manifold jobs. We entered the Moray Firth at 11 a.m., Cromarty Firth at 3.45, and anchored in between Invergordon and Cromarty at 4.30. The collier came alongside, and we rigged for coaling preparatory to starting early tomorrow morning. Found the *Hawke* and the *Edgar* and the Second Cruiser Squadron in harbour.

Thursday 17

The ghastly and revolting atrocities of the German fiends on the defenceless Belgians make me boil with rage. Rape, Ravage, and Rant are the German watchwords in this war. Right, Revenge, and Retrenchment shall be ours. God grant the defenceless may be avenged. One of our submarines has sunk the German cruiser *Hela***. German submarines sighted in Moray Firth. Commenced to coal ship at 6 a.m, and with a short interval for breakfast, continued until 10.40, taking in 450 tons. The foc'sle and foretop holds were broken down most of the time, due to broken slide rods. Watch-keeping officers excused, and "No. 1" took our hold instead of Mr. Oxlade. Got on shore in the afternoon for a few hours, went by train to get some stores from Dingwall, and then came back to tea at Invergordon. Met several gun-room officers from the Second Cruiser Squadron, including Scrimgeour-Wedderburn and several friends of Edel's at Trondhjem. Received a welcome mail at last.

* Long-range wireless from the station at Poldhu in Cornwall.
* On the morning of 13 September 1914, SMS *Hela* was torpedoed 6 miles south-west of Heligoland by *E9*.

Friday 18

In harbour all day. Acting A.P. Cockerill, R.N.R., joined ship for passage to H.M.S. *Hawke*. The *Endymion* came in at 8 a.m. and began coaling immediately. The *Dryad* left at noon with mails for our squadron out in the North Sea. Leave to the P.O.s and C.P.O.s of the starboard watch for a few hours in the afternoon. Most of them celebrated it by getting pretty squiffy after six weeks consecutively on board. Most of the midshipmen also on shore. I took a day on board to relieve the watch-keeper. Large detachments of men from Second Cruiser Squadron went route marching.

September 18th 1914
H.M.S. CRESCENT
Flagship, Tenth Cruiser Squadron

Dear Mother,

Many thanks for letters and socks (not sox, I believe). It was very kind to ask if I should like provisions sent, but perishable goods would be no good, I am afraid, as they might be a very long time in the post; still, a few other sorts of things now and then would be very welcome. The North Sea at its best is but a dull place, and as winter begins to come on it is a most God-forsaken hole, with continual rain, mist, fogs, alternating with gales and rough weather. I believe the geography books call it the North Sea or German Ocean. "What's in a name?"

At the beginning of the war I did not expect it to last long from a naval point of view, and consequently left most of my clothes with Gieves in my big green trunk at Portsmouth.

At present, as we are evidently going to remain here for some time, I am badly in need of some, left in the trunk. I should be very much obliged if you would write to them and tell them to send the following things, which will be found somewhere in the trunk:

One pair boots, one pair sea-boots (important), half-dozen flannel shirts, and as many collars as there are, also handkerchiefs. The next time you are feeling energetic in the knitting line, woollen gloves and a scarf would be much appreciated.

By the way, the young Anderson killed at the Front, about whom I questioned you, is a brother-in-law of one of our midshipmen; it may be of interest that this fellow has nine brothers and three brothers-in-law—twelve in all; of these, three are in the Regular Army, one in the Navy, four in the Territorials, two have joined Kitchener's Army, and two have volunteered as temporary surgeons in the R.N. Volunteer Reserve. Two of the army ones are dead, and the navy one was saved from the Amphion. Our Captain's secretary, Assistant Paymaster Cockrem, was at school with Harold Wacher.

Some old benevolent "Johnny" has decided to present the Fleet with an innumerable supply of gramophones; we had already bought one, but his new records come in useful and help to amuse our gunroom, which is quite a cosy little hole when you get used to the thick atmosphere. Please thank Mrs. Drake very much for her socks; which were hers? Please send George's address. I hope the good folks at home won't forget that their first duty is to the wives and children of bluejackets and soldiers without support, even before the Belgian refugees, and certainly before German prisoners. Their atrocities in Belgium are too revolting. By the way, in future you can address letters to Midshipman Scrimgeour, Royal Navy, as the rank of acting midshipman, held since the beginning of the war, has now been confirmed.

Nearly everybody is growing beards and moustaches now, as shaving-water is a waste of precious coal to work the fresh water distiller, and also shaving is an unnecessary nuisance. If we stop here long enough, I shall get quite a good beard.

Why does not daddy get a rifle and practise firing at birds from the roof? He might be quite useful if the projected German attack on England ever comes off. I hope Jimmy and Billy are being drilled, and Peggy initiated in the mysteries of first-aid nursing.

How is our district doing in the recruiting line?

I have just remembered those lovely peaches I was going to gorge before I went away; I feel more incensed against the Germans than ever; the insolence of preventing me eating my peaches is a far greater offence than all the Belgian atrocities, I am sure.

The party leaving Swanbister deprived us of a welcome change of diet (grouse) for a bit, but several people in Scotland are sending consignments of game to the Fleet, and we get some now and then. The Germans have invented a splendid game, so our submarines tell us. They come out of harbour a mile or two, well inside their protecting mine-fields, under cover of night or fog. They then fire off all their guns, a terrific cannonade for hours; they knock a few spars, strays, and things about, possibly lowering a mast and dropping a few boats overboard. Then they return to harbour and report a huge naval victory over the British. This has had to be given up, as the German officers and men, who are really quite sound at heart and ready to come out and fight, if they were allowed, gave the show away.

By the way, in addition to letters of news, if you get any photos of things or people at home, I should find them very interesting.

Stanley and Sophie are the last people I should have expected to enjoy hop-picking; give them both my love.

I hear turkeys will be very scarce this year; Auntie Maud should do well.

No more now.

Excuse this disjointed effusion, but I write a few lines

whenever the spirit moves me. Is daddy very busy? I should enjoy his opinions on the war, especially his expert financial views. Very best love to all at Wickhambreaux.

From
TOBY.

Saturday 19

R.A. Second Cruiser Squadron shifted his flag from the *Shannon* to the *Cochrane*. *Shannon* went into the floating dock, stationed here, for repairs; and rest of Second Cruiser Squadron put to sea at 9 a.m. H.M.S. *Sappho* came in at 9.30 a.m. from Loch Ewe, and placed herself under our orders as she is to join the Tenth Cruiser Squadron; she will put to sea on Monday. Hands aired night clothing after divisions. Lieut.-Commander Beasley relieved Lieutenant Wilson as officer (in lieu of Sub-Lieutenant) for gun-room duties. Completed with stores during the afternoon. N.C. Day from *Sappho* (Exmouth term at Dartmouth) came on board with official papers and had a drink in the gun-room. We weighed and put to sea at 5.30 to return to our patrol. Received a broken thermos flask by post (I don't know who sent it) from Junior Army and Navy Stores.

Sunday 20

It is rumoured that Germany intends to attack London with a gigantic aerial fleet. I hope we are properly prepared. Bad news of the loss of the depot-ship *Fisgard* off Portland in a gale comes through. She was bound with dockyard stores for Cromarty. A very rough night. We took several big seas in. Those sleeping on deck had to go below. Joined the squadron at 10 a.m. The gale continued all day. Conditions most uncomfortable. The *Edgar* proceeded to Cromarty and then to Newcastle to dry dock. The routine with regard to ships of our squadron proceeding to Cromarty to coal will continue in turn as at present. The *Endymion* goes next.

Monday 21

On our patrol all day. The gale continued, and, although the barometer rose, got but little better. G.Q.s in the forenoon. Rigged a net at loader to safeguard practice cartridges, and fitted a range dial on port side after-bridge.

Exchanged stores with rest of squadron during the dog-watches, although the lowering of sea-boats was very difficult owing to the big sea running. Physical drill at 4.30. Wireless via Poldhu says Battle of the Aisne is still raging.

Tuesday 22

Better weather today. The *Sappho* joined Flag at 8 a.m. Exercised after control starboard side firing all the forenoon 1-inch aiming tube and rifle. The First Lieutenant was quite a success for the first attempt. Plenty doing all day. Received a weird collection of wireless fragments, the only intelligible news being that either the *Hogue* and *Aboukir* have been sunk or have sunk something. But we have no confirmation or repetition. Physical drill in the dog-watches very amusing, as the old Admiral, the Secretary, and the Captain joined in, and we had great fun wrestling, cock-fighting, and jumping the horse. The Second Destroyer Flotilla, supported by Second Cruiser Squadron, will attack the German patrol at mouth of the Ems tonight.

Wednesday 23

Loss of the *Hogue* confirmed, also *Cressy*; *Aboukir* uncertain. A great disaster, as they were excellent ships, just older than the *Drake* class. Most of the snotties were of the Grenvile term, a year junior to us. Do not know whether they were all killed or not. Believe young Cameron was one of them. The Admiralty postponed the attack on the Ems patrol due to bad weather. All British warships withdrawn from North Sea temporarily, as it is infested with German submarines, except our squadron, the Tenth, or "ragtime," who thus hold a very distinguished but dangerous position. Captain Hyde-Parker of the *Endymion* is making quite a name for himself by the stupid antics of his ship. They were in trouble as usual today. Squadron scattered for target practice. Nine a.m. we lowered two targets, but both were destroyed by the choppy sea, and we had to give up the idea of firing, which was disappointing. Gym on quarter-deck in dog-watches as usual. Most of ward-room and gun-room rolled up, had good fun with horses v. bucks, skipping, single-sticks, boxing, fencing, cock-fighting, etc.

Thursday 24

The Battle of the Aisne still continues—in point of view of duration, it easily beats the previous battles of this war viz. Haelen, Mons, Altkirch, Lunéville, Cambrai, Compiègne, and the Marne. The Russians have captured Jarolslav, and the Serbo-Montenegrin armies are all around Sarajevo, capital of Bosnia. It is reported that the *Breslau* and *Goeben*, sold some weeks ago to Turkey, are being remanned by Germans sent overland. I hope the Mediterranean Squadron will not make a second mistake. On our patrol all day. Usual routine. A great game of twos and threes on the Q.D. in the dog-watches. It appears from wireless messages received that the *Aboukir*, *Hogue*, and *Cressy* were sunk between Rotterdam and Harwich by a flotilla of four German submarines, two of which were sunk*. There is some danger of hostile divers obtaining our secret signal code-books, so these are being removed. The Japanese have allowed the German China Squadron to escape from Kiao-Chao, and they will be a great nuisance. Submarine A.E. lost by an accident on patrol with thirty-five lives off Sydney.

Friday 25

Patrolling as usual. Destroyed a mine by rifle fire. Light Q.F. gunfiring with night defence control stations in the forenoon. Poor firing, although certainly the weather was bad. Skylarking as usual in the dog-watches. I had a row with Tottenham in the gun-room. A small German squadron crept over to our coast to support submarine attacks on Cromarty and Rosyth, but they were chased back to the Ems; unluckily we were not fast enough to catch them. We are still the only squadron at sea, a risky honour. Armed German liner *Spreewald* captured by the *Berwick* in the North Sea. The German cruiser *Emden* has bombarded Madras and badly damaged our Indian Ocean trade.

Saturday 26

Patrolling as usual. Overhauled more ships than usual. News came through that the Russian cruiser *Bayan* in the Baltic has sunk a German cruiser and two German destroyers**. Later the news that the whole German High Seas Fleet has put to sea in the Baltic, probably to attack the Russian coast. I wish we could get at them. There is a rumour of our sweeping either the Sound or the Great or Little Belt and so running through into the Baltic. This would be possible, as Denmark and Sweden are neutral. Lists of officers lost and saved from the *Hogue*, *Cressy*, and *Aboukir* came through.

---

* HMS *Hogue* was sunk with her sisters, *Cressy* and *Aboukir*, by a single German U-boat, *U-9*. More than 1,000 lives were lost.
** The Russians captured the German code books – a priceless asset.

Delmege, Corbyn, W.A.H. Harrison, and Froude are among those drowned.
We captured a suspicious-looking trawler fitted with wireless, and though
Dutch, with German papers.

September 26th 1914
H.M.S. CRESCENT

Dear Mother,

How are you all getting on at home? I am so glad Uncle John and
Auntie Connie are going to Quaives. I hope they enjoy themselves.
Very many thanks for the woollen goods you have sent. Daddy's
vest and the socks are most useful, as it is exceedingly cold by
night on watch even now, and in November and December and the
early months of next year it will be far worse.

Among my books brought back from the Cornwall you will find
a big brown leather book, "Inman's Nautical Tables;" also a
green book, the 1914 "Nautical Almanac;" I should like these
sent as soon as possible; also, by the way, Sennet and Oram's
"Marine Steam Engine."

Have you got any walnuts this year? If you have plenty, I should
love some; apples are another thing that would be much appreciated.

Do you mind getting me some more visiting-cards printed when
you have time. I will give you an example of what I want; no
bigger, as that enclosed is just a convenient size. Did I ask you
for George's address last time I wrote? Anyhow, will you send it
me sometime. Thank daddy for his splendid long letter.

I have noticed that several friends and relations are rather apt to
treat you as a sort of exchange for domestic servants. I wonder if
you could look out for a job for me (not me personally). The
man I recommend is aged forty-five, a retired naval petty officer,
a teetotaller, guaranteed a very capable and reliable man, for
whose trustworthiness I will vouch. He is married, with no
children, and wants a job as caretaker or lodge keeper or

something in that line. Only a very moderate wage, as he has a pension. I don't expect it is much good asking you, only I thought you might possibly hear of something.

Daddy asks if I want any money. I do not at present, unless it is with which to feed the fishes, as we have nothing to spend it on, except messing, and my pay just covers that. Still, I should like my allowance to accumulate while I am away, as it will go pretty fast, I imagine, after the war.

I am thinking of volunteering to go to the Front with the Naval Brigade when they go, as this is such dull, dry work till the Germans come out. But I am afraid they won't let me go, as active service officers are much needed afloat, and the Naval Brigade will be officered chiefly by Reserve officers and Volunteer officers who know very little about Service life afloat and would be far more useful on shore.

I hope you are all on the lookout for spies. The father of one of our officers arrested, or caused to be arrested, his butler on suspicion, and he proved to be a dangerous alien spy. (This has been passed by the Press Bureau, I don't think!)

Is George only a private? I should have thought that with his experience of the South African War they would have made him a corporal.

Is your camera in working order? If it is I could take some snaps which would be very interesting when the war is over and the censorship removed.

Please don't send any clothes other than what I ask for, as space is very limited for stowing surplus clothes away. If you want to send things, send food of sorts.

No time for more now.

Very best love to all.
From
TOBY.

Sunday 27

It is feared that the submarine *E4* has been lost off Heligoland. The Battle of the Aisne continues. The Germans reinforced by troops from East Prussia have regained ground lost on the right wing at St. Quentin. Russian investment of Przemsyl. On our patrol as usual. The *Sappho* and *Dryad* were temporarily detached from squadron and sent to Scapa on special service. Captured a four-masted German barque three months from Brazil.

Monday 28

A filthy night, very big sea running this morning. We were going into harbour today, but cannot get there before nightfall, and as we are only allowed to enter by day, we shall have to wait until tomorrow. The officers' commissariat has given out, and we are living on salt pork and ship's biscuit. Conditions altogether most unpleasant. More submarines missing, but it is hoped they are sheltering from the storm in some of the more deserted of the Norwegian fjords. German submarines supposed to be sheltering on our coast. First Light Cruiser Squadron and two destroyer flotillas searching for them. Our battleships are now based on Poolewe.

Tuesday 29

Came up the Moray Firth at full speed to lessen the danger of attacks by hostile submarines supposed to be sheltering here. Anchored in the Cromarty Firth at 7.30 a.m. Three submarines and three seaplanes have been based here for defensive purposes within the last three days. Coaled ship, taking in 480 tons. It was a double-derrick collier, and we had a most efficient coaling. I had a row with "Guns" over "Empties," always a source of trouble between foc'sle and foretop holds. The gunnery staff brought out a scheme for the modernisation and re-armament of H.M.S. *Crescent*; personally I consider it not worth while. Other ships in harbour—Second Cruiser Squadron, *Endymion* of the Tenth, *Argyll* of the Third, and depot-ships. Snow in the distance on Ben Wyvis; this helped to create gorgeous sunset.

Wednesday 30

Received good mail from home. The *Argyll* went into the floating drydock. *Endymion* weighed and proceeded to sea 7 a.m. *Royal Arthur* came in 10 a.m. Route march for our starboard watch in the afternoon; very good exercise for them. The Second Cruiser Squadron have done it whenever in harbour for a long time. Eight miles stiff walk inland over the moors and

H.M.S. "CRESCENT"

Sketch Plan shewing Armament

two pints of beer at the end, then straight back to the ship. First Lieutenant in charge, also Lieutenant (G.) and four midshipmen. A very humorous affair, but ship's band a great success. Old "Pops" has but little idea of managing a large quantity of men, and "Guns" was two cuts above helping him. Cobb motor-biked to Dingwall with despatches for the naval victualling agent. Ran over two hens, one dog, and a sheep. Stood him a bottle of fizz to commemorate it. Gun-room wine store just received twelve dozen fizz.

September 30th 1914
H.M.S. CRESCENT

Dear Auntie Ethel,

Very many thanks for your letter and for Auntie Dora's enclosed; I hope you will drive out of her head the lingering idea of sympathy for the Germans, with which her point of view seems stricken. The Kaiser is mad, but that is no excuse for the appalling atrocities committed in France and Belgium, quite apart from vandalism, such as at Louvain and Rheims— the guilt for these crimes is indelibly inscribed on the judgment-hooks of the impartial critic, against the German military officers and N.C.O.s who have instigated their men and have themselves committed the ghastly orgies of drunkenness, destruction, cruelty, and rapine.

I am proud to belong to a nation whose bounden duty it is to stamp out the military caucus and displace the depraved dynasty who have caused these disasters to civilisation.

Before the war I admired and respected the Germans as an honourable and enterprising nation, although quite realising their lack of scruples in international affairs. Although our naval opponents have shown considerable proof of that chivalry with which the Franco-English encounters of the past were usually tempered, yet the hypocritical behaviour of the military forces of a nation professing culture makes one gasp at the brazen audacity of the perpetrators in pursuing their career of crime against humanity. Enough of hot air!

It is very kind of you to make woollen goods for us; it certainly is very cold and unpleasant in the North Sea, and will get far worse as the season advances, but the Admiralty are showing better organisation than in the past, and the men are getting plenty of warm clothes. Personally I am quite well off for woollen clothes, as mother sent me a lot.

Daddy also keeps our gun-room supplied with papers. Eatables are really the most acceptable presents, as tinned meat and ship's biscuit and salt pork are our chief staples of diet, except for a few days after leaving harbour, when we go in periodically for a few hours to coal and reprovision.

Unluckily, being an old ship, we are not fitted with refrigerators, and nothing will keep very long.

We all love chocolate, which is very nice in the long night watches; but do not bother about us too much, as the army are having a very severe time, I expect. We can do nothing until the Germans come out, except keep the seas clear for commerce, although, of course, there are plenty of submarine attacks and destroyer raids on both sides. In two years Percy Scott will be right—submarines and seaplanes will drive the battleships from the sea. Beresford was also right when he raised his cry of "Speed!" unavailingly; if we had built more fast cruisers, the Emden could never have committed the depredations on our commerce in the Indian Ocean that she has done. The cry of "If" leads one on to think of what might have been if Lord Roberts' ideas and warnings had been listened to, but "ifs" are worthless things; our conduct has exceeded all my highest hopes; the Government have done well because they are full of capable men (scoundrels if you will). The immediate appointment of Kitchener was remarkable, as if they realised, as we did, that he was essential to the War Office, why was he not sent there years before?

The war has made men out of thousands of monkeys, and is undoubtedly a much needed tonic to the British Empire. I am afraid you anticipated matters in addressing me as lieutenant; it is a rank which cannot be attained in the navy until long technical courses have been gone through in the various subjects of engineering, gunnery, navigation, seamanship, and torpedo; at present I am a midshipman. I expect you were misled by the rank of lieutenant in the army. I will give you a list of equivalent naval and military ranks, which may be of interest, and you will see that a lieutenant in the navy ranks with, but before (as the navy is the senior service), captains in the army.

NAVY

Admiral of the Fleet
Admiral
Vice-Admiral
Rear-Admiral
Commodore
Captain
Commander
Lieutenant-Commander
Lieutenant
Sub-Lieutenant
Midshipman
Naval Cadet (sea-going)
Naval Cadet (Osborne and Dartmouth)

ARMY

Field-Marshal
General
Lieutenant-General
Major-General
Brigadier-General
Colonel
Lieutenant-Colonel

Major
Captain
Lieutenant (First)
Lieutenant (Second)
Subaltern
Military Cadet (Sandhurst and Woolwich)

I hear that all my friends at home are joining the army. George Wilson was offered a commission after the South African War, but refused it, so it is very sporting of him to enlist as a private again. I volunteered for the Naval Brigade to go to the Front, but they are only sending Reserve and Volunteer officers who are of little or no use afloat, and as far as possible no active service naval officers are going, so that is off for me.

I'm afraid the German Fleet won't ever risk a fleet action, so it will be a matter of submarines, unless the unexpected occurs.

Now I must turn in and go to sleep, as sleep is a valuable commodity to us.

Don't suppose I shall get a chance to write again for some time. Very best love to all in your district, including Tentworth, etc.

From
TOBY.

OCTOBER

Thursday 1

The *Emden* is doing considerable damage to our trade in the Indian Ocean, and there are still several other cruisers at large. The *Cumberland* is doing excellent work off the Cameroons and has sunk a gunboat and captured nine large valuable German liners. The Canadian Expeditionary Force is due to leave in a few days. The Battle of the Aisne still continues with varying success. Klück's army on the German right is their weak spot and is reported unofficially to be in a bad position. The fighting is fierce and continuous. The Germans in Belgium are operating with a view to the siege of Antwerp. The German army has advanced right into Russia and is attempting unsuccessfully so far to cross the Niemen. Meanwhile the main Russian Army threatens Breslau and Cracow, is besieging Przemsyl and finishing off Austrians. Main scheme is to advance simultaneously on Berlin and Vienna with 5,000,000 men while leaving a masking force in East Prussia. Another route march for port watch under Lieut.-Commander Beasley, Torps, and four snotties. I went again. Got three hours' leave afterwards, and got introduced to a very nice little girl, Mina George. Also met an awful good subaltern in the Camerons, a real good sort. Midshipman Florence of Sturges' Exmouth Term came on shore from the *Drake*. She has two guns out of action from a collision with a Danish merchant vessel. Russell A.S., Murdoch, and P-Pinhey from *Royal Arthur* came to dinner in our gun-room, and we had a very festive evening. Drambuie much in evidence. Second Cruiser Squadron went to sea 6 a.m. *Drake* came in 7 a.m. The Third Cruiser Squadron came in 10 a.m., and the *Devonshire* changed places with the *Argyll* in the floating dock.

Friday 2

Weighed and proceeded to sea at 7 a.m. Went out through the Moray Firth at full speed. Joined the squadron at Rendezvous P3 at 5 p.m., and then continued our patrol work. The minelaying squadron—*Apollo, Andromache, Naiad*, etc .—have been put under the orders of our Admiral; so that, in addition to the eight ships of the Tenth Cruiser Squadron proper, he now controls three armed liners on the Shetland–Norway patrol, eleven minelayers, and the *Dryad* and *Sappho*. We communicated and distributed mails when we met the squadron at 5 p.m. Very much improved weather, although there is a heavy swell.

Saturday 3

A big combined sweep from Scotch coast across to Norway for all cruisers in the North Sea and for Second and Third Battle Squadrons under Vice-Admiral Warrender, ships working in pairs. This is to prevent the escape of a German cruiser force, said to be going to attempt to escape into the Atlantic via the Norwegian coast, in order to attack the Canadian contingent, which is about to leave for Europe. The weather has taken a decided turn for the worse and is most unpleasant. The loss of submarine *E1* is now practically certain. The Battle of the Aisne continues, now having lasted three weeks. In many places the Allies have forced back the Germans to the Somme. The Russians are before Cracow, where the Germans and Austrians are under Hindenberg.

Sunday 4

The Battle of the Aisne, the Russian advance on the Cracow-Przemsyl district and the German siege of Antwerp continue. Russian troops have been landed to reinforce the Antwerp garrison, but the very heavy German siege guns are sure to be dangerous later on, although at present they have had no success. The 1st cruiser squadron in the Mediterranean has been disbanded. The *Black Prince* and *Duke of Edinburgh* having been dispatched to the Indian Ocean to help run down the *Emden* and the *Defence* has gone to join the *Leviathan, Cornwall, Hyacinth* and *Astrea* under Admiral King-Hall at the Cape, while only the *Warrior* remains in the Mediterranean. The big sweep of the North Sea continues without incident in very nasty weather. A German seaplane sighted off the Dogger Bank, fired at by destroyers, and disappeared in a fog. It is a funny coincidence that the ill-fated *Cressy, Hogue,* and *Aboukir* were all named after battles won against our allies the French.

Monday 5

Filthy day. Divisions on the cable deck. No G.Q.s, much to the chagrin of "Guns." We were concerned in various operations in the North Sea, the exact nature and object of which is known alone to the Rear-Admiral, Secretary, "Flags," and the Skipper. Exchanged signals with the *Russell* of the Third Battle Squadron at midday. The Admiralty have not yet confirmed the loss of *E1*, but all hope has been given up definitely. The *Emden* still at large.

Tuesday 6

We have gone on to another wireless wave in direct communication with the C.-in-C., secret code, and are no longer on the commercial code, hence for the present we shall get no news of the war from the Poldhu station. The extensive operations continue. I think they are merely another method of sweeping. The first fruitful result is that a disguised German store-ship with oil fuel and stores was captured off the Scotch coast. Bad weather continues as usual. The Germans are reported to be going to try and creep down the Dutch coast, up the Scheldt, and so attack Antwerp from the sea.

Wednesday 7

German destroyers sunk off Dutch coast. The sea went down, but a thick North Sea fog set in. The senior naval officer at Loch Ewe, which has been used as principal base for all our battle squadrons since they left Scapa to obviate the danger of submarine attacks, reports German submarines sighted in vicinity. Consequently all colliers, store-ships, oil-ships, and depot-ships have been ordered to leave, and a new battleship base will be chosen in a remote spot in the Hebrides. We were suddenly ordered to chase on a given course at 4 p.m., but after a quarter of an hour at full speed we received "Negative chase." Object of first signal unknown.

Thursday 8

Learnt from *Albemarle* that the Russians under Rennenkampf have badly defeated the Germans and driven them back into Prussia. The Battle of the Aisne still continues. In the western end of the line, both sides are attempting to outflank the other. Thick fog made our operations hard to carry out, although occasional snatches of sunshine came through. Sea an oily calm. Owing to incorrect dead reckonings in both ships, we spoke to the *Albemarle*, now of the Third Battle Squadron, late Fifth, about midday and exchanged news. We attempted to communicate with the *Hawke* before she leaves for Invergordon, but failed. Had a wireless from the *Gibraltar*, who is retrieving her picket-boat at Scapa, that she will rejoin tomorrow. *Dryad* sighted suspicious sailing craft, proving to be disguised German minelayer from Brunsbuttel, and so sank her.

Friday 9

Fog became thicker than ever; you could not see fifty yards from the ship. We passed several tramps perilously close. The operations closed at 2 p.m., and we made back to our old patrol between Aberdeen and Denmark at six knots. Guns' crews stood by the guns all day. All signalling with rest of squadron, who rejoined, done by siren Morse. By luck we made the *Grafton* out from Cromarty and got a welcome mail. C.-in-C. asked our Admiral for a reliable cruiser, fit for a long steam, and he selected the *Gibraltar*, which has been forthwith detached. Much conjecture as to what she is to do. Personally I think it is to relieve the *Theseus* at Archangel in the White Sea.

The *Drake* has been sent to Spitzbergen to destroy the German fishing settlement there.

Saturday 10

On our patrol all day. Communicated with torpedo-boat No. 027 at 4 p.m.; she is acting as Admiralty despatch vessel, and brought us out the new Navy List. Very disappointed to find that gun-room officers have already been appointed to most of the new ships due to commission this month, such as the *Queen Elizabeth* and the *Tiger;* many of the midshipmen are junior to us, and we are learning nothing but sea-going experience in these old ships. All the Dartmouth cadets who have been made midshipmen have gained from six months to two and a half years, but I suppose it will all be squared up after the war. My opinion is that the Captain does not take nearly strict enough measures with regard to the boarding of neutral vessels.

Sunday 11

Very stringent regulations have been issued with regard to neutral shipping in the North Sea, all fishing craft being prohibited anywhere there; this is a good step to end minelaying. The Germans have started laying mines disguised as periscopes, to make us ram them and so hit the mines (this information gained by spies). On our patrol as usual. Nasty weather again. Met the *Liverpool* and *Southampton* with two destroyers chasing a German supposed to be in this area.

Monday 12

Came up the Moray Firth in the early morning and anchored in the Cromarty Firth 9 a.m.; found the *Hawke* and *Endymion* and Third Cruiser Squadron in harbour. Coaled ship 600 tons; foc'sle hold jolly good; a very dirty coal, owing to the high wind, which blew dust everywhere. We had a practical example of the German spy danger, as a large portion of the coal was soaked in benzine, and several detonator fuses were found, which, if successfully ignited, would soon have demolished both us and the collier; luckily they were detected. This must have been the work of German spies. A mishap to the whaler while being lowered; a rotten fall parted, and one man broke his arm and another his collar-bone; both were disobeying regulations, and were before foremost fall. Received an excellent mail. News of the fall of Antwerp received with disappointment; jubilation at the exploits of the great Marine-Naval Brigade; sorry to hear some of them interned in Holland. A very jovial evening helped along by Drambuie; Messrs. Bacon, Oxlade, and Buddle and "Flags" were gun-room guests, and damned good ones, too. Wrote a note to Mina. Midshipmen applied for appointments to a new battleship, but the Captain refused to sanction application, as he could not spare us. This was disappointing, but nevertheless a compliment to the midshipmen, who undoubtedly have a large share in the responsibilities of the ship. Then I personally applied for an appointment to the Naval Brigade, but received the answer that no active service officers can be spared, only Reserve and Volunteer Reserve officers being sent. I thought that I might possibly see more service on land, but perhaps it will be better to go on with this job.

October 12th 1914
H.M.S. CRESCENT

Dear Mother,

Very many thanks for all letters and parcels. I returned the thermos (broken) to the stores, and received a communication some days later to the effect that it had not arrived, but will wait and see for the present. The things you have sent are most useful and welcome, but send no more clothes for the present, as I am full up in my sea-chest and no spare gear is needed. It was very kind indeed of Mrs. Sillars to knit me the scarf; it will keep me wonderfully warm, and I am most grateful. Please thank her very much from me, and I will try and write myself if I can spare the time. Also do the same to Aunt Arabella; the sterling worth of her regard is more ethereal than worldly, as I am of agnostic tendencies and by no means a strict Christian, believing the Bible quite good enough without extracts in book form; nevertheless, she is a worthy soul, and I appreciate her point of view. Thank Bob very much for his letters, which interest me greatly, and tell him that as I now regard him as one of the family he must not expect regular answers (I am always rude to near relations), and he can demand to share the news (what little there is) in my effusions to you, should he be so inclined.

This letter must seem almost as mad as some of Auntie Ruth's
(it must run in the family).

Give Jimmy and Peggy my very best love and thank them
both many times for their letters, which are splendid, especially
Peggy's.

Burbery must be a great loss; give him my good wishes when
possible.

Owing to the burning of a naval mail-waggon some days ago, I
have probably lost some of your letters, but doubt if there was
anything of importance, as I have noticed no great gap in the
dates of those I have received.

Give everyone at home my love, and also Aunt Do and Uncle
Jack, if you write to either. (I am afraid I am in Uncle Jack's
black books, as I have not heard from him for a very long
time.)

You seem to have been having a very gay time at home.
Extraordinary how you manage to enjoy yourselves whenever
I'm out of the house. We always get on so well by post; I seem
to act like a wet blanket on all your ideas of enjoyment as soon
as I come back—sack all the servants, all the children
infectious, no guests, swollen livers, and constipated stomachs.
Directly I go, lurid letters of enjoyment, shooting house-
parties, frivolous evenings, open bowels, etc. An Englishman is
never happy without a "grouse." This is my grousy page. I
enjoy the descriptions of your gay times.

What a pity Joko has not got longer hair; it is so very short.
(Mum's the word.) (Not passed by the Censor.)

Who is the pretty girl you mentioned as having arrived at
Wickhambreaux, possibly a Belgian. Details, please. This is
more interesting to a naval officer aged seventeen than details
of the milk-giving propensities of the new Jersey cow, or how

many eggs the old hen has laid. The man I asked you to look out for a place for is ineligible until after the war, as he is still on active service. Will give you his address when needed; at present he is chief gunner's mate of this ship (he was petty officer of my term at Osborne).

Good luck to everyone. Excuse this extraordinarily weird letter and weirder writing, but I feel in a sketchy mood just now.

Germans!

Your dutiful son,
ALEXANDER SCRIMGEOUR.

Tuesday 13

Route march for the starboard watch, eight miles stiff walking. Called on Mina afterwards, found the whole family down with the measles. Went on to the Royal Hotel, where the Camerons officers' mess is (the Cameron Highlanders' recruiting base is here), and had several drinks with Lieutenant McLeod, an awful good sort. The *Antrim* reports that she was attacked by German submarines 205 miles east of Rathsay Head three days ago, but their torpedoes missed. The Germans are having a good time just at present, as a Boer rebellion has broken out in Cape Colony, the Russian cruiser *Pallada* has been sunk in the Baltic, although the *Bayan* and *Admiral Makavoff* escaped, and the Russians have abandoned the siege of Przemysl, and spies are doing good work at home. Received a fine consignment of goods from daddy. Betted L.E.J. £5 I am a skipper before he is.

Wednesday 14

The store-ship *Alcinous* came alongside at 10 a.m., and we took in a large supply of Paymaster's stores and other gear.

Tested the 9-2 sights*. Route march for the port watch. I went to have tea with Mina afterwards, and found her very sweet indeed, but with a nasty attack of measles. I expect I shall catch them, too, now. Several other

---

*The 9.2in gun on the *Crescent's* quarterdeck.

people went out for trips on the local motorbikes. Found two fellows in the local hotel talking suspiciously broad Scotch, and they tried to pump us carefully. So we told the police to shadow them. Two Zeppelins were reported over Fort Rose last night, also at Delny. Personally I don't believe it. Tested the range-finder before sunset.

Thursday 15

The crying necessity of our Empire at present, more than 20 Dreadnoughts, 50 submarines, 500 aeroplanes, or 50,000 men, is to stamp out the German spy peril now rampant in the British Isles, which is a continual source of great danger to the nation, both by information supplied to enemy and by damage done to us. Let's hope the Government will soon realise this. Churchill has made an awful hash of the Antwerp show. His business is at the Admiralty and not dabbling about on land expeditions. If Kitchener needs any assistance, fully equipped naval brigades should be supplied him to do what he likes with, and not played about with by Winston Churchill. Anyhow, no skilled ratings should be wasted in naval brigades, owing to their value afloat. Landed for two hours at nine, and started riding a small 2½h.p. Humber motor-cycle and thoroughly enjoyed the first attempt. *Hawke* and *Endymion* put to sea, and the *Grafton* came in, both between 9 and 11 a.m. Took in more ammunition and shell from the ammunition lighter. Weighed and left harbour at 4.30 p.m., the boom being specially opened for us to pass (the boom has been fitted while we were at sea last time). A gorgeous sunset— a fitting close to a glorious day like midsummer.

Proceeded to make our squadron out in the North Sea at fourteen knots through Moray Firth. I got in the soup with "No. 1." Panic caused on the bridge in the first watch by a trawler firing a signal rocket.

Friday 16

Theseus reports being unsuccessfully attacked by German submarine, which was observed by seaplanes later to be moving in direction of Cromarty. Nothing has been heard of the *Hawke* since she put to sea and parted company with *Endymion* (was escorting German steamer *Nordsee* into Lerwick). Either her wireless has broken down or else she has been sunk by submarines. We were to join the squadron at 11 a.m., but this order was cancelled and we were told to proceed to a rendezvous fifty miles due east of Lerwick, a position back in the old Iceland patrol.

At midday we passed through a large number of pieces of wreckage and saw some lifebuoys floating about, so we stopped to examine, but could find no clue. The wreckage may be possibly that of the *Hawke*, or otherwise some steamer blown up by a mine. G.Q.s in the morning. "Guns" quarrelled with the Captain, Commander, and "No. 1" in turn, but received considerable moral support from the Admiral. Join squadron 6 p.m. *Edgar* in the soup for using her searchlights.

Saturday 17

The object of our cruising up north is to form a complete cordon, from Shetland across to Norway, in company with Third Battle Squadron, Second Cruiser Squadron, Third Cruiser Squadron, and the armed liners attached to us. Thus the oil-ships bound from U.S.A. to Germany should be captured. Four of them already have been sent to Lerwick with prize crews. All hope of the *Hawke* has now been given up. It is reported that only four officers and sixty men were saved. German submarines are particularly active just now, as the *Antrim* was again unsuccessfully attacked today. At 4 p.m. we sighted a big steamer and chased for three hours, when we overhauled her, and she proved to be the *Proper III.*, a valuable prize with foodstuffs for Germany. We sent a prize crew of six A.B.s under Lieut.-Commander Bacon, R.N.R., and Mr. McLachlan, the junior boatswain, on board her, with orders to take her into Lerwick; I should have loved to have gone. *Theseus* captured *U.S.A.* and let her go through ignorance and could not catch her again, so the armed liner *Alsatian* was sent in chase. During the day the new system of blockade has captured ten food-ships.

Sunday 18

H.M.S. *Crescent* was attacked by submarines. At 6.30 a.m. the bridge lookouts reported an object on the water about five miles off. This was made out by glasses to be a submarine on the surface. The day had broken and light was getting strong, but the submarine had not sighted us. The O.O.W. woke the Captain and the Admiral, and we immediately notified the C.-in-C. and our adjacent ships fifteen miles distant either side—viz., H.M. ships *Edgar* and *Endymion*. It was decided to attack the submarine, and we altered course towards it, ringing down for full speed, fourteen knots being almost immediately forthcoming. "Repel torpedo attack" was sounded off (as night defence stations were considered more suitable for action with submarines even in daytime), and the guns' crews on watch closed up and loaded. About five minutes later, when about 8,000 yards away, we were discovered, and the submarine submerged. The order was given to fire, and the two foc'sle guns opened at 8,000 yards, the shot going over. By this time the Gunnery-Lieutenant had arrived on the foc'sle with myself and his assistant, and he took over control from Lieut.-Commander Oxlade, R.N.R., who was on gun-watch at the time.

From the movement of the periscope of the submerged submarine through the water, she appeared to be moving towards us with the intention of attacking, but we were not caught napping, as the previous ships who have fallen victims to submarines have been. The guns now firing on her were the two foc'sle 6-inch (A1 and B1), also the two forward battery 6-inch (A2 and B2) and the two forward cable-deck six-pounders. The shot were falling about the periscope, the necessary range having been attained (the rate of change was very high, approximately twenty knots), but none hit. Suddenly a white streak came at us broadside on, and passed fifty yards under our stern. It had been fired from another submarine, which had been lying submerged and had not been previously sighted by us. The port battery guns opened fire on the new enemy, whose periscope was visible, but the first salvo was badly short, showing that the torpedo must have been fired at long range. Our first submarine was now getting so close (for we were still steaming towards her at full speed) that the foc'sle guns could not be depressed enough to bear. Realising that we intended to ram her, she submerged completely, and only just in time. She had been unable to fire a torpedo at us, owing to the fact that we never gave her time to turn broadside on, and the class of vessel to which she belongs is only fitted with broadside tubes. The port guns continued to fire, when suddenly the masthead lookout, who had gone aloft at daybreak, reported a third submarine on the starboard side. The starboard guns were slow in picking her up and never opened fire, as she soon submerged, and opinions differed as to whether she had ever fired a torpedo at us. All three submarines had now disappeared, and we steered S .72°W. full speed (the engine-room had now got us up to seventeen knots) to meet the *Edgar*. A wireless message was sent to Admiral Colville, commanding officer in charge of the Shetland defences, and two of the Scapa seaplanes, which by luck were at Lerwick, came out about two hours later to search for the submarines, while we warned all our ships in the vicinity of their presence. At midday they were sighted submerged steering S.37°E., and a destroyer flotilla was sent from Scapa in chase, but they were not seen again. The time from our first seeing the submarine to when the last one disappeared was twenty minutes, perhaps the most exciting I have ever spent. The men behaved well, and any excitement shown was due to over-keenness. The foc'sle guns and port battery fired well, the laying and training being good, but efficient spotting was impossible, due to the semi-daylight with the rising sun in our eyes and the minute size of the periscopes, which were an extremely small object and at first could scarcely be distinguished with the naked eye. The starboard battery were so engrossed in watching the firing of the port side that they were unable to open fire when the third submarine appeared on their side.

And this, and the fact that the "Klaxon" alarms did not work, were the only incidents that could be found fault with. Contrary to my expectations, the officers all went to their groups without any of the muddle which the obstinacy of J. Kiddle has so often caused in exercise actions. The Captain made a speech after quarters, congratulating the ship's company on their prompt answer of the bugle when turned in, and their general behaviour. It was the most exciting incident I have experienced. Some people think we sank the submarine on the port side, but I am convinced we did not actually hit her at all; if we had done so, it would have been entirely due to luck. In consequence of this attack, the line of blockade was changed from the north of the Shetlands (Muckle Flugga), north-westerly across to the Faeroes, and then across to the Norwegian coast. Only one ship captured today, and that by the battleship *Russell*. Details of the loss of *Hawke* received; seventy-five officers and men saved.

Wireless messages say that H.M.S. *Undaunted* and a flotilla of destroyers destroyed four German destroyers at the mouth of the Scheldt. She was only commissioned two months ago. This is a pleasing set-off to recent losses. On our patrol all day; quite dirty weather.

Note on the loss of H.M.S. Hawke

Apropos of the loss of the *Hawke*, it is interesting to note that 2 hours before she went to sea on her last trip, Capt Williams came on board to ask for 2 days extra in harbour to repair his engines. This was refused as he could still do 10 knots. In order to obviate the danger of submarine attacks it is customary for all our warships to leave and enter Moray Firth at full speed, minimum speed 17 knots. The *Hawke* could not possibly at forcing power do more than just over half this speed. Capt Williams realised the extreme danger of this, hence his personal appeal to the Admiral. His last words to the Flag Lieut. when leaving the Q.D. of the *Crescent*, were "it is pure murder sending the ship with over 500 officers and men on board to sea in this state."

His words proved correct in a disastrously short space of time. The story of the *Hawke* being stopped for boarding a ship, when hit by the submarine, was invented by the Admiralty to prevent unpleasant questions and a public outcry. She was attacked going out of the Moray Firth at maximum speed viz: 10 knots, and an extra 5 knots would have probably saved her. Those five knots could have been attained by an extra 2 days in harbour.

The above is strictly confidential, and were it discovered at the present time would lead to my dismissal from the service, but it is a point that may be of interest in future years.

Monday 19

On our patrol all day between Muckle Flugga and Foula. None of the required submarine oil-ships were met with, and none others were boarded, although I think we might have done so with advantage, as I am in favour of stricter measures. The Captain evidently does not want to give submarines a chance of firing at us when stopped, although we probably shall not meet any here. Yesterday's affair proves the theory that the German submarines do not work singly, but in groups of three or more. The battleships of the First Fleet are now based jointly on Tobermory and Stornoway, but submarines are reported in the Minch, so they will probably move south to Greenock or somewhere in the Clyde. Reports say two Zeppelins and aeroplanes have been seen over the Moray Firth coming from the west of Scotland. Personally I don't believe them and think they are the imaginings of overwrought brains. Transferred two signalmen to the *Alsatian*.

Tuesday 20

Had a row with "Torps." Divisional drill, loader, and deflection teacher in the forenoon. Fitted up the anti-aerial three-pounder on the Q.D. capstan. The mounting has been built to the Commander's design by the armourer and his crew. The *Dryad* is once more under our orders. She joined at noon and reports having sunk a submarine off Scapa southern entrance, which is excellent news. There is also a rumour that four other German submarines have been sunk. The destroyer *Hope* has been ashore off Mull, and is to be docked in the Clyde. German submarines reported off S. Ronaldshay, Wick, Banff, Peterhead, and Aberdeen. We have abandoned the North Sea for big ships, and are only leaving destroyers, submarines, and aircraft there. The German submarines are very daring; two German minelayers have laid mines in the Firth of Forth; it is to be hoped they will be caught. After quarters, firing tests were carried out with the anti-aerial three-pounder, which were most satisfactory, the mounting holding splendidly, in spite of the pessimism of "Guns." Maxim (anti-aircraft) drill after the three-pounder firing. The Northern Lights are very bright at night now, and so is the comet, which has an exceptionally fine tail.

Wednesday 21

Trafalgar Day anniversary. Very bad weather. *Endymion* captured grain-ship. At 4 p.m. we sighted a big petroleum ship with no colours, seventy-three miles N.N.W. of Foula, and altered course to examine her. Suddenly several shells whistled over the masts. The apparently unarmed merchant ship was armed with three new 4.1-inch guns, and was evidently a commerce marauder and also a submarine oiling-ship. We sounded off G.Q.s at once, and "Guns" decided to use the after-control, but before we were ready she had fired several rounds, but owing to the big swell her shooting was bad. One shot cut the port main shroud and passed through the maintop, and another cut the forestay. Then we opened fire at 7,000 yards, and more by good luck than good management hit her in the bows first time. This apparently set alight an oil-pipe, for she burst into flames, and after we had fired another salvo, which went over and to the left, she hoisted a big white flag as a token of surrender. It was too rough to lower a boat, so we signalled to her in the international code to consider herself a prize. She managed to put out the fire in about twenty minutes, and then we convoyed her to five miles north of Muckle Flugga, where we told the *Dryad* to take her into Lerwick.

Thursday 22

The *Dryad* rejoined at 7 a.m. and reported the prize (now safe in Lerwick) to be a Norwegian steamer bought two months ago by Germany, to be used primarily as a long-distance submarine depot-ship, and has very likely been used by those in the west of Scotland. She has been badly holed in the bows, and it is unlikely that it will be considered worth while repairing her. The loss of our forestay means that we shall have to remove one of our wireless aerials, as the strain on the foremast will otherwise be too great, and consequently our wireless range will be reduced from 1,700 to 250 miles; this will mean less news and only transferred communication with the C.-in-C. It was very exciting yesterday when we were fired on. None of us have been under gunfire before. I was in the gun-room having tea at the time, and was too busy to notice much else when the bugle sounded off G.Q.s for action. Detached the *Dryad* again 11 a.m., and in the evening she sent a message to say she was on shore at Offness Skerries; two destroyers were ordered from Lerwick to go to her assistance, but owing to the very big sea running nothing could be done; anyhow, with the rise of the tide she managed to get off at 4 p.m. and is proceeding to Scapa to repair damages. A very nasty gale got up during the night, and yesterday's bad weather is really far worse today. Made an attempt to get a sight, but all efforts were absolutely futile. Two of the forward funnel guys carried away, and it is considered possible that the funnel may topple over, as the sea is so big, like those of the *Edgar* of this class did ten years ago in the Bay. Two stokers run in for gambling. A.J.S.R. in the soup for not discovering them during "rounds." John Kiddle very objectionable. Rigged a temporary forestay.

Friday 23

The sea got very big in the night, and when we altered course at 10.45 we heeled to about 45°. Everything got adrift; chairs, tables, chests, and boxes went careering all over the place. In all the offices everything was chaos. In the gun-room the table was smashed in half. Two anchors broke loose on the booms and swept about the upper deck. All the guns on the starboard side under water. Fifteen casualties on deck and twenty-one in the engine-room. Nine cases of concussion. All the gear in the gun-room smashed, including gramophone and records, and the majority of the crockery in the ship. The weather improved at daylight. G.Q.s and shrapnel tests; three boxes did not explode, due either to damp, old age, or faulty construction. They will be returned to the dockyard. A marine reservist got three days cells for fooling the Censor.

Saturday 24

At sea on our patrol as usual all day. Assistant-Paymaster Cockrem, Clerk to the Secretary, went sick for a day, and I took on his job, and so learnt all the most interesting confidential signals. Heard that the *Badger* has sunk a

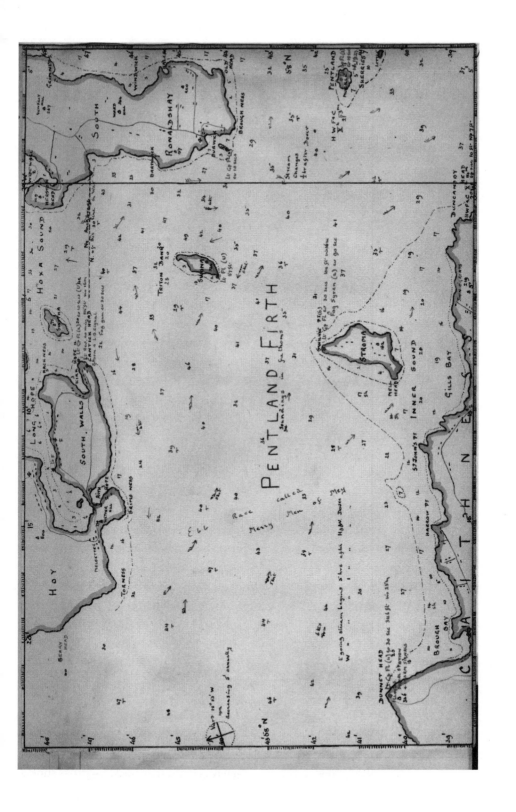

German submarine. Two more British submarines lost, the *E3* and another of B or C class, in the Pentland Firth. The Dover Patrol flotillas and monitors *Severn, Thames,* and *Humber* are doing the most excellent work on the Belgian coast harassing the Germans' right wing, and have been unsuccessfully attacked by German submarines. Boarded two steamers, but nothing of interest; one was Russian with rubber goods and stationery from Brindisi to Archangel, and the other Norwegian with fish from Newfoundland to Tromsö.

Sunday 25

Left the squadron at midnight and entered Busta Voe at 7 a.m. Busta Voe is an inlet in the west of the mainland off the Shetlands, a deserted spot which is being used as a naval base now for our squadron. It has a post-office, a kirk, and four houses. It is twenty-two miles north-east of Lerwick, but thirty miles by road. Very pretty scenery with the sun rising over the hills. Found the *Alcinous, Endymion, Theseus,* and *Zealandia* in. Midshipmen are now going to take O.O.W. in harbour to relieve the ward-room officers. The Captain says it is a compliment to the efficiency of the midshipmen in this ship that they can be given this responsibility so soon. Captain of *Zealandia* came on board at 11 a.m., and they put to sea at 1 p.m. Landed at two to climb a hill and examine the surrounding country. This is a very desolate corner of God's earth. Our picket-boat to patrol harbour by night. Tottenham in charge for first watch, ran on shore three miles from his proper station, and the Commander signalled him to stop there till he could get off, as a punishment for making a bloody fool of himself. He got off at 1 a.m.

Monday 26

Started to coal ship at 6 a.m. in the dark, raining hard, strong wind, and very cold. What a happy life! Seven hundred and fifteen tons the biggest coal we have had this commission. Still, in spite of adverse conditions, coal came in at an excellent rate, and by 3 p.m. we had finished. An excellent performance, which left everyone dead to the world. The *Edgar* came in for two hours in the forenoon to land ten hospital cases, which are being sent to Lerwick by ambulance. *Theseus* left at 7 p.m. In addition to the picket-boat by night, two armed trawlers patrol the mouth of the Voe by night and day. All luxuries have run out again, so we are once more on bare rations, and are likely to be so, as Lerwick is so far away. No mail.

Tuesday 27

All sorts of weird rumours floating round about Prince Louis of Battenberg being in the Tower with Mrs. Cornwallis-West as a spy. If this is true it must be a terrible calamity in our midst, but I don't believe it. Also rumour that four German submarines sunk in Scapa Flow. The patrols and monitors under Rear-Admiral Hood still doing excellent work on the Belgian coast. Mail arrived. First for a very long time. Very welcome provisions and letters. Heard that L.L.G. is a prisoner in Germany. Much news of interest. I was employed all the morning constructing new charts of Lerwick, Kirkwall, Scalloway, and Stromness Harbours from the Admiralty originals for the use of officers taking prizes into these places. Landed with Tottenham in the afternoon and called on Mr. Fairburn, the local U.F. padre. Found him and his wife to be most hospitable and the direct antithesis of the average Scotch "meenister." They lent us two rods, and we spent the afternoon fishing in the Delting Burn and had jolly good fun, catching eleven between us, some nearly half a pound. Brown trout, of course, are out of season, but there are sea-trout, the season for which in the Shetlands goes on till November 16th. Three suspicious men were seen up in the hills examining the harbour with spy-glasses, and although they were chased they made good their escape. The *Grafton* came in at midnight. We have established a signal station on shore to be manned by signalmen of the successive ships as they come in to coal. It is in direct communication with Lerwick by telegraph. A store depot is also being established in an old barn, and Mr. White, the factor of the Busta estate, has been appointed naval store officer by the authorities at Lerwick.

Wednesday 28

Got on shore at 11 a.m. with Johnstone, Tottenham, and Mr. Kiddle. Johnstone motor-biked, Mr. Kiddle rode, and D.F.C.L.T. and I biked seven and a half miles along the Hillswick Road to Johnny O'Mann's Loch and fished all the afternoon, but did not have much luck, only getting thirteen between us, all small. Got back to the ship at 6 p.m. This part of Shetland must be one of the most deserted parts of the British Isles, as we sighted no human habitation the whole seven and a half miles between Johnny O'Mann's Loch and Brae at the head of Busta Voe. The scenery among the hills and voes is very rugged, wild, and fine indeed. No trees or vegetation, just rocks with a little smattering of grass, moss, and thin heather. The First

Lieutenant and Mr. Bacon went shooting all day and got some rabbits and a few snipe. The *Endymion* left at daylight. At 7 a.m. the whole of the Third Cruiser Squadron came in; a secret court-martial was held, sentence carried out, and the Cruiser squadron put to sea three hours later. They anchored in Olna Voe, the adjoining voe to Busta. The prisoner was a Reserve Paymaster who had been discovered to be a German spy, although an Englishman. He had attempted unsuccessfully to communicate with the Germans and was caught. He was proved guilty by naval court-martial, sentenced to death, and shot half an hour after. This is the way we do things in the Service. His crime was a blot against the honour of all naval officers, but it must be remembered he was only temporarily entered for the war two months ago and was not a real N.O. at all. An attempt has been made to lay mines by trawlers off the west of the Shetlands, but owing to the vigilance of the trawler, motor-boat, and yacht volunteer patrols, the attempt has been most opportunely frustrated.

Thursday 29

Commander Startin, R.N.R. (late Admiral, R.N.), motored over from Lerwick to see the Admiral. It is very sporting of all these retired Admirals to volunteer as Lieutenants, Lieutenant-Commanders, and Commanders for active service in the R.N.R. and R.N. Volunteer Reserve. The *Royal Arthur* came in to coal at 10 a.m. We shortened in to two cables. Raynes came on board (he is Intelligence Officer in the *Grafton*), and "Guns" of the *Grafton* came over to see our "Guns." Weighed and proceeded out of Busta Voe through Swarbacks Minn to the open sea at 1 p.m. Made for our patrol off Muckle Flugga. Saw several suspicious trawlers, but took no notice, as the *Endymion* is chasing a suspicious steamer at full speed, and we hoped to cut her off, as she was out-steaming the *Endymion*. We thought her probably to be that ship reported to have been minelaying off the Shetlands. We got up to eighteen knots in an hour, which was a feather in the cap of the engine-room.

Friday 30

The *Endymion* came up with the ship at 1 a.m. on the morning of Friday, 30th, and shortly afterwards both we and the *Edgar* arrived. The ship proved to be the Norwegian liner *Bergensfjord*, which, by the way, we boarded some weeks ago. She had a cargo of contraband foodstuff on board for transference overland to Germany, so she was sent into Kirkwall as a prize under the convoy of the *Endymion*. A large number of German Reservists were found on board from the United States, and the German Consul-General of Seoul, the capital of Korea. The President of the Norwegian Parliament was also on board, and his detention may lead to trouble with Norway. Returned to the Muckle Flugga patrol at daybreak. G.Q.s all the morning. Extremely cold weather. The Flag-Lieutenant and Lieut.-Commander Bacon, R.N.R., went sick with bad influenza.

Saturday 31

At sea on our patrol all day. Very bad weather as usual. Big sea running, squally, and very cold. "Guns" and Mr. Beasley added to the influenza sick list. In his absence I had to do "Guns" duties, and had a fearful row with Mr. Lowman, who tried to be too officious, also with Mr. Croughan. Wireless news reports that Lord Fisher has succeeded Prince Louis of Battenberg as First Lord of the Admiralty. Fisher is a strong man, though unpleasant and rather a cad; he won't be bossed by Winston as Prince Louis was. Heard that we had declared war on Turkey at 5 p.m. The Turkish Fleet with the *Goeben* and *Breslau* has bombarded the town of Odessa.

NOVEMBER

Sunday 1

On our patrol all day; filthy weather. Stopped the Danish liner *U.S.*, but let her go as she was outward bound. I relinquished my duties as Assistant Gunnery Officer and took up those of Senior Watch-Keeper, being relieved by W.S.H. We are all changing round as three months is up.

Monday 2

The weather up here is so uniformly bad that in future I shall only remark in my diary when it is good, which I expect it will be very seldom, as the only variation to the prevailing south-west gales with rain and big seas is a biting cold northerly wind coming straight down from the Arctic Circle and Spitzbergen. No G.Q.s. Thanks for small mercies! Had a long chat with Bacon, who with "Guns" and Beasley has returned to duty from the sick list. Made up the row I had with Mr. Lowman, the gunner. The *Hermes*, old light cruiser, has been torpedoed and sunk by a submarine off Dunkirk[*].

Tuesday 3
Persistent rumours that four German submarines have been sunk in Scapa Flow and that the Dreadnought *Audacious* has been torpedoed; both are unconfirmed.[**] Left patrol at 4 a.m. and went into Busta Voe at eight to get mails and land a hospital case. Found Third Cruiser Squadron, *Edgar*, and *Theseus* in harbour. In harbour two hours and then put to sea back to patrol. A sudden wireless signal recalled us to Busta to coal immediately when two hours from land. A German battle squadron have put to sea and everything is on the *qui vive*. Admiral Beatty despatched to warm the Deutsche Breechen. The whole seven ships of the Tenth Cruiser Squadron arrived before midnight and coaled rapidly, all except the *Grafton*, *Theseus*, and *Crescent*, who are stopping in to repair small engine defects. The advent of "Jackie Fisher" to the Admiralty in place of Prince Louis of Battenberg will probably put a stopper on Winnie's gambols. Fisher is a strong man, whatever else he may be, as is stated by those who are not in the "fishpond." Personally I know nothing of the split, and take no sides. I don't think anyone does in war-time. Very pleased to turn in at 11 p.m.; been on duty since 3 a.m. The Secretary and a midshipman from the *Gibraltar* dined in the gun-room. The ward-room had a very merry evening.

Wednesday 4
No news from the scene of the German squadron's reconnaissance from Heligoland. The Turkish trouble looks embarrassing, as they are preaching a holy war. The *Cumberland*, *Duke of Edinburgh*, and *Black Prince* have been ordered to Alexandria. The *Minerva* has done good work bombarding Turkish forts in the Red Sea, and a squadron of Turkish gunboats will be confronted there by the *Espiègle* and the *Odin*. I was very nearly sent to the *Minerva* at the outbreak of the war, and instead of freezing just outside the Arctic Circle, I should have been sweltering in the Red Sea. It is just about time some of these raiding cruisers were nipped in the bud. They have got

---

[*] The cruiser HMS *Hermes*, which had been serving as a seaplane tender, was sunk by *U-27* while transporting aircraft.
[**] Commissioned in 1912, HMS *Audacious* sank on 27 October 1914 after striking a mine off the northern coast of Donegal, Ireland. Initially the Royal Navy tried to keep the loss a secret, officially listing the ship as in service during the entire war.

plenty to "veer and haul on," certainly, but we have stacks of ships after them, and they are doing a lot of damage to our trade. Coaled ship, commencing 8 a.m. Took in 450 tons; finished midday; excellent work. The *Edgar, Gibraltar, Endymion,* and *Royal Arthur* put to sea before 10 a.m. Admiral Colville has transferred his headquarters from Lerwick to Kirkwall, and is now senior naval officer in chief command of the defences of the Orkneys and the Shetlands.

Thursday 5

German submarines are operating round Land's End. A.P. Gallichan, R.N.R., has been appointed to a shore billet under the Admiral commanding at Rosyth, and his place will be taken by A.P. Cockerill, R.N.R., an old friend, who has come back from the *Royal Arthur.* Took in stores from the *Alcinous.* The *Grafton* left at 7 a.m. It has been decided to erect a small fort on Muckle Roe, and an observation station with buzzer at the entrance of Swanback's Minn, also a permanent harbour officer is to be appointed, so that Busta Voe will be quite a swagger naval base. Boom defence is also to be fitted if possible. All the postal authorities in the Shetlands have been arrested on charges of treachery, so for the present all mails are held up. Mr. Wilson was arrested on shore as a spy, being an eccentric-looking fellow, so arrested the P.C. for impertinence in retaliation. Rear-Admiral Beatty failed to catch the squadron from Kiel, and they scuttled back to Heligoland after attacking the *Halcyon* and sinking a submarine. It is a long lane that has no turning. The hospital ship *Rohilla* has run on a rock and foundered off Newcastle. Things doing badly at present.

Friday 6

I took on the duties of Navigator's Assistant ("Tanky") in harbour, instead of harbour watch-keeping. Spent the day correcting charts from "Notices to Mariners." Also put some gunnery entries in my journal. German cruiser *Yorck* sunk by a mine (one of their own) off Wilhelmshaven. Rumours of an unsuccessful naval engagement off the Chilean coast. The *Grafton* came in again 7 a.m. Some of our old torpedo-boats have been told off for patrol work round the Shetland coasts, scouring the numerous voes and sounds. It has now rained for nine consecutive days without stopping. Mr. Bacon and Dr. Maxwell dined in the gun-room. We celebrated Guy Fawkes Day a day late (as we were too busy yesterday); four bottles fizz. Got up at midnight to assist Intelligence Officer, owing to press of signals.

Saturday 7

H.M.S. *Dryad* came in with mails and washing for Tenth Cruiser Squadron at 10 a.m., the first washing we have had back for ten weeks. Went on shore with L.E.J. at nine and fished in Delting Burn all day. Had a good day; caught eleven sea-trout, several about quarter of a pound. Johnstone got a nice one of just a pound. We have had five days in harbour in order that engine-room defects may be made good. The Senior Engineer says that we shall probably go to sea on Monday morning. *Theseus* went to sea back to patrol at midnight. The battleships of the First Fleet are once more back at Scapa Flow.

Sunday 8

Captain Gillespie, R.M.L.I., joined ship for wireless and intelligence duties. Officially confirmed that the *Audacious* was torpedoed sixteen days ago. *Royal Arthur* came in at daylight. All the *Dryad*'s ship's company came on board to church. Route march in the afternoon. Saw Raynes, Pears, and Lafitte from the *Grafton*. Hoisted in all the boom boats before dark.

Monday 9

Weighed and left harbour 7.45 a.m. A strong gale with unpleasantly big sea from the south-west running outside the shelter of the land. We get the full force of the Atlantic gales here. We have shifted our patrol line to the westward considerably, and the armed liners have been told off to patrol north of the Faeroes to prevent ships passing between the Faeroes and Iceland. The Admiralty have sold off a large number of the old pre-Dreadnought battleships for foreign service, and they will be attached to the various cruiser forces abroad, to act as fortified mobile bases for these cruisers. By the way, the battleship *Canopus* should have been with Rear-Admiral Craddock at Valparaiso*, and this would have made a considerable difference.

After reading the treatises and observations of several prominent civilian so-called experts in naval matters on the naval situation at the present, it seems to them to be an established fact, of which they are all convinced, that our Fleet is conducting a close blockade of the Heligoland Bight and German North Sea coast. In fact, a blockade of the type which Nelson exercised before Toulon preceding the Trafalgar campaign.

---

*The Battle of Coronel took place on 1 November 1914 off the coast of central Chile near the city of Coronel. This was Britain's first naval defeat since the Battle of Lake Champlain in the War of 1812.

It would surprise them to know that the blockade is of the "open" type, advocated by Lord Howe; or, even more so, Lord Howe's reason for favouring this type was that the efficiency of his material might be kept up. Jellicoe's reason is a knowledge that in face of hostile submarines to keep capital ships before Heligoland would be sheer folly.

The aforesaid journalists prate of the impossibility of our abandoning the North Sea. It would surprise them to learn that the North Sea has, to all intents and purposes, been abandoned by our capital ships for weeks, except for a few patrol flotillas of old gunboats and older torpedo craft, helped by yachts and launches along the coast.

The naval disposition of the Grand Fleet at present is as follows:

Before Heligoland, in the Bight, there is a constant patrol of our most modern submarines, relieving each other in turn from Harwich. Otherwise there is not a British warship in the North Sea, except for the small coast patrols before mentioned. East Coast naval bases and the mouth of the Thames are defended by port flotillas of submarines and small torpedo craft, assisted by seaplanes. The Straits of Dover are closely blockaded by swarms of small craft, French and English, submarines and torpedoes, but even these cannot prevent the occasional egress and ingress of German submarines. Off the Belgian coast there are three monitors and some pre-Dreadnought battleships, with gunboats and torpedo craft harassing the enemy's flank on shore. The Second Fleet and older battleships are based on Portsmouth, Portland, and Plymouth, and, except for occasional excursions to the Belgian coast, are unoccupied.

The four battle squadrons of most modern battleships (about thirty-two) and the Second Battle Cruiser Squadron—the Grand Fleet proper—have for the past few weeks been stationed for safety in the Hebrides, but have now returned to Scapa. The passages between Shetland, Fair Isle, Orkney, and the mainland are guarded by the First Fleet destroyers and light cruisers; while in Cromarty are the First Battle Cruiser Squadron under Beatty, ready to dash out directly the Heligoland submarines report by wireless the Germans leaving port. The original Admiralty scheme was to blockade the Shetland–Norwegian passage, but owing to the danger of attack by submarines using the Norwegian fjords as a base, it was decided on October 19th to shift the line of blockade from the Shetlands to the Faeroes, and this was to be carried out by the Second, Third, and Tenth Cruiser Squadrons. Thus all ships, wishing to evade the British blockade, would have to pass north of the Faeroes, and near to Iceland, then along a far northern parallel eastward, and then down, hugging the Norwegian coast. It was considered improbable that any ships would attempt or succeed in doing this.

The news of a naval battle off Valparaiso is now official. The armoured cruiser *Good Hope* (Rear-Admiral Craddock), with county-class armoured *Monmouth*, the light cruiser *Glasgow*, and the armed liner *Otranto*, were defeated by the *Scharnhorst* and *Gneisenau*, armoured cruisers, *Nuremberg* and *Dresden*, light cruisers. The *Good Hope* and *Monmouth* were destroyed. The result, though disappointing, is by no means disastrous, and should not be interpreted as such.

Tuesday 10

Big gale blowing, with very large seas and squalls. I had a most pleasant middle (I don't think!). Came down at 4 a.m. to find my hammock sopping with water, a whole sea having come down the hatch. Slept on the deck, and was again sopped with water. Excellent news received from the Admiralty at noon, stating the light cruiser *Sydney* has sunk the light cruiser *Emden* at Keeling, Cocos Isles; and the light cruiser *Chatham* has run the *Konigsberg* to earth in German East Africa. At 4 p.m. we heard that three German minelaying cruisers will attempt to lay mines off Foula tonight, and we with the *Edgar* and *Theseus* are to attempt to destroy them. Everyone on tenterhooks and very excited. Too rough to eat ordinary meals; everything a stand-up picnic.

Wednesday 11

A sensational night*. At twelve the Commander sounded the alarm by accident, and in two and a half minutes every gun was manned and everything ready for immediate action. Very disappointed that there was nothing doing, but the test was most satisfactory. Two hours later we heard that the minelayers had put back to Wilhelmshaven owing to the heavy gale. During the night the gale increased in intensity, accompanied by squalls of wind and hail. Big seas came in and swamped everything.

At 4 a.m. a signal came from the C.-in-C. telling all ships to take shelter if possible, but by that time we were forty miles W.N.W. of Foula, and it was impossible. With the gale increasing, the temperature and glass steadily dropped.

---

* Admiral Dudley de Chair later described this storm as 'the most appalling gale I have ever experienced in all my years at sea, and we really did not think the old ship would weather it'.

NORTH SEA

BALTIC

FLENSBURG

APPELN

ECKENFÖRDE

KIEL

NEUSTADT

DASSAU

HUSUM

SYLT

TÖNNING

GARDING

KIEL CANAL

GLÜCKSTADT

BRUNS-
BÜTTEL

HAMBURG

AMRUN

NORDERNEY

OLDENBURG

HELIGOLAND

CUXHAVEN

River
ELBE

BREMERHAVEN

BREMEN

WANGEROOG

SPIEKEROOG

LANGEOOG

NEW W-R-
SCHARHORN

River
WESER

JADE

WILHELMSHAVEN

NORDERNEY

NORDEN

River
EMS

EMDEN

JUIST

DELFZIL

BORKUM

ROTTUM

SCHIERMONNIKOOG

HARLINGEN

AMELAND

TERSCHELLING

STAVOREN

HOLLAND

ZUYDER
ZEE.

TEXEL

VLIE

GERMANY

Sketch Map of German North Sea Coast shewing KIEL CANAL.

Note

{ Towns of commercial importance underlined in blue.
Towns of { naval or military } importance underlined in red.

The gale now blowing started about 2 a.m. on Monday, November 9th, increasing gradually for fifty hours in intensity until it became a regular storm at 4 a.m. on Wednesday, 11th. It raged with its maximum ferocity then for about eight hours till midday. During this period we waged a war against the elements of a most trying and arduous nature. For eight hours the wind was logged at 10–11, and the sea at 9–10 by the Beaufort standard. It was impossible to stand on deck against the raging wind, and huge seas swept over everything.

The storm came from the westward, and the seas were exceptionally steep and high, although uncommonly short for an Atlantic storm. This shortness made it most uncomfortable, as the ship had no time to rise to the seas, and consequently she took in tons of water, which swept over the decks.

The waves averaged, at the worst time, between 40 and 45 feet in height, and at times must have reached the phenomenal height of 50 feet; thus, considering the short length of the seas, it can be realised how steep the seas must have been. Squalls and gusts every ten minutes or so, accompanied by rain and hailstorms, increased the discomfort. The barometer dropped to about 281 inches, reaching its lowest at 7.30 a.m., and fluctuating rapidly, and the cold was very noticeable.

Everything below was swimming in water, about 4 inches on the main-deck, and regular streams through the hatchway cracks and gunport lids. All the flats and ammunition passages were also soaked. The Admiral's quarters were drenched through and through, and he had to move into the Captain's cabin. The wardroom was swamped. Everywhere a filthy smell prevailed. In the gun-room we got but little water, but being outboard the motion had its maximum effect. The ship rolled, tossed, and pitched tremendously, and everything was chucked about willy-nilly. Everything breakable like crockery was smashed, and chests, boxes, hammocks, etc., floated about from side to side, banging against everyone. When the signal came from the C.-in-C. at 4 a.m. for all ships to run for shelter, we were head-on to the gale, and after consulting the Admiral and Navigator, the Captain decided that it would be impossible to turn and run before the gale for shelter, for fear of capsizing while broadside on, for even head-on we were rolling on an average 30°, sometimes going over as much as 40° either side. At 4.30 a.m. the starboard sea-boat (first cutter) was stove in, and half an hour later the port sea-boat (second cutter) was carried in and dumped on the booms, both davits carrying away. All the ready ammunition careered about the deck in a most dangerous fashion. All the

Above: Alexander's parents,
Alexander Caron Scrimgeour
and Helen Scrimgeour.

Right: The typical Edwardian boy:
Alexander dressed in a sailor suit.

The Scrimgeour family outside their home at Quaives Farm, Wickhambreaux.

Naval cadet Alexander Scrimgeour.

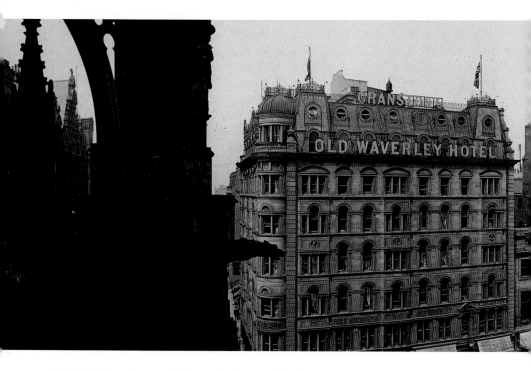

Much of Alexander's social life revolved around the theatre.
Top left: The Tivoli Theatre on The Strand, London, photographed in 1910. (Getty Images) Top right: The Savoy Theatre, photographed in 1906, with taxicabs waiting outside. (Getty Images)

Above: View down Princes Street in Edinburgh past the Waverley Hotel, 1903. (Getty Images)

Top: One of the most popular actresses of the age was Gertie Millar, photographed here in 1910 for her performance as Prudence in the musical play *The Quaker Girl* at the Adelphi, London. Alexander saw her in *The Country Girl* at Daly's Theatre in Leicester Square. (Getty Images)

Bottom: The entrance to Down Street Underground Station, photographed shortly after it opened in 1907, where Alexander met Joko for a day in London on 15 March 1915. Situated on the Piccadilly Line between Hyde Park Corner and Dover Street (Green Park) Stations, Down Street was little used and closed in 1932. In the Second World War, Winston Churchill and the War Cabinet used the station as a shelter before moving to the Cabinet War Rooms under Whitehall. (London Transport Museum)

officers and ship's company were now roused, and the Commander wanted to pass an extra lifeline to prevent the starboard sea-boat being lost altogether, as one of the gripes had carried away. The chief bos'n's mate, the midshipman of the gun-watch, and myself, the midshipman of the watch (I had the morning watch), volunteered to get into the boat and pass the line. We managed to get into the boat after ten minutes' struggling with bowlines round us, but the Commander could not get the sea-boat's crew on to the booms, so we were unable to get the line after all, and had to come back. Five minutes later the whole boat—davits and all was washed away by an extra big sea. Lucky we had left it before! Then two of the foremost cowls carried away, and all the others went later, except two, making an absolute shambles of the upper deck; a mass of ropes, wooden spars, bits of iron, cowls and projectiles rolling about in all directions, making it impossible to get about. Just before I went off watch at 6 a.m. the port sea-boat was smashed to atoms, and the foc'sle breakwater swept overboard. All such things as railings, etc., were swept away, and the quarter-deck and foc'sle were continually under the waves, and the batteries were knee-deep in water. I was thankful to get off watch, but rest or food were impossible, as all the galley-fires were put out, and we munched chocolate and ship's biscuit, and then crowded into the decoding office and the after shelter deck, except when required for duties, such as clearing away wreckage, by the Commander. The wireless aerials came untriced and streamed aft in the wind, thus cutting us off from communication. The dynamos were shut off and the ship lighted by candles below. Owing to an accidental short circuit, you got a nasty shock whenever touching the metal round the wireless office. About nine a big sea took away the whaler, and it floated off most neatly into the sea, quite undamaged. Then the depression rails on the foc'sle were bent double, and then the biggest sea of all came. It smashed the fore bridge into smithereens, breaking all the glass and woodwork of the wheel-house and chart-room like paper. All the flags and signal-books went by the board, but the signalman on watch escaped by a miracle. The Quartermaster and helmsman were badly cut about the face and neck, and the officer of the watch and the midshipman and yeoman of the watch and messenger were isolated on "Monkey's Island," and it was three hours before they were able to get down by climbing down the foremost mast ropes. All the gear in the chart-house was smashed or lost, although luckily the deck log was saved. At the same time as this occurred the whole intelligence office was swept away from the fore shelter deck, with code-books, signals, and everything.

Captain Gillespie, R.M.L.J., who joined last Monday, was inside it at the time, and everyone thought he was lost, but by an extraordinary piece of luck he clasped the starboard shrouds and did not go over the side.

The Navigator and Chief Quartermaster now conned and steered the ship from the conning-tower, as the officer of the watch was marooned on Monkey's Island, and the Quartermaster and helmsman of the watch were injured. All watches were kept in the conning-tower for the next twelve hours.

Everyone thought the foretop would carry away, and the after-funnel was very shaky, as two funnel guys snapped, but luckily both funnels and masts held, and except for the loss of the starboard fore range dial, nothing further was lost or destroyed of much importance.

During the worst of the storm we steamed eight knots (forty-two revolutions) in order to give steerage way, and could not go faster for fear of breaking the ship's back; even then we were making a leeway of about one knot.

About midday the glass began to rise, the squalls ceased, and the wind shifted to the north-west, we altering course accordingly. A watch of seamen was sent down to the stokehold to relieve the wretched stokers a little, as the wretched men were having a slave's time of it.

The storm began now to gradually blow itself out, the wind shifting towards the northward, and becoming colder than ever, although not nearly so strong. At midnight things were far better, and at 2 a.m. on Thursday, the 12th, the wind dropped completely, the gale having lasted altogether three days. The sea was nearly as big as ever, but the Captain decided to turn and run for port. There was one terrific roll when we turned, but once on our proper course we rattled off at fourteen knots for harbour and rest. A temporary wireless aerial was rigged up, and we learnt that the other ships in our squadron unable to shelter were the *Theseus* and *Edgar*, and both had been almost as badly treated as we had been, both losing several hands overboard, in which we were very lucky, as no one was lost, although several people were injured more or less.

The only other warships out were the battleship *Marlborough* and light cruisers *Nottingham* and *Falmouth*, but these managed to find shelter, before the worst came, behind Westray. The centre of the storm passed to the northward of us, and eventually must have vented itself on the Norwegian coast, while the southern limit of the storm must have been about Cape Wrath; thus luckily little damage should have been done along the Scotch and English coasts. At daylight on the 12th we sighted land and entered St. Magnus Bay and steered for Swanbacks Minn, arriving at the entrance about 8.30 a.m.

Thursday 12

Came up Swanbacks Minn and anchored in Busta Voe at 9 a.m. In harbour for seven hours. Carried out as many temporary repairs as possible. Heard that even in harbour here they had a bad time, the *Alcinous* steamboat being sunk by the choppy sea. As we came to our anchor a heavy snowstorm broke out, and by nightfall all the surrounding country was white, being 2 or 3 inches deep in snow. Ronas Hill has been covered with snow for three days. An observation station with signal staff for communication with the harbour has now been constructed on Papa Little Island, commanding the anchorages in Busta Voe, Olna Firth, and Aith Voe. Weighed and left for Scapa at 4 p.m. Big swell still running outside, and we had a most unpleasant time of it, as the ship rolled worse than ever, with the sea abeam from the N.N.W.

Friday 13

Reached Scapa at 7 a.m. and anchored off Weddel Sound to the southward of Cava Island. The whole of the First Fleet were at anchor off Flotta, and the Calf of Flotta, sheltering from the north-westerly wind. All the hills covered with snow. The Admiral visited the C.-in-C. in the *Iron Duke*. A general signal from C.-in-C. congratulating the Tenth Cruiser Squadron on their successful patrol duties, which have been conducted in all weathers, and which he says are the most arduous being undertaken by any of our squadrons, but are none the less necessary, and their labours are fully appreciated by him although there may be no immediate recompense. All the First Fleet is pleased with our work. Everyone very pleased, as we thought the authorities might be apt to forget the poor old ragtime squadron away on its lonely northern patrol. We have been ordered to Greenock to overhaul after the storm. Snowing all day, very cold; all the hills several inches thick with snow. Had a gun-room row with the warrant officers. "Torps" and Mr. Bacon dined in the gun-room.

Saturday 14

Weighed and left Scapa Flow, going out through Hoxa Sound at 7.30 a.m. Steered a course for Cape Wrath; encountered the usual bad weather, once outside the shelter of Hoy, big seas and frequent snowstorms. The Sutherlandshire mountains looked gorgeous, the snow glistening in the occasional glimpses of sunshine. Went only eight knots so as not to reach the Minch before dark, as hostile submarines have been sighted again in the Minch, and we are to go through by dark. Rounded Cape Wrath 4 p.m. and increased to fourteen knots after dark. Sighted three suspicious Swedish oilers off Stornoway; notified them to C.-in-C., but did not stop. Ran through the Minch narrows between seven and eight and shaped a course through the inner Hebrides for the Mull of Cantyre Point.

Sunday 15

Passed Oversay Light 2 a.m., and then went over to the Irish coast to communicate by flags with a signal station there, as the Belfast wireless station has broken down, and we have a message for the S.N.O., Belfast. Then came across to the Mull of Cantyre, passed Sanda (where we saw Southend in the distance, and memories of old days came back), then on past Ailsa Craig and up the Firth of Clyde to the east of Arran, Bute, and the districts round Rothesay, Dunoon, and Wemyss, looked very fine covered with snow. Ben Lomond, a great white mass towering away to the north, lost in the dark mists. Fearfully cold with a stiff south-east breeze and a choppy sea in the Firth. Came past Gourock and anchored off Greenock for the night at 4 p.m. Found the *Royal Arthur* and *Grafton* also at anchor, as they have been sent to refit also, leaving four ships up in patrol with Captain Thorpe of the *Edgar* as S.N.O. I hope we shall get some leave while the ship is in dock for her refit, and the Sec seems fairly hopeful.

Monday 16

The pilot and tugs came alongside at 7.30 a.m., and we proceeded up the Clyde. A lovely morning. Realised for the first time what a gigantic shipbuilding centre the long banks of the Clyde make. Just to mention a few of the biggest: London and Glasgow Ship Company at Govan, Beardmore's at Dalmuir, Fairfield Company, John Brown of Clydebank, Yarrow, and the numerous yards at Glasgow, Scotstoun, Port Glasgow, and Gourock. Passed several cruisers and destroyers building. Arrived off John Brown's yard at 8.45 and came alongside the basin jetty, preparatory to drydocking later on. All the dockyards are now under Admiralty superintendence, and all the authorities, with the Captain of the dockyard, came on board to make out plans and lists for our repairs. Leave for all the starboard watch and for officers. I went to Glasgow in attendance on the Admiral to see the mail and store officers, but then he dismissed me, and I went off to call on Robert at his office. He gave me tea and was most hospitable in every way. Lieutenant Wilson dined in the gun-room. Learnt with the deepest regret of Lord Roberts' death[*].

Tuesday 17

Lieutenant G. A. Wilson appointed to battleship *King Edward VII*. The dockyard hands got well to work with our refit by midday, but no estimate can be made as to how long it will take. Leave in the afternoon; called on Robert Greig, Anna, and Mrs. Greig. Learnt that Mr. Clarke, our Navigator, is an old friend of the Sandhills people. The Admiral and staff are going up to London for forty-eight hours with despatches, and on my arrival back at the ship he told me that I was to accompany him. Packed my bag at once. Left at seven, dined with the Admiral and Mrs. de Chair at their hotel, which was very kind of him. He also asked Johnstone, the second senior midshipman. Left St. Enoch 11 p.m. and travelled down to St. Pancras, arriving the following morning. The Admiral is accompanied by his Flag-Lieutenant, Secretary, and two clerks, and we had quite a good journey.

Wednesday 18

Arrived St. Pancras 9 a.m., and the Admiral told me to be at the Admiralty by one. Went to 12, Cumberland Terrace, where daddy and mother were staying. They were very pleased to see me. Went to the Admiralty at one. The clerk told me that the *Crescent* is going to be given a thorough refit and repair at John Brown's Clydebank yard, and the Admiral very kindly told me to proceed on leave until receiving further orders, and said the refit would last about a fortnight. There is to be watch and watch leave for all officers and men during the refit, which will be very welcome after our strenuous job. The Admiral is leaving for the North again immediately. Visited Aunt Do in the evening with daddy and mother. She seemed very perky. Norman Forbes Robertson, whose house this is, dined at home. I have not seen him for years. His conversation is most amusing in its way! Norman Forbes Robertson is the brother of the famous actor Sir Johnstone and in the

---

[*] Field Marshal Frederick Sleigh Roberts, 1st Earl Roberts, was one of the most successful commanders of the Victorian era. Known affectionately as 'Bobs' by the troops he commanded, Roberts died of pneumonia on 14 November 1914.

opinion of many is a more brilliant performer than his brother, and is certainly more versatile. He is a life long friend of my father's, and is intimately connected with several members of my family and is brother-in-law of my great friend George G. Wilson. He is a remarkably clever man, and a thrilling conversationalist. He is a man full of emotion, and is always on the rattle. A long thin face, with a remarkably well marked and distinguished profile, he is undoubtedly handsome. He has had not the success of his more famous brother, and wears a worried expression. His acquaintances are remarkably varied and interesting and made up of all classes and professions. He married Louie, sister of G.G.W, and has 5 children.

Thursday 19
Got up late. Daddy and I called on Jack Russell and his wife, he is brother of my friend Arthur Russell. They have some sweet little children, 2 girls and 2 boys. Went into the city with Daddy. Saw Jude Wise and Uncle John, had a very long chat with Uncle John. He seems in excellent form. Came home to dine after visiting Gieves, Matthews and Seagrove. My trunks and cases arrived from Portsmouth where they had now been stored. N.F.R. dined at the Garrick with Claude Lowther*; he and daddy wrote to the papers over the pension question. The Russian advance has been checked. There is a strong rumour in all quarters that the H.M.S. *Audacious* has been sunk in Lough Swilly; I can hardly believe this considering the signals we received with regard to the matter in the *Crescent*.

Friday 20
Lunched with daddy and John Parish Robertson at the Automobile Club. Excellent lunch, and many cocktails before and after. J.A.R is now a 2nd Lt. in the Hertfordshire Yeomanry, he was originally in the C.O.L Yeomanry with G.G Wilson, Arthur Grey, Arthur Russell, Ernest Baker, Bob Faber and Bob Kirby. E.B has now also joined the A.S.C as 2nd Lt. Went down by the 4.15 to Canterbury, bought some Oysters and supped at Westenhanger. All very surprised and pleased to see me. Mother visited P and J at Folkestone and came home later. I was also very late.

Saturday 21
Shot the Wickham Count shoot, very cold and windy. Shooting execrable. 5 guns, Governor Jack, Bing, Pongo, Baines and self. Hundreds of birds. Poor

---

* Claude Lowther was a well-known English Unionist politician and MP.

bag, 6½ brace, 3 pheasants, I have 3 rabbits, 2 duck, 2 pigeon. Lunched at
the Rectory, tea at the Kelseys. Peg and Jim came home for a night at 3, and
seemed very fit. I dined at home, and they thoroughly enjoyed the evening.
Joko has got an awful 'pash' for me now (not permanent I expect), and
fully lives up to her letters. She is a very pretty girl now, but her hair is still
not quite it. I hope for some pleasant flirtations with her this drop of leave.

Sunday 22

Mr. Oxlade whined about his bag again, what a damned nuisance he is. I
hope the devil he gets his bag. Jimmy and I went around to Westenhanger
to see Jackie who is not quite fit. In the evening I motored P and J back to
their schools at Felixstowe. Miss White, Peg's headmistress, was very stand
offish, but those at Jim's school were awfully nice. Joko came in the motor
too and we had a great time together on the way home. Daddy had
returned at midday, and he and mother dined at Westenhanger, Byron also
there. Good evening. I hope to God, the Germans have come out while the
Crescent is in harbour.

Monday 23

Everyone here is in a state of unrest. A German aeroplane from Belgium
is reported to have dropped a bomb in Canterbury and escaped unhurt.
The news is strictly classified. Called on the Drakes, and had tea with Col.,
Mrs. Baines and the boys. Little Andrew Baines is a splendid little chap.
Byron had tea at Quaives. Mrs. Drake talks Bertie's death wonderfully well.
The Westenhanger crowd, Sophie and Byron came to dinner. Quite a good
evening, all the girls being interested with my photographs of the *Cornwall*.
H.M.S. *Bulwark* blown up at Sheerness*.

Tuesday 24

Had tea at Westenhanger alone with Joko, and a very interesting flirtation
as usual. We all dined at Westenhanger in the evening, but daddy and I
were rather tired. Olive is very anxious about Henry who is at Ypres. She
leaves for Manchester tomorrow.

Wednesday 25

Mother and I went up to London in the morning; Uncle Jack and Cousin
Sittie are stopping with Aunt Do at Kensington Grove, and I spent 5 hours

---

* HMS *Bulwark* was destroyed by a magazine explosion.

there, lunch and tea. Uncle Jack seemed very well, and is rabid over the war. He and Cousin Sittie were very pleased to see me. Mother and I went down to Margate, and found the whole party over from Wickhambreaux. Norman is acting in a little piece over there, and we all went over to see him. Daddy was in poor form, and made me angry. Oysters, lobster and champagne on our return.

I went to bed early but the others stopped up later till about 3.30! Joko has grown into a very pretty girl but the old grumble remains, she has not got enough hair. What a pity it is. We are both rather taken with each other just at present. If I were 4 or 5 years older I might think of her seriously, but she is a few months older than I am, and will probably be married before I feel like settling down. She dreams of going on the stage, and might be a success as she acts well and has a nice voice.

Thursday 26

Woke up late and had rather a rumpus with daddy, and consequently stayed at home all day, wasting a precious day like an ass. Daddy went over to the shoot, taking Bing, Pongo, Baines and Gracie, Drake and the Dr. They got doz pheasants, doz partridges, 3 hares, 17 rabbits, 1 pigeon, 1 duck, 3 woodcock, 1 moorhen. I wish I had gone as I should have thoroughly enjoyed it. What a fool I am to waste a day's shooting. Daddy came home in good form and we made it up.

Friday 27

Motored over to shoot again at Aldington. Daddy, myself, Jack, Pongo and Gracie, Baines, Drake and Selby Lowndes. Got 19 brace 'pheasants', 3oz partridges, I have 5 woodcock and 24 rabbits. Excellent lunch, thoroughly enjoyed the day. Shot Jack and old Pilcher, the farmer, by mistake. He was concealed behind a bush, still it was my fault. It did not really do him much harm. Had tea at Westenhanger. Uncle John, Aunty Connie and Capt. Orton-Palmer arrived for the weekend.

Saturday 28

Left at 8.30 to shoot at Smeeth. Daddy, Uncle John, self, Jack Robertson, the Dr., and Jack Russell, whom with his wife we picked up at Ashford. Mother and Auntie Connie came too. I was sick that Daddy had not asked the Robertson girls. An excellent morning's shoot, followed by an excellent lunch. I shot very well. Good bag, 6 doz pheasants, 3 woodcock, 5 hares, and 42 rabbits. Saw several foxes. Cullen, U.J.'s keeper, is an excellent fellow, and very sick that U.J. is giving up his shoot next year. Our keeper Smith is too noisy. Large party to dinner, 4 Robertsons, 4 Kelseys, and 2 Stubbs, which with our 6 guests in the house, made 19. Most excellently good evening, singing, dancing, etc.

Sunday 29

Harold Wacher is a conceited swine and just now I loathe him. I suppose he is not really a bad fellow, a good doctor and a very clever amateur actor. His affair at present in full swing with Dolly. I make a point of blackguarding as he is a married man with children, but the real reason I dislike him now is that he is acting in a play with Joko and makes violent love to her. I, like an ass, am jealous. Everyone played squash at the Drakes all the morning. Uncle John and Auntie Connie left after lunch. Jack Russell and I had lunch with Joko and Toots at Westenhanger. Mrs. Champion from Sarne came in, Jack Russell and Daddy left for London at 6.0. Auntie Isabella came to stop the night. Malcolm, who is in the Surrey Yeomanry, came over from Faversham to dine. Gracie and Pongo to tea.

Monday 30

Had a wire at 9.0 telling to rejoin morn. Thursday, most disappointing as I had hoped to stay till following Monday, and had agreed to hunt tomorrow at Godstone, and then pay a visit to Pigeon Hill, with a dinner party at Westenhanger on Friday. Rather down in the mouth. Still, you can't really enjoy leave when you think of the trenches and the North Sea. Spent the day at Westenhanger with Joko. Went into Canterbury in the evening for her rehearsals with the Wachers. Harold Wacher came out in the evening to rehearse with Joko, and I insulted him but he took it lying down. Dined at Westenhanger. Had a long chat with Joko. She is very discontented at home and she and Nita get on each other's nerves dreadfully. She wants to leave home and go on the stage. She ought to get married as I think she would make a good wife and a sweet mother. If I were a few years older I am not so sure I might not. Told her some of my perplexities such as U.J. and A.C's ideas with regard to me and Esther. I also told Dora and her mother. No young man should marry under 30, but I am sure I shall fall.

DECEMBER

Tuesday 1

A much better day. Sophie left for London early. I motored to Folkestone with Joko, we had an excellent champagne lunch at the 'Metropole', which was terribly empty. Called on Peg and Jim at their schools and saw Jim playing football (by the way Miss White has humbly apologised for the contempt of last week). Took Doris out to Geronimo's and went with her, Joko and Jack whom we met in the cinema. Called on Miss Carey then motored home. Saw Frank Goodson (he should have gone to the front). Said goodbyes all around, preparing for tomorrow's departure. Tootie arrived with Mother at Quaives. I am afraid I am rather neglecting darling Mother. I dined at Westenhanger. The Kelseys were there. Had a quiet evening with Joko. Very close together, but a tender farewell to all especially her. Long chat with Byron. All very depressed about old Henry at Ypres.

Wednesday 2

Left home at 9.15. Affectionate farewell to all at Westenhanger. Travelled up by the 10.40 to town with Mother. She tells me that the Robertsons are absolutely on the rocks again without a penny. I suppose daddy will help them out. Mother is going to the manager of the "palace" to try and get Jack a hearing. Joko cannot get on with Nita and thinks of going on the stage permanently. She is pretty sharp, but it is a hard life I am afraid. A huge family gathering at 12 Cumberland Terrace to bid me farewell. Besides daddy, Mother, Aunt Adelaide, Billy & self, there was Norman Forbes Robertson, Uncle John, Auntie Connie, Esther, Aunt Maud, Bella Forshall, Auntie Ethel and Auntie Ruth. They all stopped to tea and Jack, Aunties Maud and Ethel stopped the night. Esther looked extremely pretty. She has the most wonderful pink complexion I have ever seen. What an awful effort it will be having to marry anybody, as there are so many other nice girls left behind. I wish one could marry 3 or 4 wives. I left for Clydebank by the midnight from St. Pancras.

Thursday 3

Arrived Glasgow St. Enoch 9 a.m. and went straight down to Clydebank to join the *Crescent*. Found everything in pandemonium. She is to pay off tomorrow. The new Tenth Cruiser Squadron will consist of twenty-four armed liners, flagship the *Alsatian*, with Rear-Admiral de Chair still in command. All the gun-room officers of the *Crescent* are appointed to the *Alsatian*, and some of the ward-room officers as well. The *Alsatian* will be far more comfortable, as she is a fine liner, but it is the same miserable old patrol. Packed up everything of our belongings in the ship and left during the afternoon. Miserable wet weather. Went up to Glasgow again, after saying goodbye to all the officers who are going to other ships. Went to 18, Lynedock Crescent, to stop the night with Anna and Mrs. Greig. Robert and Margaret came to dinner there, as they were going on to a lecture at the Royal Geographical Society afterwards. Anna and I went to the Glasgow Alhambra and saw Ethel Levey. Quite a good show, which I thoroughly enjoyed. Got to bed pretty early. Wrote to mother and Joko, Aunt Do, and Christabel. I hear that Drs. Buddle and Maxwell and Lieut.-Commander Oxlade and Bacon are not coming to the *Alsatian*, which is a pity.

December 3rd 1914
St. Enoch, Glasgow

Dear Mother,

Arrived Clydebank early this morning, and found the Crescent is paying off today for a long refit, which will take some months; she is then going to be used as an armed transport for troops during the war, and as a training-ship for boys afterwards, as her career of active service is over. The Admiral is shifting his flag to the Alsatian. She was a liner before the war, and is now armed as a cruiser; she is a fine big ship, fast, and much more comfortable than the old Crescent, though of course, as she was built for a liner, she has no armour. I would rather have gone to one of the big new battleships, but this is better than nothing a good deal. Nearly all the old cruisers of our original squadron are now doing the same as the Crescent, and are being supplanted by armed liners.

I am going to stop the night with Mrs. Greig tonight, and shall go down to Liverpool to join the Alsatian tomorrow. Please tell anybody who is likely to write to me that my address is now

"H.M.S. Alsatian, c/o G.P.O."

I hope you got my wire in time not to send the keys to the Crescent, as if you did it will be some time before I get them. Have you found the card-case yet?

I hope the manager of the Palace will prove lenient and lend you a gentle ear.

Very best love to all.
From
TOBY.

P.S.—Please discourage people sending parcels, as the Alsatian, having a far bigger coal capacity than my last ship, only comes in to coal and get mails once a month, and they say a chance of parcels being lost is very large.

The Alsatian is having more guns mounted, so I might possibly get a few more days' leave before she goes to sea.

Friday 4

Went to the Superintendent at the Central Station to try and get my lost warrant travelling money refunded. Then I went to call on Aunt Maggie Harvey. Robert's four daughters came to lunch—sweet little things. Left Glasgow at two by special train to Liverpool. Left a handkerchief and a book marker of Joko's by mistake. I had them as mementos. Travelled via Carstairs, Carlisle, and Preston. Arrived Lime Street Station at 9.30, and were then shunted round to Canada Dock. Arrived on board the *Alsatian* about eleven and found everything pandemonium. The staff confidential books arrived under the protection of a squad of marines with rifles and Glanvile with a loaded revolver, looking very fierce; he had slept all the way in the train, and any enterprising German could have snitched the lot. The *Alsatian* must be a palatial ship in peace-time. All is muddle now, as a large portion of the woodwork is being removed, and the most modern mark of 6-inch guns are being put in. Got an excellent meal on board and then turned in, in someone else's cabin—evidently having a night out. We shall be pretty comfortable here, I can see, but it will not do our training much good, as we ought to be in a battleship.

Saturday 5

Excellent breakfast. The Captain came on board at 9 a.m. and gave us all leave again from noon until further orders when the ship is ready again for sea, which may be anything from three days to a fortnight.

Spent the morning trying to find my way about the ship; every luxury in peace-time—gymnasium, swimming-baths, lovely suites of rooms, sitting-rooms, lounges, saloons, etc. Much of this is being destroyed, but still, even then she should be very comfortable. The ship is crowded with R.N.R. officers, including eight R.N.R. midshipmen. Lunched on board and left Liverpool by the 2 p.m., arriving Euston at 6.10. Went home to 12, Cumberland Terrace. Found them all at home, and "Sweet Alice," as they call Lilian Hore. Very surprised to see me again so soon. I am not any too keen on getting all this leave now, as I feel I ought to be doing something more active. After the war, when I want leave, I probably shan't be able to get it.

Sunday 6

Too lazy to get up early enough to go to Quaives. Spent most of the day playing the pianola. In the evening we all went to a concert at the Palladium; not much catch, but I quite enjoyed it.

Monday 7

Went down to Quaives by the 10.45 from Victoria to Bekesbourne. Lilian Hore left early. Everyone very surprised to see me again so soon. I feel quite hypocritical turning up again after all the loving farewells. The Westonhangcr crowd all in a ferment about the show they are giving at the Canterbury Theatre, Thursday, Friday, and Saturday, in order to get funds for supplying tobacco to our troops at the Front. I think Joko was really very pleased to see my ugly fizz again. We hit it off excellently now. Saw Babs and Missie at the Kelseys. Supped *zu hause* and went to bed early.

Tuesday 8

Spent the day doing nothing. Bob turned up in the morning; he is on sick leave from bad eyesight and expects to get invalided out. I advised him to join the A.S.C., as daddy will be furious if he does nothing. He says George is very cantankerous and has been having the most awful rows with everyone. I spent the afternoon at Westenhanger, Joko in a rather bad mood. I pulled her up about her awful spelling. They have a rehearsal on at Westenhanger tonight, and all the Wachers are motoring over, so in the circumstances I refused their invitation to dine. Mother came down.

Wednesday 9

Drove the pony into Canterbury in the morning and did some shopping, and went to have a tooth stopped by Westron, the dentist. Saw Nita; she had motored in with Byron to see about the dresses for their show, which they are all in an awful state about. Rehearsal at the theatre after tea. Joko and I supped together at the "Rose" grill-room (lobsters and champagne) and then went on to see "What-Ho Tango" at the theatre. Thoroughly enjoyed ourselves at supper. I am getting quite stupid about Joko just now. She is really quite pretty with cheeks and lips made to be kissed.

Thursday 10

Heard the news of the successful naval action off the Falklands*. I had heard rumours of this when in the *Alsatian* last week from the Admiral's staff. Motored down to Ashford and picked up daddy, Uncle John, Captain Orpen-Palmer (O.K.), and went to shoot at Smeeth; seven guns in addition to those above. Pelting rain all day ruined chances of good sport. Called on the theatrical brigade at the theatre, rehearsing in Canterbury, on the way home, and decided to come in and see the show tonight, which the Robertsons and Wachers and Kelseys are getting up to get money for a tobacco fund for the "Buffs." I have got the box tonight. So daddy, mother, and I motored in. The show consisted of three parts, first a play called "The Patriots," then recitations by Harold Wacher, then songs and dances by the seven girls—three Kelseys, two Robertsons, and two Champions. That little shit Crow, the manager, assisted by another crony, attempted to chuck me out for riotous behaviour, in giving tremendous applause; but, assisted by G. Green, I crushed all opposition. We all supped

---

* Battle of the Falklands: after their loss at Coronel, this was a resounding victory for the Royal Navy over the Germans. British forces intercepted a group of German cruisers attempting a raid on the coaling station at Stanley in the Falkland Islands. The Germans, led by Admiral Von Spee, were soundly defeated, and Von Spee and his two sons were killed during the battle.

on oysters and fizz at Harrison's afterwards. All the girls very tired. Margery Champion and Joko looked very pretty. I went and had a chat with Byron till two.

Friday 11

Had a wire telling me to rejoin noon Monday. A splendid morning. Jack and I motored down with Drake to Cullen's cottage, where we met. The others motored together. Auntie Connie and Lucy Godfrey, O.K.'s fiancée, motored from Godstone. Shot the Brabourne coverts. Seven guns—daddy, self, U.J., O.K., Jack, Drake, and Boosey, a friend of Jack's. A very enjoyable morning's shoot, but in the afternoon it came on to pelt, and we all got fearfully wet and cold. Found the girls very tired still on arriving home and not keen on acting again. They hope to get a better house tonight. I dined at home, and then when daddy and mother went to bed I went round to Westenhanger to meet them on their return. Nita with a fearful headache. The show not a great success, I am afraid.

Saturday 12

Started early and motored down to Smeeth. Met at Harringe Farm and shot Birches Huff in the morning and lunched at Smith's cottage. Shot Rabbit Wood, Round Wood, and Partridge Wood in the afternoon, and also some partridge drives. A very amusing day, which we all thoroughly enjoyed. Got fifteen brace pheasants, seven and a half brace partridges, four woodcock, eleven hares, and seventy-six rabbits; six guns daddy, self, Jack, Pilcher, Fuller (the estate agent), and Cullen, Uncle J.'s keeper. All the three Pilchers are good chaps, the farmer being most amusingly superior to his brothers. Motored home together. In the evening Stanley and I went to Canterbury, supped at the Rose grill-room; he in excellent form as he thinks his khaki contract is coming off. Then on to the theatre. I made it up with Crow. A very good house, and easily the biggest success they have had. A collection amounted to £8. We all went to the Kelseys at Wickham Court afterwards.

Sunday 13

Went round to Westenhanger early, found them all very exhausted in bed. Daddy and mother went to London by the five. I spent the day at Westenhanger with Joko. Olive returned. Said goodbye to the old people at the Rectory and to Stanley and Sophie, but owing to a mistake in the time could not go to the Kelseys. Very wet day. Bob lunched at Quaives. He is making desperate efforts to get into the A.S.C. I left by the 7.54 from Bekesbourne. Joko came to the station with me in the motor. I have gone the whole hog and am head over heels in love with her now. She is very sweet with me. The train was an hour late getting to London. Supped with daddy at the Automobile Club, and got to bed about one.

Monday 14

Left for Liverpool by the 8.30 train, arriving 12.33. Rejoined the *Alsatian* in Canada Dock, found we are to sail tomorrow. Everything in a very muddled state on board, as they have not really finished fitting her out, but want to get us to sea quickly first. I spent a very dissipated day with W.S.H., J.H.C., and L.E.J., and spent the devil of a lot of money. Remembered to send Joko some nice chocolates. The Midland Adelphi Hotel is a gorgeous place, claiming to be the most luxurious in the world, including lounges, saloons, billiard-rooms, tennis, racket, fives courts, American bars, swimming, Turkish and Russian baths, shooting ranges, etc. But it is damned expensive, as we found to our cost after various "clover clubs," "egg flips," Turkish baths, etc. Went to see "My Harem" at the Olympia in the evening after a huge dinner, and then a sort of big public dance, in aid of some fund for Belgian relief. Arrived on board very late.

Tuesday 15

I turned out early at 5 a.m. to attend on the Captain while we left harbour. Warped out of dock and made fast alongside Huskisson Wharf at 7 a.m.; left the Mersey at 8.30 and proceeded out into the Irish Sea for gun trials of the eight new 6-inch guns we have got. Some staff gunnery officers on board from Admiral Stileman's (S.N.O., Liverpool) staff. Anchored off the Mersey Bar at nightfall. We have eight R.N.R. snotties. I shall have a hard job as a senior snotty, with our eight active service fellows as well. The officers who have come on from the *Crescent* are Rear-Admiral de Chair, Captain Trewby, Lieut.-Commander Kiddle, Lieutenant Kenyon, Lieutenant Clarke, Lieut.-Commander Robinson, Eng.-Lieut.-Conimander Fletcher, Fleet Paymaster Lawford, A.P. Cockerill, R.N.R., Staff Surgeon Walker, Captain Gillespie, R.M.L.I., all the midshipmen, and no warrant officers.

December 15th 1914
H.M.S. ALSATIAN (A.M.C.)
c/o GPO

Dear Mother,

Just a line while I can, as I may not have an opportunity for
some time of writing. I arrived here all well yesterday with all
my tins, etc., and spent the day and most of the night on shore in
Liverpool, as they gave us further leave till 2 a.m. on rejoining.
We left Canada Dock at 5 a.m., some of us a little sleepy, as you
may imagine, and have been testing our new guns in the Irish
Sea most of the day. The tests, we hear whispers, are not
considered entirely satisfactory, and possibly we may have to
return to dock again. So it is just possible that I shall see
Cumberland Terrace before the North Sea, but it is unlikely; and
we should all be very disappointed to still further delay our
return to the rigorous patrol duties in the North. The dockyard
people had not nearly finished the ship, but the Admiralty wish
to get us to sea as soon as possible, so everything on board is in a
"topsy-turvy" condition, although nothing actually affecting the
efficiency of the ship is adrift. My job in this tub is one of four
decoding officers; one with plenty of responsibility, as all the
confidential codes and ciphers are in our charge, and we have to
code and decode all signals received and sent by wireless. There
is always one of us on duty, and frequently, when there is a press
of signals, two, three, or even all four are working together.

I do not like the job as much as the two I had in the Crescent
(assistant gunnery officer and then assistant navigator), as
although it is quite interesting being in possession of all the
confidential news and secret signals, yet it is of no material
help to me in gaining any technical experience and training in
the various branches of the profession. We have got several
R.N. Reserve midshipmen (apprentices in various liners in
peace-time) on board, and they are rather uncouth in their
manners and hardly what the world calls gentlemen, although I
dare say most of them are all right really. However, they rub

Plan Shewing arrangement of Turbines & steam pipes in Engine Room

H.M.S. "Alsatian"

*   = should read P.L.P.

———   = Steam Pipes

a = Manœuvring Valves
b = H.P. Regulating Valve
c = I.P.   "   "
d = Strainers
e = Screw Down Valve (H.P. to I.P.)
f = Self Closing Valve (H.P. to L.Ps)
g = Balance Pieces
h = 36" Self Closing Valve (I.P. to L.Ps)

Note —: The difference in arrangement from ships built for the Navy
will be noticed, especially that here the L.P. Turbines are
inboard, & the Main Condensers in another compartment aft of E.R.

most of our active service people up the wrong way, and I shall
have quite a nasty time preserving the peace in the gun-room,
as I am still senior G.R. officer, there being no Sub-Lieutenants
on board, worse luck.

By the way, in the cloak-room at C.T. you will find an oilskin of
mine, with a long gash in the skin. I should be obliged if you
would mend it (the best way is with sticking-plaster inside, or
else like a puncture). You need not send it me, as I have another.

A Merry Xmas to you all, in case I cannot write again. Please
give Gertrude a wedding present from me, should she marry
while I am away.

Very best love to daddy, yourself, and all the family.
From
TOBY.

Wednesday 16

The gunnery trials of yesterday declared unsatisfactory, as much of our
framework was strained, so we shall not get back to our North Sea patrol
for some time. Came into the Mersey again and anchored between the
Mauretania and the *Lusitania*, with the giant *Aquitania* towering away in
dock in the direction of Seaforth. The dockyard people and the gunnery
experts had a confab, and it was decided the mountings will have to be re-
riveted, a job which will take about a week. The Captain gave the ship's
company a speech after quarters, and laid stress on various points,
complimenting the work of the *Crescent*, and saying with pride she had
done more sea time during the war than any other warship of the British
Navy. He realises he has a different crew to deal with here, naval reservists
instead of Fleet reservists (merchant sailors instead of retired navy men).
At 8.30 we went into the basin leading to Canada, Nelson, and Huskisson
Docks, and steamed alongside the outer jetty, preparatory to the refitting
of our gun-plates tomorrow.

Thursday 17

I believe that after all the *Audacious* was sunk in Lough Swilly, and without loss of life; the Admiralty have done their best to keep it quiet, even from the navy themselves. I strongly deprecate this policy. Apparently we have taken over two battleships building for Chile. They will be renamed the *Audacious* and *Canada*. I hear that those lucky dogs in the *Grafton* and *Royal Arthur* have gone to the *Marlborough* and *Iron Duke*; perhaps we should be there were it not for the fact that the Rear-Admiral and skipper seem to have taken such a fancy to us. At present John Kiddle seems a great success in this ship as First Lieutenant, and is exhibiting qualities quite unknown in the *Crescent*, dormant, evidently, since the days of youth. He has a very difficult job, as the Reserve Commander does nothing, and Kiddle has to organise everything. At present it appears "Guns" is going to have a pretty slack time as gunnery staff officer, not nearly so strenuous as Gunnery-Lieutenant of a ship. By a funny coincidence, Roxburgh, my old Dartmouth friend, has a brother on board as temporary surgeon. All the details of the bombardment came through. Scarborough, Whitby, and Hartlepool were the towns to suffer.* The German naval force consisted of four battle cruisers, *Seydlitz*, *Moltke*, *Von der Tann*, and *Blücher*, with some attendant destroyers. I am afraid that this raid will considerably shake public confidence in the navy. I can quite understand their squadron getting here, but am very disappointed they were allowed to get back; and, in spite of the fog, I think they should have been caught. The action of the patrol destroyers, old as they were, was very plucky in attacking such a superior force, although, of course, it was bound to be unavailing. The dockyard people commenced work on our guns. Most of the people are having a pretty slack time in harbour, but our wireless is going all the time, so we coding officers have plenty to do, as signals are coming and going frequently.

Friday 18

It is rumoured that some German battle cruisers are going to try and escape, to carry on the work of Von Spee's squadron. The wireless petty officer is by repute a very clever operator. Apparently he discovered all the names of the

---

* Bombarding the coastal towns of northern England, the Germans initiated the first engagement of the First World War on British soil. The raid killed 112 and wounded over 200. Over 340 buildings were destroyed. Based at Scapa Flow, the Grand Fleet was too far away to intercept further German hit-and-run raids. Instead, the battle cruisers were brought together from various deployments to form the Battle Cruiser Fleet based in the Firth of Forth.

German ships that were going to carry out the raid on Yarmouth, but was pooh-poohed by the Flag-Lieutenant, who did not send on the news to the C.-in-C. Again on this occasion he found out the names of their ships, but not until after it was over. He does this by tapping their messages and then juggling with the numerous code-books. The public seems to be very sick with the navy. The dockyard authorities are still hard at work on our guns and deck plating.

Saturday 19

I got a touch of the 'flu. Decoding as usual. Lots of signals. I hear the *Karlsruhe* is coming north, and is to attempt to get back to Germany by going to the north of Iceland and then down the Norwegian coast; so perhaps we shall fall in with her with luck. I went and did some shopping in the town in the evening. We hope to get to sea by Tuesday. Had some letters from mother, but several of our mails have gone adrift by error to Inverness. I have not heard from Joko. I wonder if she has written.

December 19th 1914
H.M.S. ALSATIAN (A.M.C.)
c/o G.P.O.

Dearest Mother,

I expect Peg and Jim are home by now. Wish them a happy Xmas and give them my best love. I have not heard from you yet, but all our letters were kept in London, as they thought we had gone out for good, when really we had to come back to dock to have our guns refitted again; and we are going out for further gun trials tomorrow.

The two parcels arrived this evening; I am returning the oilskin for daddy, and am also sending a sackful of dirty clothes and linen, which, when washed, you might keep at home. I have told you already it is no good sending parcels now, as it is very unlikely I shall get them (I only got those by luck). I am also sending a blue Balaclava for daddy.

The following articles I have left behind (it is no good sending them now, but you might remind me to take them next time I come): my watch, some stiff white shirts (I don't seem to have any here), and the shaving-powder box.

Please thank Auntie Jessie for her letter; she wrote me a very nice one.

A letter from you has just arrived. It is disgracefully misspelt; why this lapse from your usual correctness?

You can pay the 20s. from Uncle Jack into my bank, if you don't mind.

It is absolutely ridiculous of you to talk about going as a nurse.

Your job is at home to look after the children, not to go capering about making a damned nuisance of yourself.

Best love to you all, and a very happy Xmas.
From
TOBY.

Sunday 20

I have worked myself again up into a terrible state, because I have not heard from Joko. I do not know whether she has written, or whether her letter has been lost, but if I do not hear from her before we sail on Tuesday, I shall never forgive her. 'Flu still most unpleasant. Sunday divisions quite a funny experiment, none of the men being very expert in "dressing." Had a long chat with old Kiddle. Dined with Mrs. Roxburgh and Dr. Roxburgh at the Adelphi. She knows the Finnises very well.

Monday 21

A large number of signals in the morning, so we had plenty to do. Went on shore in the afternoon and called on Miss Housden, for want of something better to do. I am not at all fond of Liverpool; it has rained ever since I first came here! Miss Housden is a clerk in her father's office, and looks fearfully ill. She was never a great friend of mine when at Quaives, but she looked so miserable, and was in such a dingy office, I took her out to tea. I had a chat and learnt some interesting details of the Joko—Doris rivalry. What little cats women are. By the way I had my long wished for letter from Joko this evening. It did not cheer me up so much as I expected. They are going to do their entertainment again at the Canterbury barracks. Perhaps the idea of the soldiers, Alan Hardy in particular, gave me forebodings.

Tuesday 22

Heard from Byron. The much talked of gun-room pianola was hauled on board, after much swearing, gibbering, and brain-waving during the morning. The Staff Gunnery Commander came on board about midday, and at 1.30 p.m. we left Huskisson Basin to go out to do fresh gun trials in the Irish Sea. But a thick "home port" fog came down, so thick that we were obliged to anchor again in the Mersey between Birkenhead and New Brighton, and wait for it to clear a little. The tinkle of the fog anchor bells of the ships all around sounded very weird by night.

Tuesday evening, December 22nd
H.M.S. ALSATIAN (A.M.C.)
c/o G.P.O.

Dear Daddy,

Just a line to thank you very much for the gun and cartridges, which have arrived safely. I am afraid I shall be unable to ring you up, as I am very busy indeed. Everything is in a ferment, as we are feverishly trying to get to sea tomorrow. The weather outside is too gorgeous for words, and the sun makes our mouths water, but the docks are encased in an impenetrable fog of coaldust, sawdust, and every other sort of dust, also flour, paint, tar, and every imaginable sort of filth. I shall be quite glad to get to sea again, away from it all. The dockyard people are still on board fitting up our new magazine protection and repairing the wireless gear, which is in a perpetual state of breakdown. To see us at present you would not think we could sail for a month, as none of the stores are stowed yet, and cases are lying helter-skelter everywhere. Still, the Flag-Captain has sworn to sail tomorrow, so I suppose we shall.

The other day, who should I see trailing across the docks but Ambrose, Mrs. Preece, and family, embarking in a Yankee liner, the Philadelphia, for "God's own country." Our letters have arrived at last, and I see in one of mother's that May also sails by the Philadelphia. I was too busy to speak to any of them. Please excuse the scrawl.

Very best love to all of you and good luck.
TOBY.
P.S.—I may get some leave in June.

Wednesday 23

Left the Mersey 3.30 a.m. and anchored outside the Bar. The Admiral and staff dined with Admiral Stileman (S.N.O., Liverpool) and staff last night, and then left overland for Scapa to confer with Jellicoe. We are going to pick them up. Carried out our further gun trials in the forenoon, and they were considered satisfactory, so dropped the Gunnery Staff Commander, and sent a mail ashore in the tug, and at 4.30 p.m. got under weigh for the North.

G.Q.s for the first time in the afternoon. My G.Q. station is rate-keeper. Very hard at work all day, as we had a tremendous number of code and cipher signals all day. Did not turn in till past midnight.

Thursday 24

It seems awfully weird that this is Xmas Eve, and tomorrow is Xmas Day —the first Xmas I have ever spent away from home. Good luck to all at home! I hope they enjoy themselves. I cannot realise it is Xmas myself. Still very busy, as the wireless gear was at it hard, and also fully employed drilling the hands and instilling the warship feeling. Passed the Mull of Galloway in the night, and ran out to the west of Oversay. Owing to a mistake by the wireless operator, we narrowly missed running into a mine-field guarding the southern approaches to the Minch, and on altering course ran right through another mine-field two miles long, without touching a mine. This is the second time this war I have been in a ship which has come through

N.W. Coast of Scotland & the Hebrides

Var. 21° W (1910) decreasing 10'

Var. 20° W (1910) decreasing 10'

ST KILDA

FLANNAN Is. Lt Gp Fl

HASKEIR Is.

LEWIS

ROAG

LOCH ROAG

Butt OF LEWIS Lt Fl

Lt Gp Fl STORNOWAY

NORTH MINCH

SULISKER NORTH RONA

NUN ROCK

Lt Alt Fl CAPE WRATH

EDDRACHILLES BAY

ROSS-SHIRE

LOCH EWE

HARRIS

Lt Gp Fl

SHIANT Is.

LITTLE MINCH

N. UIST

MONACH Is. Lt Fl

BENBECULA Lt Gp Fl DUNVEGAN

PORTREE

SKYE

RAASAY

Lt Fl

Lt Gp Fl

KYLE OF LOCHALSH

INVERNESS-SHIRE

S. UIST Lt Fl

LOCH BOISDALE (W.T.)

SEA OF THE HEBRIDES

Lt Gp Fl RUM

BARRA

MALLAIG

BARRA Hd Lt Occ

COLL

ARDNAMURCHAN Pt. Lt Fl

TOBERMORY (W.T.)

MORVEN

LOCH LINNHE FORT WILLIAM

BALLACHULISH

TIREE

MULL Lt Fl

SKERRYVORE Lt Fl

OBAN

ARGYLL

Scale of distance

0   10   20   30   40   50   miles.

a mine-field unscathed. We passed right to the west of St. Kilda and the Flannan Isles to avoid further mines, leaving the Hebrides far to the east. St. Kilda looked very cold, dark, lonely, and desolate. Altered course at about eleven to pass to the south of Rona, and steered to clear Cape Wrath and enter the Pentland Firth from the west. So far the weather has been very moderate but very cold.

Friday 25

Came in through Hoxa Sound and anchored off Fara Island in Scapa Flow at 8.30 a.m. The Admiral and staff came on board immediately from the *Cyclops*, depot-ship, in Long Hope. The First Fleet had already put to sea, except the dummy squadron of three ships, representing the *Audacious*, *Iron Duke*, and the *Collingwood*. They are extraordinarily good models, made out of old tramps. Only a very experienced eye could distinguish them from the real thing; in fact, I don't believe I should have recognised them had I not been told. I don't quite know how they will be used, but there seem to be infinite possibilities. We left Scapa at 4 p.m. and went out through Hoxa Sound and shaped a course for the Faeroe Islands, which will be in the vicinity of our patrol. Very busy in the coding office all day. The Allan Line gave us an excellent Xmas dinner in the evening, and we had a musical time afterwards with the pianola and gramophone; and for the first time today I felt something like Xmas. Thank God the Admiral let the Allan Line mess us after all, so the food is excellent.

Saturday 26

Boxing Day. Made the Faeroes about midday. Our squadron consists of twenty-four armed liners, patrolling four patrols—A, B, C, and D. A is between Iceland and the Faeroes, B between Faeroes and Shetlands, C between Shetlands and Orkneys, D off St. Kilda. The *Alsatian* is in A. A nasty gale sprung up, and we had some very dirty weather, combined with extreme cold and interrupted our wireless. The Admiral is living up to his nickname of "Old Make-a-Signal," as he is making reams and reams of wireless messages to everybody. "Flags" and Gillespie, the intelligence officer, at their wits' ends, as we cannot get any of the Admiralty messages through, and there is a congestion in the wireless office. All the coding officers working night and day.

Sunday 27

The Admiral's signal craze continues, and we hardly get a minute's peace. The gale got far worse, and we were obliged to lie to in the shelter of the Faeroes, off Strömsö. Thank God we are not still in the *Crescent*! The *Karlsruhe* is reported to be in the vicinity. The weather is so bad that I am afraid she may slip through. We are only getting five hours' daylight, and even that is pretty poor, dim sort of attempt. It gets light about 9.30 and dark at 2.30 in the afternoon again, and the sun is very rarely visible.

Monday 28

The weather moderated considerably. The precipitous snow-covered heights of the Faeroes, terminating in the bold headland of the Mingganaes, looked most imposing. It is now considered a moral certainty that the *Karlsruhe* has managed to slip through in the long hours of darkness. There are twenty-four ships altogether in our squadron of armed liners. A patrol extends one thousand miles—40 miles a ship.

Tuesday 29

Forty miles a ship is a minimum, as six out of the twenty-four are always away coaling and reprovisioning, so it makes the patrol about fifty-five miles a ship, so it is easy in this weather for anything to slip through. Our coal will last about five weeks, so we ought to go back about the end of January. That is the advantage of this type of ship; a cruiser could never stop longer than a week for need of coal. Boarded a ship, a Danish vessel, outward bound, at 3 p.m., but let her go again. She had picked up a cargo of Faeroe ponies at Vestmannshava and was bound with mails for Reykjavik, Iceland, and Upemavik, Greenland. She is the first ship we have seen since we left Scapa five days ago, so that shows what a lonely spot this is. I spent all the day, when not on watch, in the engine-room examining the engines. The Admiral issued a set of war orders to the squadron which took three people five hours to code.

Wednesday 30

Gun drill 9 a.m. A nasty dirty choppy sea, not big enough to affect a ship of our size much, but just enough to make boarding a very tricky process. Boarded another Danish ship, a trawler, and Ward, the midshipman of the boat, fell in the ditch and was nearly introduced to Davy Jones, but when nearly scuppered was hauled on board with a grapnel in the seat of his breeks, leaving a rent the size of a main topsail and more. He did not seem so grateful as he might have been. Wood managed to smash up the sounding machine very neatly, much to the Navigator's joy. "Guns" on the hop all day. Now that he is staff officer he has nothing divisionally to do with the ship, and is taking things easy, except for gun-room ferreting.

Thursday 31

G.Q.s at 10 a.m. Nothing occurred of any interest.

At midnight we observed the ancient Service custom, the youngest midshipman in the ship, Richardson, ringing sixteen bells in place of the customary eight, to ring the old year out and the new year in. All the officers in the ship turned up as usual, and the Admiral shook hands all round, commencing with the Captain and finishing with the Junior Head Steward, R.N.R., the last officer in the ship. So ended the fateful year of A.D. 1914.

This completes the eighth consecutive year of my diary without a single day's gap. Of the eight years, I think that this just completed will be found to contain by far the most interesting reminiscences. For the first half of the year is taken up by my experiences during an extended cruise to various foreign ports in H.M.S. *Cornwall* (with one exception I had never been abroad before); while the second half of the year is chiefly concerned with events occurring in and connected with my life, serving as a midshipman in H.M. ships *Crescent* and *Alsatian* in the Grand Fleet, operating in and around the North Sea during the opening months of the greatest international conflict the world has ever seen.

Several events of interest have occurred, and these I have recorded with as much accuracy as possible. Much of the knowledge contained herein is, at the time of writing, absolutely confidential, for it is strictly prohibited that officers or men of H.M. Navy on active service should keep diaries, which would in all probability give valuable information to the enemy should they fall in their hands. My opinions of various officers are also, of course, strictly private, and also will probably change, so they should not by any means be considered as permanent. I make no apology for the use of terms both technical and otherwise that are unintelligible to the uninitiated. This diary (although I hope that in future years it may be of a certain amount of interest to some of my friends and relations) is considered primarily for my own edification in times to come.

1915

JANUARY

Friday 1

This time last year Bench and I were at the New Year Covent Garden Ball. I remember vividly how we enjoyed it, and what thick heads we had next morning. What a change of surroundings a year later! And what funny things that year has brought us!

Got the Admiralty's new year promotion list by W.T.; unluckily several interruptions occurred, so we did not get the complete list, but Mr. Wolfe-Murray, the First Lieutenant of the *Cornwall*, was among the promotions to Commander. The Germans made determined efforts all day to make our wireless useless by making continuous signals of absolute gibberish in English, French, German, Russian, and Norwegian. Gun drill at 11.30. I have taken a great liking to Mr. Macintyre, one of the R.N.R. engineers. He is a very nice man. Also a great dislike to that fat swine, Jack Barton, the R.N.R. one-stripe A.P.; his manner is intolerable.

Saturday 2

We had a sing-song and quite a jovial evening last night, after a very good dinner. The Allan Line messing is excellent after the *Crescent*. The only trouble about the ship is that, practically speaking, I never get any fresh air, and the coding office is a stuffy place, as the ports can seldom be opened, the seas coming in usually during the scanty hours of daylight, and "darken ship" enforcing them being shut by night. Also the Admiral keeps us on the hop so with his signals that we are too tired to take any exercise when off watch. Henderson has got a very nasty attack of 'flu. The Captain examined our journals; judgment deferred. The *Hilary*'s barque she was towing to Kirkwall sprang a leak and sank. One Sub-Lieutenant, R.N.R., and one signalman drowned. Received news of the loss of the battleship *Formidable**.

Sunday 3

Received supplement to promotions list.

Among the new Commanders of interest are: Sneyd, First Lieutenant H.M.S. *Cumberland;* our old friend Mr. Dalglish; Holbrook of B2; Horton

---

* HMS *Formidable* was sunk off Portland Bill by torpedoes from the German submarine *U-24*. Five hundred and forty-seven men lost their lives.

of E9; Burgess-Watson, Uncle John's friend; and two cousins of Hutchinson's. The Norwegian liners *Christianiafjord* and *Bergensfjord*, old acquaintances, passed close to us in the night, as we heard them talking by W.T. at a range of less than twenty miles, but we sighted neither. I got in the soup for omitting Admiralty reference serial numbers in decoded messages.

Monday 4

Several German submarines reported off the Shetlands. A new dodge of theirs has been discovered. Apparently oil-tanks have been sunk in the open sea, either before the war or since by neutrals, in a given position, and their submarines utilise these as fuel bases, hence their big ranges of action. We detached *Teutonic*, *Mantua*, *Virginian*, to watch Trondhjem, whence contraband running is reported. All the midshipmen in the *consommé* with Kiddle for not reporting their divisions at evening quarters. Record day for signal section; no rest, enormous number of signals. Thankful to turn in soon after midnight, dead to the world.

Tuesday 5

Nasty gale blowing. Not quite so busy as yesterday. Hands painting ship. Gun drill 11.30 a.m. The *Otway* and *Cedric*'s operators both in Captain Gillespie's (squadron W.T. and Intelligence officer) bad books. "Flags" in a hilarious mood. The Staff Eng.-Lieut.-Commander (Mr. Fletcher) drivelled for several hours on gun mountings, about which he knows nix. Still, it amuses him, I suppose. The new German submarine bases are known to be in the vicinity of the Orkneys and Shetlands. Confidential Admiralty reports state the Germans intend to try and rush a battle cruiser squadron up this way. Of course, this would annihilate us, but we ought to get Beatty well on their track first, which is the chief thing. The *Karlsruhe* is reported as not yet having reached Germany, so perhaps she turned back after all.

Wednesday 6

It is reported an attempt will be made to smuggle a lot of German reservists over in the *Bergensfjord*, next trip from New York to Norway, and thence to Germany. So she is to be intercepted and searched. I took some sights in the afternoon, but the sun was refractory, and a heavy ground swell made sextant work difficult. Pretty busy all day. The *Warrior* carried out firing practice near our patrol. She is just home from the Mediterranean, where she was originally in the First Cruiser Squadron under Rear-Admiral Troubridge. She is the ship to which I was to have gone probably had there been no war.

Thursday 7

Took up a position considerably to the southward of our regular patrol, sighting St. Kilda in the afternoon. Control practice, using a trawler as dummy target in the morning. I distinguished myself afterwards by dropping the Dumaresq down the fore A deck hatch and badly damaging it. It is a big one of the latest mark, and will cost about £25 (pay stopped for several months) unless I can get the chief armourer to repair it. The ship was rolling heavily, so it was not altogether my fault. Had a long chat with "Guns." Considerable excitement caused after dark by flashes of heavy gunfire, but proved to only be the Sixth Cruiser Squadron night firing.

Friday 8

The W.T. department have fitted up a small sending and receiving apparatus in the motor-boat detailed as the Admiral's Barge. I don't know what it is for, as she hasn't dipped this commission yet, but it is quite a neat little installation. Communicated with the *Cedric* off Foula, where we had come from St. Kilda. Sent despatches on board for the S.N.O., Liverpool, as the *Cedric* returns to Liverpool in a few days to coal. Practised both after groups, 1-inch aiming tube firing in the afternoon; not bad results for first attempt. I, in my capacity as rate-keeper in the principal control, had plenty to do, as my trainer was away, and I had to train myself. The Captain very liverish and critical. Urgent signals from C.-in-C. to say *Bergensfjord* must be caught at all costs.

Saturday 9

"Guns" lectured on the theory of fire control to all the control officers and all the gun-room officers; quite an interesting lecture despite the interruptions of Mr. Schlosser. I got in the soup with Gillespie for muddling call signs and calling up the *London* off the Belgian coast, instead of the *Patuca*. At 4.30 p.m. stopped engines and buried a fireman who had died of double pneumonia. The Captain conducted the service, as we have no padre on board. It is the first sea funeral I have ever witnessed. All over very quickly. A few prayers, then the body sewn in a Union Jack and weighted with a shell, committed to the deep, three volleys by the marines, and the "Last Post," to mark that Nature had reclaimed one of her living creatures from this troubled world.

Sunday 10

Boarded a Swedish oil steamer; all correct, so allowed her to proceed. German submarines reported off Lerwick, Stromness, Aberdeen, and Flamborough Head. Either submarines or else disguised neutral ships have managed to lay mines between Sulisker and Sule Skerry. At 4 p.m. we heard the *Bergensfjord* calling up S.S. *Bergen*, about seventy-five miles away. I hope she won't get through in the night.

Monday 11

At 7.30 a.m. the *Viknor* intercepted and captured the *Bergensfjord** to the north-east of the Faeroes; she had, as anticipated, been trying to slip through to the northward under cover of darkness. The C-in-C made a signal "Well done!" to our Admiral and to the *Viknor* on hearing the news. The Admiral is not such a fool as he appears, and the disposition of our patrols to effect this capture was most skilful. Detached the *Eskimo* for special duty off the Norwegian coast. Very cold; the ships looked like great white icicles, all glistening with frost. On hearing of the capture of the *Bergensfjord*, we communicated visually with the *Teutonic* and *Orotava*, and proceeded to rendezvous the *Viknor* and her prize at full speed, coming up with them at 1 p.m. The man Spero, with the Mexican passport, was arrested with seven German stowaways, but no signs of the numerous reservists were found, although of course it would have been easy to disguise them among the 800 passengers. Spero is supposed to be the famous Baron Von Wedel, referred to in the spy Karl Graves' book, the chief of the German spying bureau. What his mission in America was is unknown, but it is of little doubt that only a tremendous bribe would have induced the Captain of the *Bergensfjord* to risk his all by contravening international law so flagrantly as to bring a man like Von Wedel across the ditch. The great importance the Admiralty attached to his capture is indicated by the fact that no less than twenty ships, the whole of our squadron not coaling, and available, were detailed to capture the ship at all costs. The fact that we knew he was coming in her shows our Secret Service

---

* The supposedly neutral *Bergensfjord* would trouble the Royal Navy on at least three separate occasions. On the first, she was found to be harbouring known German propagandist, Dr Durnberg, and on another the German Consul from Korea, as well as numerous German reservists.

to be by no means a minus quantity. Immediately on being boarded by the *Viknor*, Spero, alias Von Wedel, was arrested. He was found burning incriminating papers. He was taken unawares, as he did not expect us to know of his disguise. The *Bergensfjord*'s wireless was taken over and a prize crew put on board to await the arrival of the Rear-Admiral in the *Alsatian*. When we got there at 1 p.m. the *Viknor* was ordered to take Spero and the German stowaways on board and to escort the prize to Kirkwall for examination, as either the German reservists, reported to have embarked at New York, were hidden on board, or else they must have been transferred to other ships in the Atlantic. The Norwegian skipper cut up nasty, and the incident will probably lead to all sorts of complications with Norway. They proceeded in company for Kirkwall at 6 p.m. We left for the south of the Faeroes immediately, and boarded two Danish vessels at 10 p.m. Apparently a company has been promoted in the U.S.A. for running the blockade with food and reservists for Germany at all costs—of course, being very highly paid by the German Government. Our squadron are after several suspicious ships just now, and we are fearfully busy with signals in the flagship, of course.

Tuesday 12

Back to our old patrol off the Faeroes. Still very cold. Snow in the morning, turning into sleet, hail, and then rain in the afternoon, as the wind backed from N.N.W. to S.S.W. General quarters all the morning. Remarkably good work by the fire control. I got congratulated by the skipper for keeping an excellent rate, my rate giving clock ranges which coincided with rangefinder ranges for two whole runs. One-inch aiming tube firing for all guns. After control and local control poor, owing to inefficiency of auxiliary communications.

Wednesday 13

A variety of signals full of useless bunkum came through, and muddled us considerably, due to careless decoding in other ships. Sir George Warrender is having a most unlucky time with his Second Battle Squadron. In addition to the loss of the *Audacious*, the *Monarch* is at Plymouth disabled with serious turbine defects, and now the *Conqueror* has suffered serious damage, and has left for Liverpool to be docked. Some of us would have been pleased if it had been the *Thunderer* instead, as, by the amount of balderdash she sends out, her wireless staff ought to be throttled or worse!

Thursday 14

Received orders to detach the *Ambrose* to rendezvous the *Conqueror* off Stornoway. Much speculation as to the nature of her damage. Admiralty (to all ships) signal reported considerable activity amongst the German Fleet at Kiel, apparently preparing for sea. All First Fleet ships ordered by C.-in-C. to prepare for all eventualities. *Alsatian* patrolling off the Faeroes as usual. Intercepted a Danish steamer, *Spigerborg*, from New York with oil-cake for Germany. Sent a prize crew on board under Midshipman Adams, R.N.R. with orders to take her into Kirkwall. Much wrangling in the gun-room, chiefly over the question of McNaught, his airs and manners. The Captain of the *Otway* made a bigger B.F. of himself than usual.

Friday 15

Big gale, high wind, and heavy swell from the N.N.E. I got in the soup badly for faulty coding, although, as a matter of fact, Captain Gillespie was entirely to blame. Received information to the effect that A code has somehow fallen into German hands, probably through spies at the Admiralty. They have now got A and C of our numerous codes and ciphers. C.-in-C. reported that a cruiser raid is anticipated against our patrol tomorrow night, and ordered us to shift patrol line one hundred miles to the west; thus the Germans will find, instead of several moderately weak armed merchant cruisers, two strong cruiser squadrons, with Beatty's battle cruiser squadron in reserve.

Saturday 16

During the night the Germans tried without success, by making *en clair* signals for help, to induce us to betray our position. "Guns" settled the R.N.R. dispute satisfactorily. He gave a further lecture on fire control, which unluckily I was too busy in the coding office to attend. Still a nasty gale from the N.N.E., although the swell diminished somewhat. Frequent snow-storms. The *Viknor,* with Von Wedel and the German prisoners on board, is now three days overdue at Liverpool; grave fears are expressed as to whether she has been blown up by a mine. It is inconceivable that Wedel has managed with the other prisoners to overcome his guard. German cruiser raid came off, but weather was so bad that no one saw them, and they saw nobody, so nothing occurred.

Sunday 17

Gale abated somewhat. Sighted and spoke the *Patia* at 4 p.m. Very cold. Argued learnedly (sic) about advantages of rangefinder control.

Monday 18

Last night after I had turned in the gun-room held a rowdy sing-song to celebrate Cobb's birthday, and the promotion of Glanvile from Assistant-

Clerk to Clerk. The Admiral objected to the din as it was Sunday, and I got scrubbed this morning in consequence. The joys of being senior midshipman are not unalloyed. The *Digby* reported a steamer she could not catch at midnight, so we shaped a course to intercept her, and did so at 3.30 a.m., the *Digby* coming up half an hour later; but she proved to be only a Russian carrying volunteers from U.S.A. to Archangel. Our senior wireless officer, Captain Gillespie, R.M.L.I., in the soup with the Fleet wireless officer of the *Iron Duke*.

Tuesday 19

Learnt that a German submarine expedition has just left to operate against our armed merchant cruiser squadron, and so, if possible, to relieve the blockade. A great compliment to the efficacy of our patrol. It is said that the exports of copper and food from America to Germany via Scandinavia have dropped enormously since the armed merchant cruiser squadron started its duties properly last December, and in consequence the Germans are beginning to feel the pinch. Detached three ships for a patrol of the Romsdal Fjord on the Norwegian coast, as the ships coming round the north of Iceland are said to enter the fjords here and work their way south, thus evading the examination of our blockade. The C.-in-C. reported that bodies and wreckage, presumably of the *Viknor*, had been washed ashore at Portrush, so all hope has been given up. She had Von Wedel on board and all the prisoners. I hope Von Wedel did not escape. The disaster is the irony of fate, after their success, and the Commander was practically sure of promotion. By a funny coincidence we were the last ship to sight the *Viknor*, as was the *Crescent* with the *Hawke*. Whether the *Viknor* was mined, or foundered in a gale, is still a complete matter of conjecture[*].

Wednesday 20

Heard through the British Minister at Christiania (my old friend Mr. Findlay) that a big German steamer, the *Marie* from Apenrade, had arrived at Frederikstad; she will attempt to reach Thamshavn near Trondhjem to bring back a cargo of copper. She intends, apparently, to work her way up

---

[*] Count Botho von Wedel was Privy Councillor to the Kaiser and Chief of the German Spy Bureau before and during the war. Dr Armgaard Karl Graves, a German spy turned traitor, frequently mentions von Wedel in his book *The Secrets of the German War Office* (1914). Little is known about von Wedel's death, although it is widely accepted today that HMS *Viknor* struck a mine off north-west Ireland, all on board going down with her.

inside the fjords via Vobervig, Hangesund, Alesund, etc. We warned the Norwegian patrol to look out for her. Received news of the German Zeppelin air raid over the Norfolk coast. I expect the Hemsby people had some excitement*.

Thursday 21

Continuous snowstorm all day. Intensely cold, thermometer below freezing-point; the ship looked like a great white iceberg. A strong wind drove the snow down at a great pace, and a very nasty sea got up. One of the after wireless aerial braces carried away, but did not interfere with our signalling. The Yankees have been making all sorts of complaints about their ensign being hauled down when sent into Kirkwall for examination, and the Captain of the *Cedric* is going to get it in the neck.

DESCRIPTION OF 10TH CRUISER SQUADRON PATROL WORK, MIDSHIPMEN'S JOURNAL JANUARY 21ST

The primary object of the 10th cruiser squadron (cruiser force B) patrol is to stop the traffic in contraband-of-war, intended eventually for Germany, and shipped from America to Scandinavian ports. A similar patrol is being maintained at the entrance to the English channel in the south by other cruiser forces. In the north 24 armed merchant cruisers under the command of R.A. de Chair (H.M.S *Alsatian*) have superseded the 7 old cruisers of the *Crescent* type which were carrying out the patrol duties previously. The advantages of the new patrol are manifold, the ships being more numerous, better able to keep the sea in any weather, and having coal capacity for considerably longer periods, which in many cases the ships are newer and faster; the conditions of living for officers and men are also considerably improved.

It is the duty of the patrol to intercept all ships passing to the north of Scotland or between Orkneys, Shetlands, Faeroes or Iceland. In view of the order closing the North Sea and various arrangements, described later, made with neutrals, all neutral vessels, whose arrival has not been notified, should be regarded with suspicion. Thus all eastward bound vessels should be sent in with prize crews to Kirkwall for examination by the customs authorities. These ships should not be treated as prizes, but with courtesy, being allowed to fly their

---

* On the night of 19 January 1915, the first airship raid on Britain took place. Zeppelins of the Imperial German Navy Airship Division dropped bombs on Great Yarmouth and King's Lynn, killing 5 people.

own colours, in order not to offend the susceptibilities of neutrals. If however contraband is found onboard, the authorities will exercise the right of confiscation. Certain vessels of neutral shipping lines, have been granted special permits to use the north about route provided they call at Kirkwall, and it is unlikely the privilege will be abused, as this would entail the withdrawal of the permit. It is also possible to obtain clearances from other British ports. British and allied vessels may use the north about route, but if from foreign to Scandinavian ports, must call at Kirkwall.

The present regulations with regard to west bound ships are that they should be advised in their own interests to go to Kirkwall for examination, but force must not be used to turn them back. Few vessels take this advice however, and it is probable that in the near future stricter measures will be taken, as it is easy at present for these vessels to escape examination of any kind, especially when bad weather prohibits boarding, and so to slip through the blockade. Thus mines can be easily got through, concealed under a cargo of salt or some other such commodity. Vessels westward bound are directed to Lat 60°N Long 3°W, whence they should keep to northward of 60° parallel until they reach 3°W, and then to Kirkwall. Eastward bound sailing ships should make Faeroes, and then keep 50° north of the Shetlands. Stornoway has been suggested as an examination port for westbound ships to reduce the amount of ships going to Kirkwall. Kirkwall and Fair Island passage should be made by day, as there are no lights by night. The Pentland Firth passage is prohibited at all times.

It is probable that as the pressure of the patrol is increasingly felt in Germany, bigger commercial inducements will be offered to smuggle through copper and other contraband. In consequence, the duties of the patrol are likely to become harder rather than lighter.

Friday 22

On patrol as usual today. Snowstorm continued unceasingly, and thermometer lower than ever—several degrees below freezing-point. Intercepted some signals from the *Minotaur* and *Hampshire*, so discovered they have returned from China; thus the old "Bird" (C.T. Wilson) is knocking about near home again. This means Kenneth is home also, I suppose, unless he remained at Hong-Kong in the *Triumph*. McWilliams on the sick list with influenza.

Saturday 23

Left patrol off the Faeroes and proceeded to Rockall for firing practice. Rockall is a conical rock 80 feet long by about 50 feet high, sticking straight up out of 400 fathoms of water, in the middle of the Atlantic, about the most desolate place in God's earth; it is four times as far west from the Hebrides as St. Kilda, and St. Kilda is considered about the loneliest habitable spot in the British Isles. Firing practice; fire control, seven rounds practice each side, with two rounds common. Results satisfactory, but nothing to enthuse over, as several things went wrong. Afterwards proceeded for Barra Head.

Sunday 24

Proceeding to Liverpool to coal. Made Barra Head 8 a.m. All lookouts double-banked, as these waters are mine infested. Much better weather. First sun for some weeks. The extra daylight down south here is most welcome. Passed the *Calyx*, *Clan MacNaughton*, *Otway*, and destroyer *Swift*. The Captain of *Otway* is taking charge in our absence. Passed Oversay and Dhub Artach, making Mull of Cantyre 3.30 p.m. Great excitement in the evening. I did eight hours consecutive watch-keeping. The *Hibernia* reported hostile submarines off Lame, though how they got there the Lord only knows! Later they were reported on our starboard beam, about three miles off, but immediately we increased to twenty-two knots—full speed—and escaped.

Monday 25

Anchored off Mersey Bar at midnight. Too foggy to go up the river before 10 a.m. Docked in the evening. Very exciting day. Intercepted all sorts of wireless news; apparently the First Battle Cruiser Squadron with some destroyers engaged the German battle cruiser squadron which had ventured out of Wilhelmshaven*. We sunk the *Blücher* and sent them scuttling back to port, with the *Seydlitz* and *Lutzow* badly damaged. On our side the *Lion* was damaged, and so were the destroyers *Liberty* and *Meteor*. I celebrated five weeks' abstinence by drinking more than was good for me and getting a head like a hen. It is quite funny being in port again, after five weeks continuously at sea. Received a bumper mail, also first for five weeks. Some very interesting letters. The majority of the

---

* Battle of Dogger Bank, a battle cruiser action between Beatty's Battle Cruiser squadron and the German First Scouting Group. The German objective was to attack British patrols and fishing vessels in the Dogger Bank area – a shoal lying about 60 miles east of the coast of Northumberland. Thanks to a series of decoded radio intercepts, the British had advance knowledge of German intentions and were waiting for them. Thinking they were outnumbered the Germans turned for home under a barrage of long-range gunfire.

officers went on leave, but they kept some of us on board, self included, to run the ship while she is being coaled. Shut up the wireless office at twelve noon; they are going to fit a new set. We are going to change duties next month. Four other midshipmen are going to take on coding officer. I am going to be Navigator's assistant again, as I was in the last month in the *Crescent*.

Tuesday 26

Took over my duties as "Tanky." Cobb is going to be my extra assistant in harbour. Spent most of the day correcting charts and winding chronometers. Most people have a pretty slack time in harbour, but I seem to have more to do than ever. There is simply heaps to be done. All the sailing corrections to light lists from N. to M.s, etc., with several clocks and chronometers to look after. Went ashore in the afternoon, did some shopping, and called on Miss Amy Soderströme, a Norwegian girl I met in Norway, and then had tea with Mrs. Roxburgh at the Adelphi. Worked up till midnight at chart correcting.

January 26th 1915
H.M.S. ALSATIAN

Dear Daddy,

Best love to you and mother and the rest of the family; please thank mother for all her letters. We arrived in port to coal yesterday and anchored for the first time for five weeks; we have not seen any terra-firma, except occasional glimpses in the distance, since December 23rd. Christmas and New Year at sea. So you can imagine we were pretty pleased to be at anchor again, especially as we have had no news or mails whatever since we left, except occasional fragments intercepted by wireless. I don't think we have ever appreciated letters so much before. We are going to sea again at the end of the week. Nearly all the officers have gone on a few days' leave, but about six of us are left on board doing the work of the other fifty. I have got 200 charts to correct, all the chronometers to overhaul, and a hundred and one other things to do, as the Navigator has gone, so I don't expect to see much of the shore. One of our midshipmen has just been appointed to the battle cruiser Australia, and I should not be surprised if we all get to battleships and battle cruisers before long. If all goes well, and I am still in the Alsatian, I hope to get down to London for a few days next time we come in, which will be roughly about March 6th—12th.

We are far more comfortable than in the old Crescent, but are kept a good deal busier, for as there are twenty-four (now twenty-three) ships in the squadron, there is the devil of a lot of staff squadron work to get through, in addition to the ordinary watch-keeping and work of the ship.

I should be very much obliged if you would tell the people at the bank to send me some sort of account occasionally. I should have thought the beginning of the year would have been a suitable time. Mother should have paid £1 for me, which Auntie Enid sent as a Christmas present, but either she forgot or else she omitted to inform me that my request had been carried out. I am sending them £12 of my pay by post, and if they don't acknowledge it they will lose my custom. It won't make much difference when my pay is £31 a year, but when it is £5,000 a year for First Sea Lord, perhaps they will buck up a bit.

We have had quite an interesting time, though a bit monotonous at times. It has been bitingly cold where I have been, with snow the rule rather than the exception. I expect you read of the Viknor's loss; she belonged to our squadron. "A tale hangs thereby" of remarkable interest, which makes the old saying that truth is stranger than fiction appear remarkably true. The whole affair is shrouded in mystery. After the war, when censorship is dead, I think the loss of the Viknor and the events leading up to it will be found to be one of the most dramatic stories of the struggle, on the naval side at all events.

Best love to all.
From
TOBY

Wednesday 27

The Navigator, Mr. Clarke, the Captain, and the Commander went on leave. So I am senior navigating officer on board. Still more work to do. I am no shirker, but I can't possibly get everything done in three days. Robinson got an appointment to the battle cruiser *Australia*, so our gun-room mess was broken up. He is very pleased, naturally. Johnstone went to London on thirty-six hours' leave. The Captain of the *Caribbean*, a Commander, R.N., and Commander Wardle, Captain of the *Calyx*, came on board. Mr. Croughan, another old *Crescent* friend, also of the *Calyx*, whose gunner he is, also on board. Dined in Birkenhead with Tottenham and a Reserve A.P. from the *Orotava*, and then went to the Argyle Theatre. Returned to ship at midnight.

The mystery of the *Viknor*'s loss, with the fate of Von Wedel, and the events transpiring on the capture of the *Bergensfjord*, seem likely to remain unsolved. Whether the ill-fated vessel foundered in a gale, ran ashore, struck a mine, or was destroyed by the agency of the German prisoners on board, it will probably never be ascertained. There is considerable pathos attached to the event, as the *Viknor* was coming into harbour after a long and weary sojourn on patrol, and her officers and men were looking forward to a rest in port, and leave to their homes for many. She had, by intercepting the *Bergensfjord*, scored a notable success and been congratulated by the C.-in-C. Thus Commander Ballantyne, her Captain, must have felt sure of accelerated promotion to the rank of Captain. Then when almost in safety she was swallowed up, and another record imprinted in the vast list of unsolved mysteries of the ocean. It is a point of some satisfaction to feel that in all probability Baron Von Wedel (alias Spero), the arch-spy and schemer of the German Secret Service, with his fellow-prisoners, perished with his captors. True, the foreign newspapers report the arrival of Baron Wedel in Rome with important documents; but this is almost certainly a blind to mislead the ignorant on the part of the German authorities, chagrined and frightened at the loss of their chief spy. Nevertheless, the report has given rise to a theory that Von Wedel actually escaped, either by bribing a neutral in the *Bergensfjord* to impersonate him, and so escaping to Norway, or else as a lone survivor of the *Viknor*. The first idea is remarkably improbable, owing to the fact that however large the bribe offered, the man must have known that he was taking in exchange death or at least imprisonment for life; while the likelihood of the well-guarded and valuable prisoner being the sole survivor of the doomed

ship is practically nil; for even had he escaped the wreck, how could he have landed and fled the country, unnoticed and unthought of.

No! There can be but little doubt that though in the loss of the *Viknor* we suffered a sad loss of valuable lives of officers and men, yet the blow to the German spy system, in the almost certain death of its prime mover, cannot be overestimated in its importance.

Thursday 28

A day of catastrophes. The auxiliary steam pipe burst in the engine-room, and we were in complete darkness for half an hour, as the dynamos stopped, and no one could find any candles. No hot water, and a cold dinner, the worst we have had in the ship, because we had a guest, I suppose. H.M.S. *Natal* came in for a refit in the morning and secured astern of the cargo liner *Hesperian*. I did not go ashore. I spent most of the forenoon with Cobb wrestling with the chronometers. Corrected a large number of charts. Went on board the *Natal* and had some drinks in the gun-room. They are to be in a fortnight, and hope for five days' leave each. The A.P. came on board and had five cocktails, and Greenland came to dinner. A pretty rowdy evening, liquid flowing freely.

Friday 29

The Captain and Navigator returned from leave. Three hostile submarines reported off Bardsey Isle. H.M.S. *Natal* went into dry dock, in place of the S.S. *St. Paul*, a Yankee liner. Two stokers broke out of the ship and deserted. More charts arrived for correction. Submarines reported off the Bar at midday, probably the same as those seen earlier at Bardsey. The brutes seem to be everywhere. One actually fired at the Barrow forts. It will be pretty dangerous work getting in and out of the Mersey now. How I envy those devils in the battle cruisers! Everyone does. They get all the fighting, and not nearly such hard work as we do.

Saturday 30

Hawkins and Martin came on board from the *Natal*. Met old "Tweedledum," our signal instructor at Dartmouth three years ago; he is in the *Caribbean*, in which ship is also C.P.O. Lobb. Went to the Adelphi in the afternoon, after working all the morning. Spent most of the afternoon imbibing cocktails, also had a shooting pool with Bench and Ikey, and took 5s. off each of them. Met old Hole, who was surgeon at Dartmouth with us; he is now senior medical officer of the *Bayano*. Pleasant reminiscences of old days. Dined with the Captain and A.P. Cockerill (his secretary) at the Adelphi. Tottenham was also invited, but couldn't come. We had a box at the Empire and several drinks afterwards. The skipper behaved like a brick, and the dinner was excellent, so was the wine. I went on a tour with Cockerill afterwards—he is not nearly so wet as he appears—and did not get back on board till two. The German submarines, of which one is *U-21*, sank three merchantmen off the Bar.

Sunday 31

Eleven more merchant ships sunk; the matter is getting very serious. All sailings of H.M. ships cancelled, so we shall not leave tonight. Ships of the Tenth Cruiser Squadron coming in to coal are being diverted by wireless to the Clyde, and all the big liners to Southampton. The enforced inaction of several ships in Liverpool will weaken our patrol badly. Later news states that the authorities have declared the port of Liverpool closed to all shipping. This will seriously damage trade. We are under sailing orders, but shall not leave for two or three days, when we shall probably try and slip out in the dark, which will be very exciting, especially as we know three submarines are waiting for us.

FEBRUARY

Monday 1

The despatch of a torpedo-boat flotilla from Pembroke to attempt to waylay the submarines is anticipated. All officers and men returned from leave except the Captain and the Admiral. I worked all the morning and afternoon. Several trawlers, yachts, motor-boats, and fast Isle of Man packet-boats have been commandeered by the authorities, and are being sent out armed with six-pounders to hunt down the submarines. There is little doubt they are oiling from neutral vessels, which have previously received British clearances under false pretences. The *Natal's* picket-boat also went after the raiders. I went on shore in the evening, did some shopping, dined with Johnstone, met old Hole. Then went to the "Whirl of the Town" at the Olympia with Ward and Learmont. An excellent show; Wilkie Bard, Daisy Wood very good, and a very pretty chorus. Daisy Wood sang recruiting songs exuberantly, with a very naughty twinkle. House crowded with naval officers. Got back on board midnight.

Tuesday 2
Working all day as usual. Broke leave in the evening. Went on shore with Ward to the Olympia again. Havers and Rae from the *Natal* both there. The "Whirl of the Town" is the best show I have ever seen out of London. Supped with Olive Russell and Ninon Oste afterwards, two very nice and chic little girls. Ninon Oste has got about the second most important part. Got back at 2 a.m. I am beginning to feel rather a wreck with this enforced inactivity in harbour working all the day, and on the spree all the night, no sleep.

Wednesday 3
Usual routine, worked all day. Heard from Joko; not much of a letter. "Drippie" P. Porritt with a friend, and Little from the *Natal* to lunch. Porritt is now in the King's Liverpools and leaves for Canterbury shortly; I must inform the people at home. Went on shore with Ward and took Olive and Ninon out to tea. Came back to the ship to dine. The *Calyx* took fire at anchor—cause unknown; still burning at midnight. On shore again after dinner, and to the second house of the Olympia. Havers and Rae there as usual. Took Olive and Ninon to supper at the "Exchange." Very hilarious.

February 3rd 1915
H.M.S. ALSATIAN

Dearest Mother,

We are still in harbour, a week extra owing to the fact that there are some submarines waiting for us outside, so I am taking this opportunity of writing. We hope to slip out on a dark night and so get back to our patrol, which will be quite exciting. The devils would have had an excellent chance of bagging us, but for the fact that they were foolish enough to betray their presence, of which we were unaware, by sinking some merchantmen, as I dare say you have read in the papers. I was very busy the first few days in harbour, but finished all the work on hand by attacking it ferociously until midnight two or three times. Since then I have been very nice and lazy, and have spent most of my spare time pleasantly, but not too wisely, with more amusing objects than charts. There is an excellent revue with a first-class chorus (for looks) at one of the theatres here; so possibly you can guess our amusements. A large number of us will go to sea "broke," so perhaps certain members of the caste or company or whatever it is of the revue will have heavier purses.

Prospects of leave in the immediate future—that is, for a month or so—are nil, but I will write again as soon as we return to harbour in a few weeks' time. Best love to all.

From
TOBY.

Thursday 4

Last night, at the Olympia stage door, whom should I meet but old Dean, Eng.-Lieut.-Commander of a destroyer refitting in Albert Dock. I have not seen him since Osborne days. He was not waiting for a fairy, but for Wilkie Bard, whom he knows. The "Whirl of the Town" is practically entirely monopolised by the Services now. H.M.S. *Macedonian*, armoured merchant cruiser on foreign service, proceeded to Sandon for half-tide basin. At 10.40 we slipped and proceeded in charge of pilot and tugs also to Sandon half-tide basin; this is a sign that we shall sail soon, submarines or no submarines. Secured alongside the Cunard liner *Mauretania* in Sandon basin at 11.40. I spent the day on board, recuperating and doing a little work. Left the Olympia girls to themselves for a change. By the way, there is a big dance on at the Adelphi, but I am too much of a wreck to go.

Friday 5

Usual work in the morning. Since the submarine scare, the remainder of our ships (Tenth Cruiser Squadron) have been using Loch Ewe and Glasgow as coaling bases instead of Belfast and Liverpool. Went on shore in the afternoon and up to the Adelphi. Ran across Olive and Ninon, and had tea with them under the disapproving glances of Commander Wardle of the *Calyx*. Met their friend, Mrs. Carmichael, a jolly good sort, and also the stage manager; several cocktails with him, and he said if I came tonight he would put me up to all the best of the charms, behind the scenes, I don't already know. So I determined to break leave and have the time of my life. Tottenham and Glanvile dined with the Captain, and Richardson with the Admiral. Wood and Learmont had three girls on board to tea, and McNaught one to dinner. But bad luck dogged me; just as I was leaving the ship bound for Olympia, looking forward to a tremendous night with the girls, I ran right into Lieutenant Kenyon's arms, and he nailed me and stopped my leave, of course. I expect I shall catch it tomorrow. A damned nuisance! I was very disappointed, but put the best face on it and did some more work instead. It was a proper walk-over. If Jellicoe catches Tirpitz as well as Kenyon did me, he will do well.

Saturday 6
Cast off and left Sandon basin at 2.35 p.m.

Found the *Lusitania* and H.M. ships *Calyx*, *Caribbean*, *Orotava*, and *Bayano* in the river. Anchored for an hour off New Brighton, after passing the *Aquitania* in dry dock. Weighed later and proceeded to sea. Dropped the pilot off the Bar Light and proceeded at eighteen knots. Much speculation as to whether we shall evade the numerous mines and submarines and get back to our patrol. Ran past the Mull of Galloway and out of the Irish Sea during the night.

Sunday 7
A fire broke out during the night in the fore starboard fan-room, but was easily extinguished. Passed Oversay at 6 a.m. Very dirty weather, and thick, consequently came in unpleasantly close to Skerryvore and had to alter quickly to clear the reefs. Shortly before noon a mine was sighted. The starboard six-pounder was manned and a firing party of marines got up to sink it. But there was a very high wind blowing, and owing to the bad weather we lost sight of it. Cruised about for half an hour or so, but failed to find it again, so continued our course. Passed Barra Head and outside St. Kilda. *Bayana* reported more mines off Skerryvore.

Monday 8
Arrived back on patrol, and took over command once more, after fifteen days' absence. Dirty weather. Spoke the *Bayano* in the forenoon. Went to

G.Q.s, and spotting table practice afterwards. No sun, but just managed to snap a time azimuth to get a deviation. I like my job as Assistant-Navigator (Tanky). Sighted Sydero 5 p.m. and altered course to the south-west. No news has been heard of the *Clan MacNaughton* since the 2nd instant, and bodies are said to have been washed up*. She is the second ship of our squadron to be lost. With her goes Commander Jeffreys, her skipper—he is our *Cornwall* Jeffreys cousin—and dear old Lieut.-Commander Popham, our First Lieutenant in the *Crescent*. Very bad luck, as he was an awful good sort; married, with one child, to whom he was absolutely devoted.

Tuesday 9

Very busy all day. There is heaps to do in this job, but it is excellent experience, and I get good sleep, as night hours are fairly slack. Swung ship roughly in the forenoon and compared the four compasses. Mr. Green issued a large number of Service text- and work-books, etc., to the gun-room. The loss of the *Clan MacNaughton* is now to all intents and purposes certain, but whether she was blown up by a mine, torpedoed by a submarine, ran ashore and broke up, or foundered in a gale, remains a mystery, as with the *Viknor*. Wreckage has been found far out from land, presumably hers. Communicated visually with the *Hildebrand* in the afternoon. Fine, sunny day, very nice after Liverpool fog; still a big swell, and gale got up again after dark. I have got into the Admiral's and Skipper's bad books just lately. Stopped up late and finished correcting charts. Great game of deck hockey in the "dogs."

Wednesday 10

Took advantage of moderate weather to play more deck hockey on the lee side. It is very nice to be able to do this, after the cramped decks of the *Crescent*. Intercepted a Danish barquantine bound for Troon with timber; she proved to be the *Esther* of Marshal. Let her proceed. Had a long chat with old Outram. He is a dear old chap, and talks in a gruff old voice; very interesting some of his anecdotes are. It must be rather unpleasant for him, as the Commodore of the Allan Line, now being only a Commander, R.N.R., and junior to our skipper and the Rear-Admiral, and treated as practically a nobody. He is a fine old seaman.

---

* It is believed that HMS *Clan MacNaughton* was sunk off the north coast of Ireland on 3 February, 1915 after striking a mine during a storm.

Thursday 11

The armed boarding vessel *Caesarea* has been detached for service with Tenth Cruiser Squadron, for bringing out prize crews to their ships. I like Lieutenant Clarke, the Navigator, my chief, very much. He is a quiet, methodical sort of devil, a great favourite of the skipper's. Reputed very good at games. Rather apt to be a bit short-tempered, but on the whole a d__d good sort. Very fair weather on patrol. Worked both sounding machines forward, also the *Empress* after one, in the forenoon. The *Cedric* reported unsuccessfully chasing a big steamer at dawn, which drew away from her at sixteen and a half knots. We told off all our patrol to intercept her and went south ourselves. She was intercepted in the afternoon and proved to be the *Frederick VIII.*, a Danish liner; examined and allowed to proceed. Several Scandinavian liners are suspected of smuggling Germans across from U.S.A. Took an Eiffel Tower time signal at 11.45 p.m.* A great game of deck hockey in the dogs. Very ferocious play.

Friday 12

Very wet and unpleasant all day, although the sea and wind kept down fairly well. G.Q.s in the forenoon, 1-inch aiming tube firing, with the starboard guns, the proper guns' crews closing up first, and then the corresponding part guns' crews taking their places. The firing was fairly good considering the blinding rain. The skipper had a row with "Guns," much to that individual's annoyance. The imperturbable Clarke was nearly drawn in, and, of course, old J.K. had to have a jolly good gas about it.

Saturday 13

The *Otway* intercepted the Norge-Amerika liner *Trondhjemsfjord* during the forenoon and sent her into Kirkwall with a prize crew. A close watch is being kept for the *Oscar II.*, which is supposed to be carrying German officers and men of the Reserve to Copenhagen. The Captain inspected our journals; only very cursorily, however, and made but few remarks. Apparently he didn't see my plans of the steering arrangements, which would, I think, have interested him. Tottenham very much to the fore; could not understand why his noon sight was 300 miles out, having used a 1914 "Nautical Almanac."

---

* Throughout the war, the Eiffel Tower in Paris, which was sending out wireless time signals for the Navy, sent out two additional sets of 'scientific' time signals at 11.30 p.m. and 11.45 p.m. GMT.

Sunday 14

Evidence now obtained seems to show that the *Clan MacNaughton* was very probably torpedoed by *U-21* returning from her raid on the Mersey shipping. The *Cedric* reported intercepting the *Oscar II.* and sending her into Kirkwall with a prize crew. We stopped the Norwegian sailing ship *Olav*, cleared from Falmouth with bran; very probably intended for Germany; sent her into Kirkwall with a prize crew under Midshipman Evans, R.N.R. Stopped a trawler after dark, but let her go after examination. All the R.N. snotties in the soup. Had a long chat with Clarke about game, the Greigs, etc.

Monday 15

Suspicion has fallen on the Falmouth Customs authorities, who are said to be giving neutral ships false clearances with contraband, intended ostensibly for neutrals, but in reality for Germany. Submarines sighted off Loch Ewe and Stornoway. They are reported to have unsuccessfully attacked the store-ship at the Stornoway naval base. More wreckage of the *Clan MacNaughton* discovered. Sighted H.M.S. *Digby* in the forenoon. She was "told off" by the Admiral for having bungled his instructions *re* the prize crews at Stornoway. Germans are said to have lain mines off Lerwick, which the *Benbow* narrowly escaped. One trawler patrol ship sunk by them. Sighted the battle cruiser *Australia* doing night firing. I wonder how "Fober" Robinson likes his new ship.

Tuesday 16

The *Caribbean*'s urgent demands for coal resulted yesterday in her being sent to Loch Ewe to coal, instead of Liverpool, much to her disgust. Very cold day, a snow blizzard in the morning watch, but it cleared up beautifully in the forenoon, and we had some gorgeous and most welcome sunshine. How we value the sun now, when a year ago it was nothing! Communicated with the *Cedric II.*, visually, and sent a mail by her into Liverpool, as she is off to coal. "Guns" got his leg badly pulled, trying to read the *Cedric*'s semaphore. "Guns" trousers are quite a by-word now in the gun-room. G.Q.s and rate of change practice in the forenoon. Passed the Second Light Cruiser Squadron under Rear-Admiral Napier coming back from firing practice. H.M.S. *Glasgow*, of Valparaiso and Falkland fame, among them. They looked like great long greyhounds, but were making very heavy weather in a sea which didn't even move us.

Wednesday 17

The battle cruiser *Tiger* and light cruiser *Active* passed the patrol for firing practice. During the night there was a sudden change for the worse in the weather. The glass dropped steadily all day, and the wind blew a full gale from the south-east, backing gradually. A very big sea by noon. By dark there was a regular storm, the worst we have experienced since I was in the *Crescent*. The *Alsatian* is an excellent sea-boat, but nevertheless we were none too comfortable, and all the smaller ships must be having an appalling time. The Admiral heard by wireless that information concerning our patrol is leaking out, consequently he is thinking of stopping all leave next time we go to coal, and anyhow the strictest reticence must be observed. He issued a memorandum to the commanding officers of the squadron *re* this.

Thursday 18

Germany's threat to torpedo all merchant shipping in British waters, regardless of loss of life, comes into action today. I am afraid the effect will be more serious than is generally anticipated. As a forerunner of what is to come, five German submarines were sighted at noon yesterday off Cape Wrath, proceeding to the south-west, probably bound for the Irish Sea. Thirty trawlers are reported to have left the Kattegat full of German mines, and the First Light Cruiser Squadron and some destroyers have been sent to look for them. An oil-ship has escaped unexamined from the Manchester Ship Canal, and it is feared she will oil the submarines. Considering the Russian military situation, things are looking rather black in general just at present. Weather moderated a little, but still very bad, high wind and very big sea running. All the R.N. snotties in the soup with J.K. again. He is getting very bumptious now as Acting Commander; very different from the devil-may-care sort of chap that he was when a mere watch-keeper in the *Crescent*. Stopped and boarded the Norwegian steamer *Sisland* from Christiansand to Baltimore at 11 p.m. Allowed her to proceed.

Friday 19

Sighted two more steamers during the middle watch, but weather prohibited boarding. Gale continued all day, getting considerably worse towards nightfall, and we hove to. Went to G.Q.s in the forenoon. Very cold, and a very high wind from the E.N.E. to N.N.E. The Second Light Cruiser Squadron have been sent to support the First Light Cruiser Squadron and destroyers, sweeping down to the Kattegat for the minelayers, but little can be done in this weather. The First Cruiser Squadron, composed of some of the China and Mediterranean ships home from foreign service with "B" patrol of the Tenth Cruiser Squadron, will sweep east on a line north from Muckle Flugga, and so catch the minelayers if they have not already escaped up the Norwegian coast.

Saturday 20

Gale still blowing in all its fury; seas mountainous, running right down unchecked from the North Cape and off Spitzbergen. Miserable day. The Signal Bos'n sounded off the alarm by mistake after breakfast, and we all rushed to our action stations, thinking a scrap was in sight at last, and were very sick to find it a false alarm. It reminded me of the false alarm on the *Crescent* when Commander Wardle sounded off by mistake. The old man gave the Signal Bos'n what for. He has a nasty liver this morning. Merchantmen and trawlers report submarines off the Faeroes; they are probably after us, but they won't like this weather. We are shifting temporarily from the south-west to the south-east of the Faeroes, about half-way to the Shetlands, to support "B" patrol.

Sunday 21

Two German disguised minelayers will leave the Norwegian port of Bergen tonight. Owing to the submarine menace, all our patrols are to be moved about a hundred miles to the westward by noon tomorrow. Gale continued without abating one jot. Communicated with the *Digby*, who reported sinking mines off Sydero. Sighted two trawlers, apparently British; too rough to board.

Monday 22

Gale went on like blue hell, but continuous snow supplanted the rain squalls we have had previously. Wind shifted to of the northward. Very big sea running. Cold intense; the coldest weather I have yet experienced since I joined the ship; average height of thermometer 16° F., 16° below freezing-point, although at times it has dropped considerably lower. The spray flying over the bows froze before it reached the bridge, and cut your face with the force of the impact. All the decks not actually awash were as slippery as ice. Intercepted and examined the S.S. *F. Heredik* of Hangesund for the second time in a fortnight. She is bound from Goole to Reykjavik, and appears to be taking her time over it.

Tuesday 23

A great controversy—Lieutenant Kenyon and the gun-room officers, R.N., versus Lieut.-Commander Kiddle and the gun-room officers, R.N.R. Result, a draw in their favour. Woke up and turned out on deck to find the decks covered in snow, inches deep. The gale abated, and sea went down a little. Snow-storms all day, and still fearfully cold. Made Sydero early, luckily near Sunbö Light, otherwise we might have fetched the Munken. Stopped and examined a trawler from Iceland to Sorvang. She looked more like the icing off a wedding cake than a real live ship. Went to G.Q.s in the forenoon, but too cold for target practice and too rough to lower target.

Wednesday 24

Not quite so cold and weather better. Fears expressed for the safety of the *Patia* and *Orotava*; they have not been heard of for three days. We met the *Changuinola* and *Columbella* at a rendezvous in the forenoon, and got back our prize crew with Midshipman Evans, which took in the *Olav* ten days ago. They spent three days in Kirkwall, and went to St. Kilda in the *Caesarea*, and finally went on board the *Changuinola* and so back here. Ben Evans brought back some messages from old Shearer at Kirkwall. The *Digby* and *Hilary* both reported sinking mines.

Thursday 25

McNaught's twenty-first birthday celebrated in great style. The famous *Dacia**, which has been taking such a front seat in the newspapers of late, is reported to be in wireless touch with Valentia. Whether she will try the north or south about route seems uncertain. The *Ambrose* has three prize crews away and cannot send any more. We are leaving our patrol off the Faeroes and coming south for a bit. Several changes are now being made in the constitution of the various patrols. The *Changuinola* has been despatched to the Flannan Isles. The safety of the *Patia* has been ascertained. We intercepted a Norwegian sailing vessel, the *Glen Lora*, and sent her into Kirkwall for examination with a prize crew under Midshipman Renfree, R.N.R. Also we stopped the Swedish steamer *Drotting Sophia*, but allowed her to proceed. I was employed superintending fitting out of after-control.

---

* Belonging to the Hamburg-America Line before the outbreak of war, the *Dacia* flagrantly carried contraband from the USA to Germany throughout the early part of the war. The French eventually seized her, loaded with cotton, at the entrance to the English Channel.

Friday 26

More bad weather experienced. Stopped and boarded the S.S. *Overdia*, bound from Baltimore to Malmö in Sweden, and sent her into Kirkwall for examination with a prize crew under Midshipman Elliott, R.N.R. The *Dacia* has been heard calling by wireless, but her route is still uncertain. We altered course to the north-east to stop a ship, making for the Shetlands, that the *Digby* had failed to catch. Took an Eiffel Tower wireless time signal at 11.45 p.m. "Little things annoy great minds"—the amended proverb. The Admiral searched for a stump of pencil the Flag Captain had lost for three-quarters of an hour; accused everyone of stealing or hiding it, and finally found it in his pocket.

Saturday 27

Very cold again, snowing all day. No news of the *Dacia*. I hope she hasn't got through, though it is quite possible, as the snowstorms prevent us seeing more than a few cables from the ship, and she might slip through unobserved. Sighted Sydero early, and spoke the *Hilary* and *Digby* later. I had a row with Henderson over physical training. Tottenham logged our course S. 84° W. instead of N. 84° W., and put our 8 p.m. D.R. twelve miles out. He got scrubbed by all four O.O.W.s, and was very anxious that the Navigator and skipper should not know, as (he said) it would affect his certificate, which, however, in our opinion, must be already so bad that it can't be worse.

Sunday 28

Heard by wireless that the *Dacia* had been captured in the Channel by a French patrol. Mustered the hands by Open List. Big gale blowing, usual weather, heavy snow, large seas, and very cold. Still to the south-west of the Faeroes.

MARCH

Monday 1

Weather as per routine, glass well below freezing again. An American ship refused to be boarded by the *Ambrose*, who thereupon applied to the *Patuca*, the senior officer of her patrol, for instructions. Shots were fired

Sketch Map Shewing disposition of Patrols of the 10ᵏ cruiser squadron on March 1ˢᵗ 1915

"A"

"Mantua"

Thorshavn
FAEROES

Trangisvaag

"B"

MUCKLE FLUGGA

Balta Vos
SHETLANDS
Lerwick

FOULA

Var. 22° W (1912) decreasing 10' annually

"Motagua"

"Teutonic"

"C"

"Patia"

"Cedric"

"Alsatian" (Flag)

"Virginian"

"Oropesa"

"Hilary"

"Changuinola"

Var. 20° W decreasing 10' annually

Fair Isle

Var. 18° W decreasing 10' annually

North Rona

Sule Skerry

ORKNEYS

Suliskey

Kirkwall

"Ambrose"

"D"

"Patuca"

Butt of Lewis

CAPE WRATH

Flannan Isles

Loch Roag

Thurso

Wick

Stornoway

SKILDA

HEBRIDES

SCOTLAND

MINCH

Lochewe

MORAY FIRTH

Ships detached for Coaling, &c

"Otway"	"Hildebrand"
"Columbella"	"Caribbean"
"Orotava"	"Calyx"
"Bayano"	"Eskimo"
"Digby"	

Not joined yet
"Laurentic"

Sunk
"Viknor"
"Clan Macnaughton"

across the Yankee ship's bow (the *Navahoe* her name was), and she then hove to. A boarding party from the *Patuca*, who had come up, was sent under our old *Crescent* friend, Lieut.-Commander Bacon, R.N.R., and she was taken into Kirkwall as a prize for examination, in spite of the vehement protests of her captain and crew.

Tuesday 2

Heavy snowfall all the forenoon; better weather in the afternoon. Went quite close to Sydero, the black heights of Sunbö Head, topped with the glistening snow-white hills behind, looked very fine. Sighted H.M.S. *Cedric* at noon and cruised in company during the afternoon; communicated by boat and exchanged several signals. She proceeded south-east to her patrol at 4 p.m., and we went back to ours to the south-west of the Faeroes, from ten miles to two hundred miles distant from Sydero. The *Patuca* reports the death of her Commander. I had a row with Clarke; he accused me of being abrupt, and we argued thereon.

Wednesday 3

Sea and wind moderated, but steady rain and thick fog all day. Went to spotting-table in the forenoon. "Pompous Percy" in his element. John Kiddle ranting about the gun-room doing 6-inch loader, but no one listened. The ward-room started a backgammon competition, and the Secretary tried to arrange a concert for Saturday night; success patchy. Sighted a steamship, the *Jemtland*, at 9 p.m., examined her, and allowed her to proceed; then went full speed ahead to deceive her, altered course, and came around astern unobserved, and followed her throughout the night to find out if her intentions were genuine.

Thursday 4

Neutral vessels are now taking the precaution of having their name and national flag and port of register painted on their sides. In spite of the unfavourable predictions of "Guns," the Secretary's concert is advancing apace. The ship's company have several turns, and a gun-room septette are singing "Old Uncle Tom Cobleigh." The gun-room will also provide "When Irish Eyes Are Smiling" and "A Capital Ship," and McNaught is going to give a piano solo.

Boarded the *Jemtland* at 7.15 a.m., and as everything was found all right she was allowed to proceed, as she promised to call at Kirkwall for full examination. Personally I think she should have been sent in with a prize crew. Came up to the east of the Faeroes to act in conjunction with A and B patrols, in order to catch a Danish ship laden with whale-oil, trying to get through from the Faeroes to Germany. Sighted H.M.S. *Martian* 5.30 p.m., and at eight boarded and examined an Aberdeen trawler.

Friday 5

Boarded, examined, and allowed to proceed, the Norwegian steamer *King Haakon*. Went back again to the south-west of the Faeroes. Heard that a Yankee ship with foodstuffs for Germany has succeeded in slipping through down the Norwegian coast. Carried out rate of change practice in the forenoon, and target firing practice in the afternoon. The firing was quite good, especially with the 6-inch guns; although the six-pounders were not so good, we did not manage to damage the target much, but succeeded in deafening everybody, which always seems a great objective of gunnery experts. Tottenham and the Signal Bos'n had a long argument over a pair of spotting-glasses. They were so surprised by hearing the first gun go off that they dropped the glasses and smashed the prisms, 25s. each; language unprintable.

Saturday 6

Worked the after sounding machine successfully. Had a last rehearsal of the concert in the afternoon. Weather fair, but very cold indeed. The concert came off at six. Rather early, but if it had been later it would have disturbed the night watch-keepers. A great success. About fifteen turns, all the gun-room ones being excellent, especially "A Capital Ship" and "Widdicombe Fair." The Admiral seemed very pleased, and the skipper expressed approbation in his usual philosophical manner. With the exception of the Secretary and Staff Surgeon Walker, the ward-room did nothing, which was awfully flat of them. Individually they are a very nice set of chaps, but as a mess they are the dullest I have ever served with; no go or guts at all. It is the same in everything. Very busy all day clearing up generally, preparatory to going into harbour early next week.

Sunday 7

Left patrol for the south to go to Liverpool to coal. Stopped a Danish steamer with cotton from Galveston to Goteborg, and sent her into Kirkwall with a prize crew under Midshipman Wood, R.N.R.

Communicated with H.M.S. *Patuca* visually and by boat. Examined another sailing vessel in the evening.

Monday 8

Passed Barra Head at 8 a.m. Later Skerryvore, then Oversay, and then across to the Irish coast. Turned all our boats out and kept a very close lookout for mines and submarines, with which these waters seem infested. Passed between Rathlin Island and Portrush, then rounded Fair Head and ran down into the Irish Sea.

A whole network of trawlers minesweeping between the Mull of Cantyre and Larne, also the Gunboat *Skipjack* and patrol despatch vessel *Tara*. The longer light and extra warmth down south again most welcome. Arrived off the Bar at 12.30. A very busy and exciting time. On the bridge all night. Coincident with our return the German submarines have arrived again, and two ships were sunk tonight within three miles of us, although fog prevented us rendering any assistance. All hands drowned.

Tuesday 9

Anchored in the Mersey off Pier Head at 2 a.m. A very welcome mail came off at six. Stacks of letters for me, and, tired as I was, I waded through them, taking about two and a half hours. A wasted day spent dawdling about in the Mersey, as the docks are so full of shipping. Very busy clearing up in the chart-house, although feeling dog-tired from want of sleep. Secured alongside in Canada Dock at 8 p.m. H.M.S. *Columbella*, the only other ship of our squadron in, leaves at dark. Another submarine victim just outside Bar. Passed H.M.S. *Devonshire* in dock. Landed 8 p.m. Had some cocktails at the Adelphi and proceeded on leave by the 10.45 p.m. train.

Wednesday 10

Arrived London 4 a.m., went to Cumberland Terrace, and turned in. Claude Lowther and Jack Russell dined here last night. Spent the forenoon in bed, then went to call on Aunt Do after lunch with Norman. Daddy, Uncle John, Auntie Connie, and Esther also there. Went to call on Sophie; met Fanny Hallowes and Olive. Went home in a fearful hurry, stopping at Gieves for a cap on the way, when I saw dear old Humphrey Legge for a minute. Rushed off, dined with Olive at the Tiv., then on to "Peg o' My Heart" at the Globe. Rotten play, but Peg excellent. Norman and Claude Lowther there. Took Olive to sup at the Cri., and then home about midnight. Old Norman has been to see "Peg o' My Heart" nearly twenty times.

Thursday 11

Got up late, went and shopped most of the forenoon in Bond Street, also went to my bank in Russell Square. Norman accompanied me at first. Came home to lunch. Olive to lunch. Gertrude and Aunt Amy arrived about three, but I had to leave directly afterwards to go to Victoria to catch a train to Canterbury East, arriving 6.10. Got some oysters at Harrison's, and then went to Quaives to get some fizz. Loved being home. Stopped the night Westenhanger. The oysters and fizz a great success. Poor old Jack arrived very late, about twelve. Toots in bed with a breakdown; she has been doing too much. I had a long nocturnal chat with Joko from our bedroom windows. I find myself worse than ever over her.

Friday 12

Got up late, went round with Jack and Joko to see Grannie at the Rectory; saw Byron, Dolly, and Gwen Cohen, who is stopping with the Kelseys, and has developed into a very pretty girl now. After lunch called on Mrs. Kelsey and had several drinks with Bob, the Doc, Jabez, and Frank Goodson at the Tank, then went on to Quaives to get some gear. Left at four, motored to Ashford with Joko. Gone over her completely again, and very jealous as she is very keen on two damned carabiniers, Dent and Charlesworth. How I long for the dear, safe, dull old Buffs again! Went by train to Godstone. Met Malky and Miss Judd at the station. Stopped night at Godstone with Uncle John. Auntie Connie, Grannie Greig, Malky, and old Uncle John Thomson also there.

Saturday 13

Hunted; met at Oxted with the Old Surrey. Cecil Leveson-Gower out and in great form. Not much of a day; killed a lame fox early on, and then did rottenly. May Gould out; a very nice girl, and quite pretty, or rather picturesque; Malky raves about her. Uncle John Thomson left, and Mike, Mog, and Beg arrived in the evening. Old "Doc" Paterson came in with Cecil to tea. A tremendous game of billiard bowls in the evening after dinner; Malky tremendous fun. I sat up very late swigging whisky-and-sodas and talking to Mike, and as I did a bottle of fizz for dinner, felt quite happy. Old Grannie Greig not at all well.

Sunday 14

Went up by the 11.10 train to town. In the afternoon daddy, Jack, and Mrs. Russell, with their children and Billy and Donald Hugh and I all went to the Zoo. Donald Hugh Ellis is a little boy of Billy's age, who is living with us during his parents' absence in India. He is a grandson of Admiral Finnis, my old friend. Jack R. invited me to dine at the Berkeley with him, but I could not go, as Joko came to town and I met her. We dined at the "Troc.," then to a concert at the Palladium, and then home to Sophie's. Poor old Stanley laid up with a broken ankle. On my return home at one, found a wired leave extending Tuesday till Saturday.

Monday 15

Got up late, went to meet Joko at Down Street Station, and then we shopped together in Regent Street, Oxford Street, and Bond Street. Lunched at the Café Royal. Then called on Aunt Do and had tea. Then went to see Henry, who is wounded in hospital and looking awful. Olive was with him. Also called on the Buchanans, but they were out. Then Joko went home to dress, ditto me. Met her at Piccadilly Station, and we dined at the Savoy. Then went to "The Country Girl" at Daly's. Excellent show; Gertie Millar* and W.H. Berry excellent. Mabel Sealby, the girl J.P.R. was engaged to, was acting. Went back to the Savoy for supper and stopped for two or three hours' dancing. Thoroughly enjoyed every minute of it. Went home madly in love.

Tuesday 16

Got up late again. Joko came to lunch. Then she and I went to Madame Tussaud's and called on the Phelps and Woodwards. Then we both went home our ways. Izzie Phelps to tea at home. Joko and I dined with Johnstone at Prince's. Then went on to "Kings and Queens" at the St. James's Theatre. Marie Löhr** acted wonderfully well, but the play was rather too tense. Afterwards we met Florence Lomax, and then went to supper, the four of us at the Piccadilly Restaurant. Then on to dance at the "400." I was very disappointed with the "400," as were Joko and Johnnie, although we all enjoyed ourselves. Got home about 3 a.m.

---

* Gertie Millar was one of the most famous stage actresses of the era, renowned for her performances in musicals.
** The actress Marie Löhr would later go on to have a long and distinguished film career in Britain.

Mother and daddy dined with the Finches. These days with Joko are a beautiful dream, I am madly in love with her. I wonder if I shall ever get over it. She is very fond of me, but I am afraid would not marry me anytime for many years. I fear people will begin to talk about us being so much together soon.

Wednesday 17

Got up late again, and Joko came to lunch again. Then in the afternoon we went to the "Flag-Lieutenant" at the Haymarket, which she thoroughly enjoyed. Queen Alexandra there. In the evening daddy, mother, Joko, and I dined with Mr. and Mrs. Russell at the Bath Club, and then went on to "Business as Usual" at the Hippodrome; Harry Tate* very funny, and quite a good show. I took Joko home afterwards. Heard that Henry is very serious now. I told Joko that although I have enjoyed these days with her more than anything on earth, I don't think they ought to be repeated, as people are beginning to talk about us. Oh, that I was a few years older and could ask her to marry me, as I am sure we should hit it off well together. I think Joko is fond of me, but not enough to promise anything at present, so I shan't ask her. I feel helplessly miserable as I shall hardly see any more of her. Oh why at 18 must I suffer the troubles of men 5 years more my senior.

Thursday 18

Joko rang up about 11.0 to say she would come round in the afternoon to see Norman about getting a job. So I was looking forward to seeing her for the last time, when imagine my chagrin to find she rang up again to say she could not come as she must stop with Olive as Henry was undergoing a very serious operation. She never let me know what train she was going home by with Jack, consequently I felt absolutely miserable and wretched at not seeing her again. I learnt too late from Sophie that she had gone down by the 7.45 with Jack. I was nearly off my head with misery. Norman, Louie and the two little girls, Olivia and Jill, arrived home from Torquay from stopping with the Blackers. Daddy and mother persuaded me to go and dine with them with Dr. and Mrs. Handfield Jones, but I was too miserable to enjoy it.

---

* Harry Tate was a Scottish comedian who performed in musical halls and later in films. He died in 1940 as a result of injuries he sustained during the London Blitz.

Friday 19

Went to the Automobile Club, met daddy, and went to call on Admiral Finnis at the Naval and Military Club, but he was out. Then went up to see daddy's searchlight position on top of Oceanic House. Saw the model of the *Alsatian* in Trafalgar Square. Went on to the city, called on old Alex Thompson, saw Jack Russell and his Uncle Jeph, saw Blunt and Uncle John and Charley Tatham. Lunched with daddy at the City Canton, then went to see Aunt Do, and on to Sophie's at Earl's Court. Unluckily Stanley and Olive out, but Sophie said Henry was better. Muriel Stubbs and Miss Fell called. Went home. Little Olivia, Norman's eldest girl, is a wonderful character, years older than she really is, and an awful flirt. She quite fascinates me. Dined with daddy and mother at Gennaro's. Then went on to see "The Man Who Stopped at Home;" quite good. Denis Eadie very clever, and Isobel Elsom* very pretty. I wish Joko had seen it.

Saturday 20

Daddy got a bad cold. Packed, wrote letters, etc., and settled up my affairs generally. I am leaving my diary at home for safety, and shall write it up on my return. Left for Liverpool 6 p.m. Said goodbye to little Olivia and went up to Liverpool; travelled with Johnstone. Arrived on board about eleven. Lots of interesting chatter. Rumours of an attack on Heligoland in the future. H.M.S. *Calyx* and *Eskimo* of our squadron have been paid off, being too small for the work. During my absence the prize crews had joined up. Elliott had had an interesting experience, being chased by a submarine off Westray. A drastic blockade policy, which has been decided on by Government as retaliation against German submarine policy, has resulted in 120 being stopped and sent in during our absence from patrol.

Sunday 21

Found H.M. ships *Devonshire*, *Virginian*, and *Victorian* in harbour. The latter may join our squadron later on. A gorgeous day. Wrote to mother, Aunt Do, and Joko. We went out into the river at 1 p.m. and left the Mersey at 11.30. A submarine reported right ahead off the "Chickens," and we made a detour southwest and saw nothing; Micky Freer looking very ferocious with a huge cutlass and two revolvers.

---

* Isobel Elsom was a notable actress of stage and screen, and would later go on to enjoy a long and illustrious career in Hollywood.

March 21st 1915
H.M.S. ALSATIAN

Dear Mother,

Just a line in a hurry, before we sail, which will be soon, I
expect. It is a gorgeous day here, quite hot and bright sunshine.
I hope daddy's cold is better; don't let him go back to duty until
he has got rid of it. When he is up again, please remind him to
leave a card at Admiral Finnis's club.

No news; give my best love to all, and a kiss for Olivia.
TOBY.

P.S.—We sail at midnight tonight (Sunday). This will be
delayed two days in transit.

Monday 22

My job this trip is gunfire control officer. There are four of us aft and four
forward, each in four watches. Dropped the pilot at Formby, and left the
Bar Light Vessel 1 a.m. convoyed by H.M. destroyer *Dove*. Strict lookout
night and day owing to submarine and mine menace. Boats turned out in
case of accident. Hostile submarine reported off Corsewall Point. Went to
general quarters in the forenoon. Got safely out of the Irish Sea without
mishap. The *Dove* left us at Oversay, and by evening we were past Barra
Head and out of the danger area. On passage back to patrol. Had a long
chat with "Pompous" Williams.

Tuesday 23

Back on patrol south-west of the Faeroes. The fine weather we have
experienced down south still continues, but the drop in the temperature
is very noticeable. Rendezvous with H.M.S. *Cedric* at 4 p.m., and took over
charge of Tenth Cruiser Squadron from Captain Benson. She reports
having experienced the coldest weather of the whole winter in our
absence. I had a row with Lance-Sergeant Powell, R.M.L.I., and told him

off. John Kiddle is said to have suffered serious financial losses lately owing to the war; hence his temper, which is phenomenally bad.

Wednesday 24

Two prizes sent in during the day, both Norwegian, one Galveston to Stavanger, and the other Norfolk Island to Aalborg. Midshipman McNaught, R.N.R., in charge of the first, and Midshipman Ward, R.N.R., of the second. Very cold still, glass below freezing-point. A strenuous game of deck hockey in the dog-watches. In the first watch "Pompous" Williams continued the story of his multitudinous experiences in Yankee-land.

MIDSHIPMEN'S JOURNAL DAILY LOG MARCH 24TH TO MARCH 27TH

On Patrol
Rough extent of patrol ground   {Lat 60°-62°N.}
                                   {Long 10°-13°W.}

On 25th sent in Swedish S.S. *Centric* to Kirkwall with prize crew under Midshipman Adams R.N.R.

APRIL

MIDSHIPMEN'S JOURNAL DAILY LOG MARCH 28TH TO APRIL 3RD

On Patrol
On Sunday 28th shifted our patrol position to "A" between the Faeroes and Iceland. Sighted the Icelandic coast at 10.0 am. The great snowy mass of Oraefajökell (6900ft) appeared most imposing.

The Captain read letters of congratulations, to the ship's company, from the Lords of the Admiralty and from the C. in. C., Admiral Jellicoe, to Rear-Admiral de Chair, on the work of the 10th cruiser patrols.

A large number of fishing ketches are met with in these waters, returning from and going to the Icelandic fisheries. On the 28th we challenged in error the small Danish

S. 519.—Revised, May, 1914.

JOURNAL

FOR THE USE OF

MIDSHIPMEN.

_____

Mr. *A. Scrimgeour.*

H.M.S.*hips "Crescent" + "Alsatian"*

From *Aug 2nd 1914*

To

_____

LONDON :
PRINTED FOR H.M. STATIONERY OFFICE BY WATERLOW & SONS LIMITED.

1914.

CW 13762.
11.

Sta. 45/14.

THE LOCHS ROAG

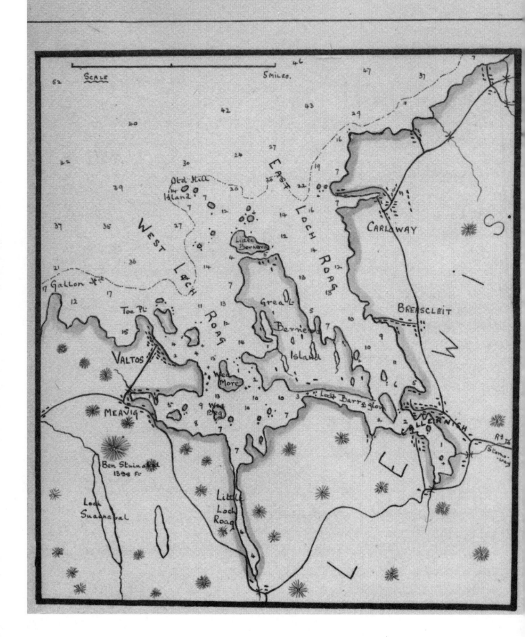

fishing Gunboat *Islands Falk*; but on discovering her identity, apologised, and allowed her to proceed. The Norwegian S.S. *Bergensfjord* has again been caught with several German Reservists onboard, and she has been sent to Kirkwall by H.M.S. *Otway*.

On Friday, April 2nd, we regained our 3 prize crews from H.M.S. *Digby*, whence they had been transferred from H.M.S *Patia*, who brought them out from Stornoway. They were conveyed from Scapa to Stornoway in the Armed Boarding Vessel *Duke of Cornwall*, which has succeeded the *Anglia* and *Caesarea* on 10th c.s. prize crew duty. While at Scapa the prize crews were accommodated in the *Cambria*, lying at Long Hope. The officers in charge of the prize crews report that the major part of the Grand Fleet is lying at Scapa. Whilst in the *Duke of Cornwall* they were fired on by the Armed Yacht *Vanessa* off Cape Wrath, owing to an error in the challenges.

MIDSHIPMEN'S JOURNAL DAILY LOG APRIL 4TH

After receiving our prize crews, we did not return to "A" patrol, but remained on "C" patrol west and S.W. of the Faeroes.

We escorted an eastward bound American S.S. towards Muckle Flugga. About noon we turned her over to H.M.S. *Motagua*, it being too rough to board; and then altered course to the S.W. to make Butt of Lewis.

Suggested New Base for 10th c.s.

The Admiralty have suggested a new base for the 10th cruiser squadron at West Loch Roag in Lewis on the N.W. coast. The object of this new base would be to minimise submarine danger, and to save time taken by ships proceeding from and to patrol while using the Mersey and Clyde as bases.

In consequence we decided to visit West Loch Roag in order that the Rear-Admiral, commanding the 10th cruiser squadron, might report personally on its suitability for a base, after examining it himself.

MIDSHIPMEN'S JOURNAL DAILY LOG APRIL 5TH

We passed Sulisker Rock, and North Roua in the forenoon, and later the Butt of Lewis. Gun control watches were set, owing to the submarine menace, a submarine having been lately sighted off St. Kilda. At 1.30 p.m., being about midway between Gallon Head and Old Hill Island, we altered course into West Loch Roag to the S.E.

At 3.0 p.m., after passing through Wea Sound, we anchored S.S.E. of Wea More Island, in the inner part of the Loch. The steam- and motor-boats were immediately lowered from the davits, the motor-boat being told off as Ship's Duty Boat, while the steam-boat did duty as Admiral's Barge.

A boat was sent off to Meavig, about 3 miles away, in the western portion of the loch, to bring off Rear-Admiral Tupper (S.N.O. Stornoway) and his secretary, in order to confer with Rear-Admiral de Chair. Rear-Admiral Tupper went ashore again at 6.0 p.m., and motored back from Meavig to Stornoway.

During the evening 2 patrolling trawlers came in and anchored close to the *Alsatian*. We sent the duty boat away with the Navigator in order to mark the position of a dangerous submerged rock in the Sound of Wea, by laying down a "Reindeer" buoy, after fixing the position by sextant angles of the cairns on top of the Wea More Island, Wea Bay Island, and the south and north extremities of Wea More.

MIDSHIPMEN'S JOURNAL DAILY LOG APRIL 6TH

A strong breeze from the mainland caused the ship to "sheer" considerably at single anchor, and as our stern was in close proximity to the lee shore of Bernera Island, we let go a second anchor, which steadied her considerably. We sent a mail ashore at Meavig, and at 6.0 p.m. weighed both anchors and proceeded out of harbour back to patrol again.

MIDSHIPMEN'S JOURNAL DAILY LOG APRIL 8TH

Sighted a large number of ships during the day, and intercepted and boarded the majority. The Steam Ships *Lapland* and *Zamora* with one sailing barque were sent into Kirkwall with prize crews under Midshipmen Renfree, Elliott and J.G. Wood R.N.R.

Received information that H.M.S. *Teutonic*, who is detached for duty off the Norwegian coast and has effected some valuable captures including that of the *Sir Ernest Cassell*, was chased last night by a ship with strange lights. The Captain of the *Teutonic* surmised that she was a German cruiser, and attempted to draw her towards Muckle Flugga to engage her in daylight. The *Teutonic* omitted to challenge her. On receipt of the news the C. in C. despatched two light cruisers to look for the vessel.

MIDSHIPMEN'S JOURNAL DAILY LOG APRIL 9TH

Considerable alterations in the patrols of the 10th c.s. are under consideration, owing to the shorter periods of darkness now being experienced with the approach of the summer. The alterations include a patrol North of Iceland, one between Iceland and the Faeroes, reduction to single line patrol between Sydero and Cape Wrath, and a patrol East of the Shetlands off the Norwegian coast. Several more ships will be required.

Details will be given later.

MIDSHIPMEN'S JOURNAL DAILY LOG APRIL 10TH TO 18TH

On the 12th we communicated with H.M.S. *Cedric*, just out from Liverpool, and on the following day with H.M.S. *Teutonic*, from whom we received two of our prize crews under Midshipmen Elliott and Renfree R.N.R.

Prize Crew Procedure

East bound prize crews take their ships to Kirkwall, except in some cases of sailing ships, which are obliged to make Lerwick. West bound vessels, when sent in, go to Stornoway. The prize crews making Kirkwall are accommodated in the *Cambria* at Long Hope. At intervals of about a week, the *Duke of Cornwall* conveys them all to Stornoway, where they are transported to a ship of the 10th c.s., which distributes them to their various patrols. Lerwick crews go to Kirkwall in a drifter, then as above.

Midshipman Wood R.N.R. who took in a sailing ship on the 8th was obliged to make Lerwick, and here assisted with his prize crew in putting out a fire, caused by a serious explosion in an ammunition shed.

On the 14th we went up north of the Faeroes to patrol in Latitudes 64° and 65°N, and extremely cold weather was experienced. On the 18th, however, we came down south again, preparatory to leaving patrol to coal.

MIDSHIPMEN'S JOURNAL DAILY LOG APRIL 19TH

Finally left patrol to go in to coal, leaving H.M.S. *Cedric* as S.O. 10th c.s., in the absence of the Rear-Admiral. H.M.S *Digby* is to be despatched to Reykjavik the capital of Iceland, to deliver despatches to the British Vice-Consul, and to ascertain the probable limits of ice in the Icelandic districts this season.

We passed Barra Head 60 miles to the westward at noon. Received news that H.M.S. *Oropesa* had been attacked by a submarine further to the south, consequently a vigilant look out was kept.

H.M.S. Oropesa's action with submarine

The *Oropesa* (Commander Stanley R.N.) was returning to patrol after coaling in the Clyde. When off Oversay a submarine appeared astern and chased. The R.A. *Alsatian* and S.N.O. Larne were immediately informed, and fire was opened with the after guns. After a time several shells exploded close to the submarine, which disappeared. Consequently the *Garry* and *Tara*, which had been sent to the assistance of the *Oropesa*, were recalled by the S.N.O. Larne.

The *Alsatian* passed the *Oropesa* at 2.0 p.m. and later in the dog watches, large patches of oil were sighted, when off Oversay. Thus the *Oropesa* may have sunk her adversary.

MIDSHIPMEN'S JOURNAL DAILY LOG APRIL 20TH

A new route was followed, and instead of going over inside Rathlin Island, the Scotch coast was hugged, and we passed the Mull of Cantyre light abeam at 9.0 p.m.

We arrived off the Mersey Bar Light Vessel at 6.0 a.m., and picked up Mr. Trenter, the Allan Line pilot, from the tug *Bison*. At 7.0 a.m. we dropped anchor off the Pier Head, Liverpool, in the Mersey.

MIDSHIPMEN'S JOURNAL DAILY LOG APRIL 21ST

Three gangways rigged, and the coal lighters came alongside, coaling commencing at 7.0 a.m. with shore labour.

When the coal lighters amidships between the ship and jetty were emptied and required to be shifted to give place to full ones, it was necessary to start the ship out from the jetty a little. To do this an 8" hemp, secured to the *Scandinavian* on the opposite side of the dock and lying on the bottom so as to avoid impeding the fairway, was brought to the capstan on the port side of the *Alsatian* and tautened up; the strain, this brought on the hemp, being sufficient to start the ship out enough to let the lighters pass, without it being necessary to interfere with the wires securing her to the jetty; these not being taut enough to oppose the motion. When the lighters were shifted, the hemp was slacked off again to the bottom, and the wind carried the ship back to her old position.

JOURNAL FOR THE USE OF MIDSHIPMEN.

1. The Journal is to be kept during the whole of a Midshipman's sea time. A second volume may be issued if required.

2. The **Officer** detailed to supervise the Midshipmen's instruction is to see that the journal is properly kept in accordance with the following instructions. He should initial the midshipmen's journals at least once a month, but should see that they are written up from time to time during the month and not immediately before they are called in for inspection.

The **Captain** is to have the journals produced for his inspection from time to time, and should initial them at each inspection.

The **Midshipman** on leaving a ship should get the Captain to initial his journal.

The following remarks indicate the main lines to be followed in keeping the journal.

Midshipmen should record in their own language their observations about all things of interest and matters of importance in the work that is carried on, on their Station, in their Fleet, or in their ship. They may insert descriptions of places visited and of the people with whom they come in contact, harbours and anchorages, fortifications; they may write notes on coaling facilities, landing places, abnormal weather, prevailing winds and currents, salvage operations, Foreign ships met with, and the manner in which Foreign Fleets are handled, Battle practices, Gunlayer's test, actions in manœuvres, remarks on P.Z. exercises. On the ship making a passage of sufficient interest, they should note the weather and noon position.

Separate entries need not necessarily be made for each separate day, but full accounts should be given of any events of interest.

Midshipmen should understand that the main object of keeping the journal is to train (a) the power of observation, (b) the power of expression, (c) the habit of orderliness.

Midshipmen should illustrate the letter-press with plans and sketches pasted into the pages of the journal, namely :—

Track Charts.

Plans of Anchorages. (These should show the berths occupied by the Squadron or ship, and if a Fleet was anchored the courses steered by the Fleet up to the anchorage).

Sketches of places visited, of coast line, of headlands, of leading marks into Harbours, of ships British and Foreign, of parts or fittings of ships, or any other objects of interest.

4. The Journal is to be produced at the examination in Seamanship for the rank of Lieutenant, when marks to a maximum of 50 will be awarded for it. (K.R. Appendix X. Part II. (13).

MIDSHIPMEN'S JOURNAL DAILY LOG APRIL 21st TO APRIL 28th

In Liverpool, alongside No. 1 Canada Dock Coaling, provisioning ship, making good minor defects and receiving various new fittings.

6 days leave to 1 watch. Received onboard various R.F.R. ratings (chiefly stokers) for exclusive duty with prize crews.

6 officers with 3 prize crews joined the ship for passage to H.M.S. *Cedric* on patrol.

Repairs and Alterations

Whilst in harbour, several minor defects were made good, and small alterations made. The wireless set, always a source of trouble, was repaired; the dynamo armature having been burnt out some days before entering harbour, this necessitating the use of the emergency set. A new main dynamo armature was fitted; and also a "direction finder," the extra aerials being supported by spars above the boat deck. This contrivance should be of great use in approximately locating ships to be intercepted, when they can be heard using wireless.

The most important of all items however, was the new magazine protection fitting. In several cases of ships being torpedoed, it has been found that their magazines have exploded, thus extra protection has become a dire necessity. Up to the present a torpedo striking the ship abreast the magazines, would only have had a narrow and thin plate to pierce after destroying the side plating; thus magazine protection was to all intents and purposes nil. The cartridges are stowed against the port side of the magazine and the projectiles the starboard side, and only the thin plating and ship's side separated them from the water. The new system of protection however is as follows:

The deck has been slightly armoured both above and below the magazine. In the case of the fore magazine two stiff fore and aft plates have been substituted for 1 thin one. They are joined at the fore end to a stiff transverse plate, and at the after end to the ordinary ship's bulkhead. The space between the outer of the two transverse plates and the ship's side has been fitted with sandbags.

In the case of the after magazine, the beam limits of which are considerably further from the ship's side than in the fore magazine, only one fore and aft plate was fitted, and was secured fore and aft to the transverse bulkheads, no extra transverse plate being considered necessary. Sandbags were packed as before between the side plating and side of the ship.

It is hoped that this will prove an efficient protection against mines, or submarines firing torpedoes, and exploding either magazine.

April 25th 1915
H.M.S. ALSATIAN

Dear Mother,

How are you all at home? We got back into harbour on
Thursday, after quite an exciting four and a half weeks at sea. I
was laid up for about a fortnight owing to a small accident, but
am quite well again now. We were very disappointed on
arriving in, to find no mails waiting; apparently they had been
sent to Inverness by mistake, and we are still awaiting them, as
so far we have had no news. Everything is chaotic on board;
most of the officers are on leave, and ourselves, the unlucky
remnant, are living in a seething mass of coal-dust, wet paint,
and filthy rubbish of every description. Dockyard "mateys" all
over the ship, as we are having special magazine protection
fitted. On Saturday (yesterday) I had to accompany the
Admiral's Secretary up to London with despatches for the
Admiralty, being in charge of his escort. We started at 4 a.m.
and got up at 8.30, and I had to spend the morning and
afternoon at the Admiralty, but managed to get off for a few
hours in the evening, and went to meet daddy at the
Automobile Club. We dined with Mr. and Mrs. Jack Russell at
the Berkeley Grill-Room, and I had to catch the midnight train
back to Liverpool, arriving at 5 a.m., pretty tired, as you can
imagine, and found myself with a "day on."

The chaos seems to have increased, but we are supposed to be
sailing on Tuesday, although I don't see how we can sail for at
least a week.

I got some of the news from daddy that you had left
Cumberland Terrace, Grannie Greig's death, etc. how are Peg,
Jim, and Bill?

Best love to all of you.
TOBY.

H.M.S. Alsation
Flagship, Tenth Cruiser Squadron

A day on board as O.O.D. at Liverpool, Canada Dock, April, 1915

Four a.m., turned out with a very thick head after five hours' sleep, threw on some clothes, and relieved Midshipman Cobb, R.N., as O.O.D., who retired with unholy glee to his bunk. Went the rounds with the corporal of watch; everything quiet and correct and remarkably dirty, coal-dust, saw-dust, straw, packing-cases, etc., lying everywhere. At 4.30 the shore gangs of dockers began to arrive, and the foreman asked permission to commence coaling at 4.45, and soon the ceaseless bang, squeak, and whine of the steam winches started, accompanied by the roar of the coal rushing down the shoots. At 5.30 they asked me to shift the ship a little to allow the coal lighter to be changed, so I called the duty part of watch on board and mooched aft with the Q.M. to haul her out by tautening our after 8-inch hemp, bringing it to the port capstan and taking the slack out of the st. wires. Tried to look happy with a pipe of ship's in the pouring rain, but my oilskin was leaking, and I have lost my sea-boots, so I am afraid I failed dismally. Called the hands at six, and was much refreshed by a boiling cup of ship's cocoa. After a stormy interview with a sleepy and bad-tempered C.O. (Lieut.-Commander Edwards, R.N.R.), I turned the hands to getting on board stores, under the auspices of Lieutenant Freer, R.N.R., who came out of his bunk like a rag-time ballet girl, I don't think! Then the short-leave night liberty men began to arrive. With much difficulty I assured the M.A.A. that it was tomorrow morning, and then he, I, and the corporal O.W., with the assistance, more or less unwilling, of several marine and seamen sentries, began dealing with the streams of shore-goers. The marines came off, spick and span, smarter than when they left; seamen roll off in an eminently seamanlike fashion, the regular nautical roll, so that you can't tell whether they're drunk or sober; in this, however, there is no difficulty with the firemen, whose sobriety or otherwise is quite apparent, usually otherwise. The M.A.A. discovered multitudinous bottles of gin, auntie's joy, etc., smuggled in trouser legs, scarves, caps, etc.; he is a genius at hide-and-seek. Put two men on Commander's report for insolence, under the influence of drink. At seven the bugler woke up and blew the Reveille, one hour late. It brought back pleasant memories of Osborne baby days, but I refused to allow his tender years to bias me, so gave him a dose of No. 10A to refresh his memory.

The clank of the steam hammers of the party fitting up the new magazine now added to the din, and the blue ether was quite indistinguishable amidst clouds of coal-dust. At 7.45 an orderly arrived from Admiral Stileman, the S.N.O., Liverpool's officer, and I made out the daily harbour leave report for him. At 8 a.m. sounded off "Stand Easy," and piped hands to breakfast. Attempted to have a wash and shave, but the water was thick with coal-dust and quite tepid, so after cutting my fizz several times with a razor, and reducing myself to a frenzy of rage and despair, I eventually gave it up as a bad job, and went off to mess. A steward, obviously suffering from "the morning after-itis," advanced after ten minutes' wait and brought me some stewed prunes, one dish I abhor, so determined to risk the eggs. The first two were past the age limit, and I had just started on the third, which showed signs of comparative youth, when a messenger arrived saying the Commanding Officer wished to see the Officer of the Day. After struggling with my sword belt, I found Mr. Edwards, the C.O., and he introduced me to a Mr. McWhirter, the contractor's agent, who had come to see about the fitting up of the new magazine protection; I spent the remainder of the breakfast hour grovelling in the magazines and ammunition hoists, and attempting to prove to Mr. McWhirter, a ubiquitous Scotsman, that the primary duty of ammunition is to be fired from a gun, and the requirements of safety, however important, should not be allowed to block the passage of ammunition to the guns on deck. Nine o'clock "Divisions" at length relieved me of Mr. McWhirter, and, assisted by Midshipman Cobb, the stand-by officer, and one or two other unfortunates, inspected the various divisions and reported them to the C.O. Marched on the Q.D., and the C.O. read prayers, briefly and in a great hurry, finishing up the last prayer as follows: "For Jesus Christ's sake—On caps," with no pause between the two sentences. Marched off the Q.D., and hands fell in. Told off the various parties for getting in stores, etc., and retired to the G.R. for a welcome smoke and a cocktail. Five minutes later a ship's corporal arrived, with a gleam as of a lion who scents his prey, to say that a stoker, obviously under the influence of drink, had assaulted Eng.-Lieutenant Fortay, the E.O. of the day, in the engine-room, and could I come to investigate the case? A pleasant party assembled on the Q.D., the prisoner, a ferrety-faced-looking individual, between two huge marines, also Eng.-Lieut.-Commander Jackson, known on the lower deck as the "slave-driver," Mr. Fortay, the M.A.A., a ship's corporal, the corporal on duty, and sundry messengers, etc. Heard the evidence on both sides, and although strongly in favour of prisoner, obliged to refer matter to C.O. as charge was brought by an officer. The C.O. was sent for, and arrived in about twenty minutes, and, after asking twenty or thirty useless questions, put the prisoner on the Captain's report. At 10.30 the Captain arrived on board from shore leave; the Bos'n's mate, of course, was adrift with his piping, and I got scrubbed by the C.O. The skipper sent for me later and asked me to dine with him that night; hearing that I should be on duty, he very kindly asked me to come tomorrow. He seemed very chatty and pleasant. On arriving back at the gangway, the Captain of Marines arrived in a fearful fury, shouting for the Officer O.D. On seeing me, however, he calmed down, and demanded an escort to be sent immediately to Lime Street Station to fetch some very valuable wireless machinery which had arrived there. I told him that there were absolutely no hands available, and advised him to go to the Naval Base Office in Water Street and apply for an escort there. He went off mumbling to himself, with one moustache bristling and the other drooping almost to the deck. The remainder of the forenoon passed without incident, except for a few minor offenders, whom I dealt with as necessary. Sounded off "Cooks" at 11.45 and attended the issue of rum to the men, the M.A.A. with an eagle eye there to prevent any man having one drop more than his proper tot. At noon piped hands to dinner and went off to mess. A most appetising menu, rather marred by coal-dust, sauce, and questionable cooking, but things looked up after a glass of port and a cigar. Cobb relieved me very kindly for two hours in the afternoon, and I had a doze in my bunk. Woke up at three, and, after dipping my head in a basin of water, went back to the gangway. I found Cobb, his lanky 6 feet 3 inches of bone shivering with rage, "putting the sergeant-major of marines in his place," as he called it (to me it sounded like a costermonger reviling a much-loathed rival). Apparently the postman, a newly fledged corporal of marines, had left the ship, reporting to the S.M., who was complaining to the O.O.D. in disparaging tones which did not please his ludship, Mr. Cobb. Cobb left on my arrival, and the sergeant-major retired disconsolately to his mess. Sounded the "Cease Fire" at 3.30, and piped liberty men to clean and shift, and then went and had a cup of tea. At four sounded off "Evening Quarters," inspected the men, reported to the C.O., and then piped hands to tea. At 4.20 inspected the liberty men and marched them over the side. A few minutes later the defaulting postman arrived with the mail, and as he had some interesting letters for me I decided not to punish him, and handed him over to the tender care of the sergeant-major. Then Hutchinson, who is now temporarily running the gunnery department, arrived with a heart-stirring appeal. He apparently wants to get one of our after 6-inch guns stripped down by tonight, and, not knowing how to do it himself, was depending on my help. The armourers are pensioners, and have never had anything to do with guns of this pattern, so this complicated matters. Rummaged in my sea-chest, and eventually found a gunnery notebook, written during my "G" course in the *Cornwall*, with the help of which I managed to show the armourers how to get to work on the gun, after smearing my best coat in oil and grease. Then left the armourers and W.S.H. struggling with the gun, and returned to the gangway. Found three ladies, apparently a sort of governess person and two girls, one about twenty-two and the other about sixteen, a flapper. They are cousins of Fleet Paymaster Lawford, the Admiral's Secretary, who is away in London on duty with the Admiral. They seemed very keen on seeing over the ship, which I had to refuse, the regulations prohibiting this in war-time. However, they came and had tea in the G.R. Both girls were quite good sorts, and the elder very pretty, but the governess was rather a stumour. Their names were Miss Sybil and Dorothy Grant, and they lived near Chester, where they had motored from. They asked me very kindly to go over and play tennis if I can ever get away. The remainder of the dog-watches passed without incident till dinner-time, which was half an hour early for some obscure reason, causing me to be three-quarters of an hour late. Quite a good dinner. What a contrast to the food in a real battleship in the Grand Fleet or at the Dardanelles! But it was spoilt by Athenry, who persisted in smoking cheap cigarettes throughout the meal, in spite of my pointed remarks that nowadays noblemen were no nearer always gentlemen, and in that a title did not entitle him to inconvenience everyone else in the mess. He continued, however, with his usual silly jokes, far-fetched humour, and everlastingly grinning face. After dinner spent half an hour with Lieutenant Freer overhauling Bos'n's stores, stoppers, nippers, hawsers, blocks, etc. At 9.45 went rounds with the C.O., and at ten the hands piped down and turned in. Feeling very sleepy, as I usually do at this time, after a day on, but managed to keep myself awake with frequent pipes and by chatting to the Q.M., a hoary old individual, who told me stirring yarns of events in the Egyptian Wars of '82, in which he apparently had played a part which should have entitled him to at least a V.C. and immediate promotion. At 11.30 went rounds again with the corporal of the watch, then signed up the rounds book, and sent the messenger to call Hutchinson, my relief, and waited in patience for twelve. Midnight arrived, but no Hutchinson; however, at ten past he slouched up; gave him my belt as a badge of office, turned over the various details in about five seconds, and went off to bed, tore off my clothes, and was asleep in half a minute.

MIDSHIPMEN'S JOURNAL DAILY LOG APRIL 28TH

Left Canada Dock 6.0 a.m.; cast off and proceeded in charge of pilot and tugs; warped through Sandon ½ tide basin gates and anchored off Pier Head.

MIDSHIPMEN'S JOURNAL DAILY LOG APRIL 29TH

Sailed at 8.0 p.m.; dropped the pilot off the Bar Light Vessel, and shaped a course to pass to the south of the Chickens Rock Light, to the west of which we met the Destroyer *Dove* which convoyed us through the chief submarine danger area. Passed the Mull of Galloway, thence shaped a course to pass Fair Head (Co. Antrim) and inside Rathlin Island. Altacarry Lighthouse abeam 1.0 p.m. The *Dove* parted company off Oversay. Speed throughout the day 18 knots, zigzag. Strict look out kept for submarines, as many have recently been sighted in the waters passed through, and only yesterday a fleet collier was sunk off the Butt of Lewis by a large German submarine. Their latest type from all accounts is of considerable size.

MIDSHIPMEN'S JOURNAL DAILY LOG APRIL 30TH

Rendezvoused H.M. Armed Merchant Cruisers *Cedric* and *India* 50 miles W.N.W. of St. Kilda. Took over charge of 10th cruiser squadron patrols from Captain Benson of the *Cedric*, who has been Senior Officer in the absence of Rear-Admiral de Chair. Transferred her 3 prize crews to the *Cedric*. The *India* has just joined the squadron, having recently fitted out in the "Thames" as an Armed Merchant Cruiser. She is very short of the necessary code books for W/T signalling.

Proceeded at 10.0 p.m. to the northward to pass to the westward of the Faeroes and back to patrol.

MAY

MIDSHIPMEN'S JOURNAL DAILY LOG MAY 1st

Arrived on patrol to the north of Faeroes, this is now "A" patrol. Communicated with H.M. Ships *Otway* and *Digby*. The *Digby* has lately returned from Reykjavik, the capital of Iceland, where she proceeded with despatches for the British Consul.

During our last period at sea, the following ships were intercepted by the 10th cruiser squadron:

MARCH 8th—APRIL 19th

Norwegian	106	West Bound	95
Danish	97	East Bound	
167			
British	82	Trawlers, locals, etc	94
Swedish	53	Not ascertained	1
U.S.A	14	TOTAL	
357			
Russian	1		
Finnish	1		
Not ascertained	3		
TOTAL	357		

Of these 129 were sent in

To Kirkwall	115
To Stornoway	10
To Lerwick	4
TOTAL	129

Disposition of the patrols of the reinforced 10th cruiser squadron as rearranged

"A" *Alsatian* (flag), *Otway, Orcoma, Mantua, Alcantara, Teutonic.*
"C" *Cedric, Patia, Orotava, Oropesa, Changuinola, Motagua, Digby, Patuca.*

"E"　*Virginian, Columbella, Andes, Arlanza.*

"F"　*Hildebrand, India, Ebro, Hilary.*

"G"　*Caribbean, Ambrose,* X.

"B"　and "D" patrols have been discontinued.
Ship X, in "G" patrol, is a cruiser to be detailed by C-in-C.

"A"　patrol must always have a minimum of 4 ships on patrol, and is to extend from the north of the Faeroes.

"C"　patrol must always have a minimum of 5 ships on patrol, and is to extend between Cape Wrath and Sydero Island.

"E"　patrol to the north of Iceland spread north from Latitude 67° N along the meridian of 15° W.

"F"　patrol to the south of Iceland spread at 150° from a position 63° 20' N 15° W.

"G"　patrol must have at least 1 Armed Merchant Cruiser on patrol, extending on the meridian of 3° E from Lat 62° N to Lat 63½° N.

MIDSHIPMEN'S JOURNAL DAILY LOG MAY 2ND TO MAY 3RD

On patrol between Iceland and the Faeroes. Stopped, boarded and allowed to proceed two vessels. Communicated with H.M.S. *Hildebrand* on the 3rd.

MIDSHIPMEN'S JOURNAL DAILY LOG MAY 4TH

Proceeded from the North of the Faeroes to the S.E. to Busta Voe in the Shetlands.

Went to General Quarters in the forenoon, and picked up some fishing buoys and jettisoned spars.

MIDSHIPMEN'S JOURNAL DAILY LOG MAY 5TH

Arrived in St. Magnus Bay in the N.W. of the Shetlands at 3.0 a.m., and at 4.0 a.m. came to with port anchor in Busta Voe. Found a squadron of 3 auxiliary armed patrol trawlers there. Received a visit from the S.N.O. Lerwick. H.M.S. *Duke of Cornwall* Armed Boarding Vessel, came to anchor at 5.0 p.m., and sailed at 9.30 p.m. after discharging prize crews for the *Patia* and *Virginian* to *Alsatian* for passage.

Day spent in examining the anchorage and considering its suitability as a coaling base for the 10th cruiser squadron.

Busta Voe has already been used as a base by the old 10th c.s., when formed by the *Crescent* class. It is proposed to use Busta Voe in conjunction with the adjoining water of Aith Voe and Olma Firth.

An important item of the question is the water supply, a plentiful and pure local source being necessary. In the forenoon an expedition consisting of the Staff Surgeon, Lt Kenyon (squadron Gunnery Officer) and 1 midshipman went in the motor-boat to examine the supply of a small burn in the Muckle Roe Island to the south of the Busta Peninsula. An aqueduct had been constructed here in November last, but was wrecked by the winter gales.

MIDSHIPMEN'S JOURNAL DAILY LOG MAY 6TH

It was intended to go round and examine Olma Firth today, but receipt of the news that an east bound oiler had eluded patrols, necessitated a change in plans; so we weighed and proceeded to the northward of Muckle Flugga, to intercept her.

At 3.30 p.m. we came up with the oiler, about 15 miles N.N.W. of Muckle Flugga, and she proved to be the S.S. *Petrolyte* of American nationality with a large cargo of oil for Copenhagen, probably intended eventually for Germany. She was sent in for investigation to Kirkwall with a prize crew under Midshipman Learmont R.N.R.

MIDSHIPMEN'S JOURNAL DAILY LOG MAY 7TH

Discharged their prize crews to the *Virginian* and *Patia*, also communicated visually with H.M. Ships *Patuca* and *Hilary*, all of "C" patrol at present. Sighted battleship *Orion* returning to Scapa Flow, after a refit at Plymouth.

MIDSHIPMEN'S JOURNAL DAILY LOG MAY 8TH TO MAY 9TH

On patrol North and West of the Faeroes.

On the 8th we communicated with H.M. Ships *Digby* and *Teutonic*, and on the next day we intercepted the Swedish S.S. *Kronprinzessar Margerat* bound for Rio de Janeiro and Santos, with German exports onboard. She was sent in with a prize crew under Midshipman Ward R.N.R.

Loss of R.M.S. Lusitania

In the Poldhu W/T news of the 9th we received regrettable news of the loss of the mammoth Cunard Liner *Lusitania*, torpedoed by a German submarine off the Old Head of Kinsale, while homeward bound. Nearly 1400 lives were lost, including that of many well-known passengers. A great outburst of indignation is reported from U.S.A, as many Americans were lost. The loss of life rivals that of the *Titanic* disaster of 1912. The Cunard Company had not previously lost a passenger's life for 80 years, and it is suggested that at the successful end of the war, they shall be compensated with the Hamburg-Amerika liners *Imperator* and *Vaterland*.

A day at sea on patrol by an officer in H.M.S. Alsatian, May 28th, 1915, west of the Faeroe Islands.

Turned out at midnight to take the "middle" watch as Midn. O.W. on the bridge. The usual "dead dog" sort of feeling was slightly lessened as I met the gun-watch officers of the "middle" going to their various stations, feeling and looking more miserable than myself. Relieved McNaught on the bridge, and he wasted no time disappearing into the bowels of the ship. "Lieutenant Chester" was O.O.W., and as he seemed in no mood for telling any of his yarns, I sent the messenger below to fetch some cocoa, and then retired to the chart-house to examine our position on patrol and news in general. It was a miserable night, a cold north-easter blowing, temperature 30°F., certainly better than recently off Iceland, but not much to boast of, as there were frequent snow and sleet squalls, and the ship was making heavy weather of a nasty sea, rolling and pitching like a cockleshell. Luckily the barometer was rising, so there were hopes of a change for the better. Cocoa and ship's biscuit were most refreshing, and, having finished my shave, I relieved Chester on "Monkey's Island" while he got his. Not all my oilskins, woollies, etc., could keep out the cold, and my hands and feet were like blocks of ice. The four hours of a middle watch always seem like twenty-four of any other watch, and at one I felt as if I had been on watch for hours; the weather was worse, the wind having increased to force seven or eight, and the sea being about six or seven by the Beaufort scale. Soon after one I went below to go rounds with the corporal of the watch—a long job in a ship of this size. First of all visited all the offices, ship's, Admiral's, Captain's, etc., to see them all properly locked up. Then looked round the various cabins and officers' messes, and passed down to the seamen's mess-decks below the Fx, groped my way along beneath dozens of hammocks emitting loud snores, with the Corporal O.W. in front with his lantern. Visited all the forward store-rooms, and tested the W.T. doors. Returned to the cells, and the sentry reported the cell prisoners correct; next visited the E.R. office, and rang up the engineer in charge in the E.R. and stokehold, who reported all correct below. Then through the marines', boys', stewards', and stokers' messes and flats. Found four stokers playing cards outside the chronometer-room. Obliged to run them in. What extraordinary people these stokers are! They work frightfully hard, and yet, instead of getting a little sleep at night, they must get in the rattle for gambling. All the after store-rooms and magazines correct. So went the rounds of the guns and upper decks. Found the various gun-watch officers more disconsolate than ever, cursing the weather, the ship, the war, and everything else in general. Looked in at the wireless office to pick up any scrap of news from the Grand Fleet, but heard nothing much of interest except the multitudinous reports of submarines from all quarters of the British Isles. Bill Adams in the coding office, struggling with a signal in an abstruse cipher, miles long, from the C.-in-C., all hot air. At 1.40 returned to the bridge and reported rounds correct to the O.O.W. The worst of night rounds is the filthy smell below, which is most nauseating. Chester, a little more communicative now, came out with his usual story about the Odessa girls and the sentry-boxes. About 2.15 the clouds cleared a little, and I managed to snap a sight of Arcturus, which should gladden the Navigator's heart, as we have not had a sight for two days. Soon after the crow's nest lookout reported a light on the starboard bow. I went below and called the Captain, and we altered course to close the light. It proved to be a small trawler, flying the British colour, steering north-west, apparently for Iceland. The sea being considerably too high to board, we allowed her to proceed. I then worked out my sight of Arcturus, which gave a position line eleven miles away from our estimated D.R. position. Dawn now began to break in the east, and just before four we fell out the night defence guns' crews and their officers. At four Lieutenant Chester and I were relieved by Lieutenant Oram and Midshipman Learmont, and cold and wet and tired I rushed off to my bunk. Turned out at 7.30 and attempted a bath, but the ship was rolling badly, and the water flatly refused to stop in it. Went into the mess for breakfast and succeeded in getting a certain amount of food down, in spite of the cups, plates, etc., doing a highland charge continually up and down the table. Quite a fine morning, except for the heavy sea and the cold north-east wind, but the sun was very cheery. Got in a hasty smoke, and then went to "divisions" followed by prayers. Then took my division at Swedish drill. I am getting quite an expert instructor at nutty exercises now, and the men, I really believe, think I know something about it, which certainly shows their lack of intelligence. The Commander, as usual, had a frightful early morning "liver," and scrubbed poor old Ben Evans for about ten minutes for some trivial matter. At nine H.M.S. *Cedric* (Commander Benson) had been sighted, and we now went to general quarters to exercise action with dummy firing, using the *Cedric* as target. The Captain got very excited with "Guns" and Williams, when they pointed out the limitations of our guns. But we continued steadily for nearly two hours till eleven, and the exercise should certainly have increased our fighting efficiency, although I doubt if it did. General quarters affords excellent voice practice for control officers, at all events. The "Luny" worked his rate of change clock much to his own satisfaction, but not to everybody else's, while Glanvile and I struggled with the Dumaresq, and McNaught sat in silent glory at the rangefinder. Having sunk the *Cedric* at least three times, we at length sounded the "Cease Fire" and the "Secure" at eleven, and I went off to help "Guns" test the sights of the fore starboard battery guns until noon, when we struggled off to get pot-luck lunch. During the afternoon the sea went down considerably, and we were much more comfortable. Directly after lunch the Sig. Bos'n gave all the midshipmen off watch a semaphore and Morse test, the Flag-Lieutenant-Commander making caustic remarks the whole time. At two the divisions went to rifle drill, followed by squad and company drill. I shouted myself hoarse trying to instil into the wooden heads of the R.N.R. seamen from Newfoundland, etc., the elementary motions of the rifle, turning, marching. This game continued most of the afternoon, until the Commander, repenting of his decision (having been woken up by the din from his afternoon nap), gave the order for us to knock off. I managed to swallow a cup of tea before going on watch again at four, when we went to "evening quarters." The Captain now decided to close H.M.S. *Cedric*, which we did, and I went away in charge of the sea-boat with despatches for her, and also for her to transmit to Captain E.L. Boty, M.V.O., of the *Otway*. Came off watch from the first dog at six, shifted in haste, and managed to get in half-hour's strenuous deck hockey, and got really warm for the first time since yesterday. Then shifted again and had dinner, after which "Guns" announced his intention of giving a lecture to any officers who felt inclined to attend, on "Lessons in Tactics learned from the Falkland Action." I was too lazy to go, as the Commander, now being in an excellent after-dinner mood, asked me into the ward-room for a chat. At nine we sighted a steamer eastward bound, and she proved later to be a big Dane. I went away in the boarding boat with Lieutenant Williams and A. Payr. Barton, as the Mid. O.W. was busy aft with the patent log. Got on board after a struggle and getting sopped through. She proved to be the S.S. *Escalonia* of Copenhagen, bound from Boston, U.S.A., to Aarhus with a cargo of wheat and oil-cake, ostensibly for Denmark, but intended no doubt for Germany. We morsed this information to the *Alsatian*, and then were told to return to fetch off a prize crew, as the R.A. had decided to send her to Kirkwall to be dealt with by the Customs authorities. Pulled back to the ship, and after much cursing and swearing got Mr. Barton on board, although he nearly dropped all the ship's papers into the ditch. A drizzling rain had now come on, which did not add to our comfort, and Midshipman Wood, R.N.R., who was to take the *Escalonia* into harbour, incurred everybody's wrath by taking about ten times as long as necessary to get ready, collecting his revolver, oilskin, love letters for the post on shore, etc. At last he arrived, and we pulled over to the *Escalonia* and put Mr. Wood and the prize crew on board, and ordered them to proceed in execution of their orders. Then went back to the ship, and the sea-boat was hoisted. I wasted no time getting down to my bunk and turning in for a few more hours' sleep; but a quarter of an hour later was woken up to hear that I was wanted to take charge of the marine firing party on the Fx, as we had sighted a mine, and were going to sink it. Apparently the O.O.W. by, after much thought, putting the helm over the wrong way, had narrowly missed ramming it and sending us all to perdition; he forgot it was not a submarine. A few rounds water-logged the mine, which luckily was an electrical contact one, and so sank quietly without exploding. Then at last, it being now 11.30 p.m., I really got off to sleep until 4 a.m. the next morning, when it was my turn to go on watch again.

JUNE

Thursday 3

Left by the 10.09 train from Haslemere with Jack, after thoroughly enjoying my visit. Called on Denniston at the Admiralty and had a chat and drink at his club, the Junior Army and Navy. Lunched with Aunt Do, Uncle Jack, and Cittie at Kensington Gore. Travelled home as far as Sittingbourne with old Edwards, who is leaving the *Alsatian*, and has got command of the armed yacht *Wildfowl*, and is off to take her over at Sheerness. Mother met me at the station, full of news, but I was rather liverish. The garden exquisite. Daddy was playing tennis at Westenhanger, but I did not go round as I have resolved not to chase Joko, unless I can possibly help it. I do not trust myself much however.

Friday 4

Tea and tennis at Westenhanger. Harry Baird there. Byron, Nita, Toots, Joko and I went to "The Count of Luxembourg" at the Canterbury theatre, and supper afterwards at Byron's club. Went to the 5th Liverpool's Officers Mess to see "Drippie" Porritt, but he was out. "The Count of Luxembourg" was very good for Canterbury, but I did not enjoy the evening much. I am an ass, an ass, an ass. Joko kept on harping on about those damned Carabiniers, Dent, Charlesworth, etc. Whether she really cares for one of them or not I don't know, but she acts quite well if not. I loathe them. She looks awfully nice! Auntie Connie's scheme for a Robertson pension seems a great success, as both girls have got new dresses. I was in a rotten mood, and made all sorts of arrangements so as not to see Joko before I go, so I suppose I shall make myself absolutely hopelessly miserable.

Saturday 5

Went in to Canterbury in the morning and saw heaps of friends, both Goodsons, old Hobbs, old John Robinson, Mac Hilton and Blake Wacher. Lunched at the Officers Mess of the 5th Liverpool's, with quite a nice chap called Keet, home wounded from the front. Afterwards, "Drippie" Porritt and I went up the town and had some drinks etc., and a long chat about the old days; he seems to be doing rather well. Another Zeppelin raid over Sittingbourne. Harry Baird motored Tootie and Joko over to Margate to see Henry and Olive. I played tennis with daddy at Westenhanger till tea, then we went round to Seaton and played with the Drakes, Miss Page, and a Capt of the 3rd D.G.s Went round to Westenhanger after supper and had a long chat with Nita. Joko there of course. I now feel convinced that she is very much in with some the Carabiniers and I am quite cut out. She is a fickle creature, as I am sure she used to be fond of me. But now all is U.P. I should love to snub her, perhaps someday the wind will change.

Sunday 6

"Drippie" Porritt motored over, and we all lunched at the Drakes. Colonel Clarke (who got on V.G. with mother) and Major Scott, both over from the Marine Depot. J.T.P. and I then motored to Dover to see Keigwein, who is a Lieutenant, R.N.V.R., and Admiral Bacon's Flag-Lieutenant. Unluckily we missed R.P.K. and went to Folkestone to find him, but he was not there. Came home and found some frightful old bores there, Colonel Lushington and another soldier. We all played tennis and then the Robertsons, Harry Baird and J.T.P. came to supper at Quaives. J.T.P. is commissioned by me to try and flirt with Joko, whom I snubbed assiduously and who seems inclined to thaw a little. Later on I went and had a chat with the Kelseys. I got a wired extension of leave till Thursday.

Monday 7

Played tennis all morning with Joko at Westenhanger, and then lunched with her alone in the garden, an idyllic scene. But so short lived, and I am sure she is in love with Charlesworth. I think now he is the one. He is very wealthy, and I believe a good fellow, although of course I loathe him with the most unspeakable loathing. Frightfully hot all day. Went up to London, dined at the Trocadero with Cobb and a friend, a man named Gass of the R.F.A. An excellent sort. Then went out to "Betty" at Daly's. An excellent show. Bench joined us and we had a first class box. Took Cobb's cousin Doris Preston and a friend out to supper at the Savoy. Winnie Barnes of "Betty" was there, very sweet; Mabel Sealby, J.P.R.'s old flame fainted during the performance.

Tuesday 8

Went home by the 10.45. Another sweltering hot day. Lunched at Westenhanger; in the afternoon motored Nita and Joko over to Margate to see Henry, Olive, and Toots. Found daddy and Harry Baird already there. I was a fool to take Nita as well, as I might have pumped Joko about Charlesworth, if we had some tête-à-tête. We dined with Olive and then all went on to quite a good revue at the Margate Hippodrome. A nice drive home—but 2's company, 3's a crowd; I wonder if Joko is really in love with Charlesworth. He wrote her a very long letter today.

June 10th 1915
H.M.S. ALSATIAN

Dear "Papa",

Just a line in haste before we sail tonight. There seems at last some slight chance of getting a different job, as the skipper has at last consented to forward my application for the submarine service or R.N.A.S. However, there is a lot of red tape to get over first, and it will be necessary for me to produce a certificate from my responsible parent or guardian saying he has no objection to my being employed on either of the above services.

I have written out the necessary wording and should be pleased if you would copy it, sign, and post to me.

My very best love to mother, and thank her for putting up with all my whims and making such an excellent valet.

Good luck and a speedy recovery from your dire disease.

TOBY.
P.S.—Excuse dirt, but ship is smothered in coal-dust.

SIR,
I beg to state that I am willing for my son, Midshipman Alexander Scrimgeour, Royal Navy (being under the age of 21), to be employed on any special service e.g., submarine or that may be considered suitable; and I should raise no objections to any such appointment that he might receive.

Signature . . . .

JULY

July 6th 1915
H.M.S. ALSATIAN

Dearest Mother,

We shall be in harbour again for a few days on the 10th July, but I doubt if it will be much of a rest, as it seems probable that all spare time is to be taken up with exercising landing operations, route marches, and field work. This points to the fact that as much experience as possible is to be gained in shore operations, evidently with an eye to eventualities that may crop up in the future. The last fortnight at sea has produced more interest and excitement than we have had for some months, due to various reasons which cannot be safely stated on paper*. But anyhow, we hope that possibly our work in the immediate future (that is to say, until the winter weather starts again in October) will not be quite so dull as heretofore. The poor old Russians appear to be getting it in the neck in Poland and Galicia; I suppose it is owing to the shortage in ammunition; or possibly it may be all bluff.

Give my love to all the various relations as you see them; and tell Aunt Do when next you meet that I have not heard from her for ages, and should love to have a line if convenient.

Please send me four or five white cap covers from Quaives, without delay, as I want to get them before we sail again; also some thin pants if you can find any. I am running rather short of woollen gloves, and have worn out my favourite pair. I think they are possibly past darning, but will send them to you, so that you may be able to patch them up, and anyhow will realise the type I like—viz., with long cuffs.

---

* The interception of the Norwegian steamer, *Kristianiafjord*. She slipped through the blockade and in trying to avoid the *Alsatian*, ran into the other ships of the patrol. She was seized, and with the 544 people on board, was sent into Stornaway with an armed guard.

Have all reasonable efforts been made to recover my watch and to find the pipe? You have not so far informed me. Except for the first page this is not necessarily private, but I am afraid contains but little news of interest.

My very best love to all.
From
TOBY.

Thursday
H.M.S. ALSATIAN

Darling Mother,

Just a line to tell you that my sojourn in this tin castle is at an end, and I have been warned to pack my things to be ready to leave for anywhere at half an hour's notice. I have not had my new appointment yet, but am expecting it very soon. You will probably see it in the paper (Morning Post, etc.) under the heading of naval appointments, in a few days' time, or perhaps it will be out by the time you get this.

I hear on excellent authority that I am almost certain to go to the Invincible, a battle cruiser of 17,250 tons. She went through the Falkland action, when Von Spee's force was annihilated, and has seen service elsewhere abroad since the war started. A short time ago she joined the Battle Cruiser Squadron in the North Sea, and is now flagship of the Third Division of the Battle Cruiser Fleet, flying the flag of Rear-Admiral Hood, or Rear-Admiral Hon. Horace L.A. Hood, C.B., M.V.O., D.S.O., R.N., as he is with all the etceteras. As I dare say you remember, he was Captain (before his promotion) at Osborne, when I was there, for one year. Up till April this year he was in command of the Dover patrols, and distinguished himself as chief of the squadron operating on the Belgian coast against Zeebrugge, Nieuport, etc. He is directly descended from the famous Admiral Hood of Nelson's time, one of the three brothers, all Admirals, Lord Hood, Lord Bridport, and Sir Alexander Hood; a nephew, son of a fourth brother, Sir Samuel Hood, was also a well-known Admiral. Thus they are about the most famous of all naval families. The member in question is reputed to be about the most brilliant of the younger school of flag officers, and is simply bulging with brains, so he is a pretty distinguished man to serve under. I expect you remember my telling you when at Osborne, that he is thoroughly Americanised, talking with a distinct Yankee twang, and having married an American millionairess. With the single exception of Beatty, he was promoted to flag rank at an earlier age than any other Captain in the last fifty years.

If I go to the Invincible my appointment will be due almost entirely to old "Duds" putting in a good word at the Admiralty. He has been very kind to all of us snotties.

I may not have time to write again, but I will try and let you know where I do go. At present I am in the throes of packing, and as we are coaling, and coal-dust rules supreme everywhere, the result is unenviable.

I am afraid that there will be no time to write to Jim, but give him my love, and good luck with the tonsils.

You can make use of any information in this letter that you require, but it rather loses its point if the Invincible does not mature.

By the way, wherever I go, please inform everyone likely to write to me ever of the change of address, as I shall not have time to do it myself.

Best love to you and daddy.
From
TOBY.

July 23rd 1915
H.M.S. INVINCIBLE

Dearest Mother,

Many thanks for your many and interesting letters. I am sorry
not to have written before, but have had no time until now. We
left several good friends behind in the Alsatian, but are all jolly
glad to come here. It is absolutely different, of course, from any
previous ship I have served in, but it does not take long to settle
down. I am still senior midshipman, as the seven snotties already
here are all junior to us. It is rather an extraordinary experience
having been senior midshipman in three successive flagships.

As far as I can judge, we seem to have a very nice lot of
officers. It is excellent being in company with a lot of other
ships, as I have already met shoals of old friends,
contemporary officers and cadets at Osborne and Dartmouth,
and shipmates of Cornwall and Crescent days.

This ship has already been in three actions this war: the
Heligoland Bight early in the war, the Falkland Isles, and at
the Dardanelles. Some of the reminiscences of those who have
been here all along are most thrilling. For example, in the 12-
inch twin turret, in which I am stationed for action, a heavy
shell from the Gneisenau actually penetrated the armour and
entered the turret without exploding, during the Falkland
action; and there are dozens of other interesting yarns.

The officer of the watch, when I joined the ship, was a certain
Lieutenant Stewart, lately promoted from Sub-Lieutenant; he
tells me that his father is in J. and A.'s office. Apparently he
lunched with daddy not long ago, and he tells me daddy was
wearing a most eccentric hat. Verily are the sins of the father
visited upon the children! He was very amused by daddy telling
him that I disapproved of the hat in question.

Yesterday I went to tea with Mrs. Hood and family; they have a house on shore near our base, with a tennis court and some excellent strawberry beds. As there are two A1 daughters of seventeen and nineteen, you can bet their hospitality is fully appreciated. There are also two sweet little boys of six and two.

Most of the married officers have imported their wives and families up here, as we are by no means constantly at sea. It is a pleasant change after the weary four or five weeks at sea on end in the Alsatian. On the other hand, leave is far more limited, as of course we are always ready to sail at very short notice, and you can only get on shore for a few hours in the afternoon when not too busy.

The Beattys are very much in evidence here; they have taken a huge place on shore in the vicinity, and the anchorage simply stinks of Lady Beatty's hospital ships, yachts, motor-boats, etc.

Our Captain is named Cay, and he seems a very good sort; he is considerably older than the Admiral, who is and looks extraordinarily young and is most energetic. We swarm with Commanders, having no less than five, an Executive Commander, a Navigating Commander, a Gunnery Commander, and at present two Engineer Commanders, although one is leaving shortly. There are also two Lieutenant-Commanders.

The Flag-Lieutenant-Commander is an extraordinary man. He enjoys the unique distinction of being the only R.N.R. Flag-Lieutenant afloat, but is quite different from most of the typical merchant service R.N.R. lot. He accompanied Scott and Shackleton in their Antarctic expeditions, and is a most versatile personage, as before the war he had just been appointed President of the Labour Exchanges, and was apparently going to instil some life into those lukewarm institutions when the outbreak of war prematurely interrupted his labours. His full name is Bill Adams; very democratic and quite the antithesis of his "boss," the "'onorable 'orace" as he is known on the lower deck.

One of the peculiarities of this class of ship is that the men live aft, and the officers amidships, while the quarter-deck, instead of being in its time-honoured position abaft the mainmast, is also amidships.

The battle cruisers correspond in most ways to, and are usually known as, the "cavalry" of the Navy. Not an unmixed blessing, as living in this ship, even in war-time, is twice or three times as expensive as the Alsatian. Still, in peace we have a reputation for setting the pace, so if we are still afloat then we shall no doubt have a good time.

Now I must "pipe down."

Give my best love to all and sundry.

This need not be private if of interest to anyone.

From
TOBY.

P.S.—Please post one pair white flannel trousers, two pairs grey flannel trousers.

Did my washing ever arrive?

July 24th 1915
H.M.S. INVINCIBLE

Dear Mother,

Just a line to ask for the following gear to be sent in addition to the trousers. The revised list is as follows: Two pairs grey flannel trousers, two pairs white flannel trousers, one pair tennis shoes, one pair nailed shoes, two pairs white socks, my tennis racket and golf clubs (also my greeny-bluey woollen waistcoat).

The last two articles should be carefully packed.

My postal address is:

H.M.S. Invincible,
c/o G.P.O.

If it is impossible to send tennis racket or golf clubs by post, they should be sent by rail.

Rail address:

Midn. Alexander Scrimgeour, R.N.,
Dalmeny Station,
North British Rly.
To wait until called for.

Under no circumstances must the words "Invincible" and "Dalmeny" appear in the same address.

I am very sorry to give all this trouble, and hope you won't mind. All the gear in question is at Quaives.

Long leave is, of course, a far more valuable and rare article now than hitherto, and is only likely to occur at fairly long intervals.

There is, however, a distinct chance of getting some shortly. In which case I shall probably go to Quaives for two days, and spend the rest in London.

I will wire daddy when I am coming if I do come. Best love to all.

TOBY.

AUGUST

August 3rd 1915
H.M.S. INVINCIBLE

Dearest Mother,

Many thanks for letters and all the gear, which arrived safely. I am so glad to hear you are having a good time at Thorney. How long will it be before you return to Quaives? I expect to get a week's leave very shortly; I shall not visit Thorney, in spite of the glowing pen-pictures you draw, artfully interweaving descriptions of an idyllic mode of life with less inanimate attractions, apparently with a view of enticing me there. It rests entirely with you and the children whether I shall see you or not. I wonder whether your maternal instinct or obstinate pride (hacked up by Aunt Crab, doubtless) will prove stronger. I am still waging a war of silence with her, which will last to eternity unless she considers my ultra-reasonable proposals.

Please thank daddy for his long and interesting letter (?). The excuse of "being so busy" on the Stock Exchange is rather flat just at present. Thank him for his news. — is doubtless a very good man at his job—viz., stockbroking, and is also probably a fairly well-read and well-informed man (like most Stock Exchange products I have met). But apparently the war has affected him like the vast majority of people, naturally sane under ordinary conditions; they either become morbidly pessimistic or else confidently optimistic, due, not to quiet and determined confidence that by a continuous sequence of energetic and sensible progressions we shall gradually overcome all obstacles and stumble home winners, but due to a laughably absurd and childishly superstitious faith in the interference of some master-factor in the art of war (this being or thing varies from God to Lord Kitchener and Mr. Ll. G.*, and from high-explosives to conscription), which will finish the war at one fell swoop.

* David Lloyd George.

These bubbles are continually pricked, but new phantasies are born in the brains of these people, and they are never tired of proclaiming, like Mr. ——, that some dramatic and sudden event will shortly spring up and devour the enemy.

I am getting on pretty well, but absolutely dread coming on leave, when we are due for our refit. There is a most persistent rumour that the Germans are coming to sea this month, and if they choose the time when we are refitting, I shall never forgive myself—or them.

We are a very cheery crowd; everybody is in the Battle Cruiser Fleet, and money goes like water. All the "nibs" of the Service from every point of view seem to collect here.

My very best love to everyone.
TOBY.

August 29th 1915
H.M.S. INVINCIBLE

Dearest Mother,

Thank you for your letters. As I write I hear that there is just a chance of my getting some leave in September after all, but it is very remote. By all means send Burberry my periscope; it is of no use to me. Aunt Do has just sent me a life-saving belt, which is very kind of her. Another Mrs. Duguid, Aunt Jessie, has written to me asking if I would visit her at Edinburgh, which I may do, although how she guessed my whereabouts I cannot think. I suppose you are the culprit, you naughty old thing.

It would interest me to hear what old —— blithered about, so you might tell me in your next letter, otherwise I am sure you will forget. Smith-Osborne I have got to know better lately, and he seems an A1 chap. He dined in the gun-room with us last night.

Amy Drummond Hay wrote to me from Orotava a short time ago; will you please thank her very much and send her my love.

I have called on Mrs. Roxburgh (the mother of two great friends of mine, one a surgeon in the Alsatian, and another a snotty in the Indefatigable); she knows Mrs. Finnis and the Elles very well.

I enclose a letter from Captain Trewby, my late Flag-Captain in the Alsatian, which I thought might interest you; it struck me as being very nice of him. He got the D.S.O. about a fortnight ago, as I dare say you saw in the papers.

I am getting on pretty well on the whole. It is an enormous advantage being able to get on shore occasionally and get some tennis and golf, instead of the long weary weeks up in the Arctic Circle. Life is pretty strenuous; I spend most of my time in a picket-boat, as I dare say I have told you before.

Please don't lose Captain Trewby's letter. My very best love to everybody.

Yours,
TOBY.
P.S.—If Johnny is still at Newcastle, please find out his address.

August 23rd 1915
H.M.S. ALSATIAN

Dear Scrimgeour,

Very many thanks for your letter of congratulations; of course, it is an honour for the Tenth C.S., and I have done no more than any other Captain. I suppose you are all green with envy of the mids. in Dardanelles and their D.S.C.s, but your turn will come one of these fine days, and all our talent is in the Grand Fleet, and you are in one of the best ships if there is any fighting. I showed your letter to the Admiral, and he wishes you all the best of luck. I expect at sea you have a strenuous time, but you make up for it by good long spells in harbour and shore leave. We are back at the same old port covered with coal-dust; a batch of new R.N.R. mids. have just joined straight from the Worcester, I believe, in your place. I expect Glanvile finds it dull in the G.R. now. I see your notepaper has the Spanish name for Falkland Islands and a penguin; I spent many an hour among the penguins down there about thirteen years ago. With all good wishes to you all, and may you smash up the German Fleet this side of Xmas.

Yours very sincerely,
GEORGE TREWBY.

OCTOBER

Friday 1

Arrived London 9 a.m. after a filthy journey, most of which was spent scrapping with Stewart. Went to the flat and found Jack Russell, daddy and Mother. Did some shopping and then went along to the office and saw Uncle John, Blunt, old Stewart (R.R.'s father) and Stanby. Had an 'A1' lunch with daddy. Things are in rather low water just at present, and we are trying to economise. I went home by the 5.10, and spent the evening with Mother at Quaives, successfully resisting the temptation to go round to Westenhanger.

Saturday 2

Went round in the morning and saw them all. Drove Joko into Canterbury and did some shopping; lunched with Cag and Mrs. O'Callaghan. Cag is now stationed here with his yeomanry. On our arrival home we were just in time to meet Lady Maud Warrender*, who is stopping the weekend at Westenhanger. Daddy loathes her, but she is a friend of Norman's, and I took to her exceedingly. Joko came round to tea at Quaives, and I dined at

---

* Friends with novelist E. F. Benson, Lady Warrender's house in Rye would provide the backdrop for two of his novels, *Colin* and *Colin II*.

Westenhanger. Poor old Mother is very funny, I believe she is jealous of my fondness for Joko.

Sunday 3

Slacked in the morning, a lovely day. In the afternoon went up to the Rectory and saw Sophie "Wasabelle," Kitty Mackintosh, and the old people. Went to the afternoon service at the church to hear the singing, which was magnificent, especially that of Lady Maud Warrender and Jack. Tea-fight at the Rectory afterwards.

Monday 4

Motored Joko over to Folkestone and had lunch at the Grand, lobster and fizz. Then we went on and took Peggy out from Miss White's; she seemed very well. Then on home. Florence Lomax arrived to stay. She is a funny girl, quite a good sort, very fast, but absolutely heartless and a bad influence on Joko I think. Joko very uppish, making £5 bets with remarkable freedom. She wanted to go off in the dark on Byron's motorbike by herself, but got a bit frightened of Harold West's ghost, so funked it. I adore the little minx, but I am afraid I am just as big a flirt as she is. Had a long chat with Mother, she was very interested by my descriptions of Stroma.

Tuesday 5

Neville Handfield-Jones killed, also Cecil Gedge, who died a most glorious death, and whose soul shall float on in glory through Valhalla to all eternity. Went round saying goodbyes to everyone; old Baird seems very well disposed towards me just at present. Sorry to leave, as my visits home are always so short, but perhaps it is for the best. Joko looked too fascinating in the morning. I am sure she is a naughty wee thing, there is not much she does not know. As I have said before, Florence is inclined to hold out glimpses of London life, which are not good for Joko's imagination. Said goodbye to dear old mother, and went up to London by the 2.28 from Bekesbourne. Joko came to the station with me as usual, and was sweet as an angel, and drove me into ecstasies of adoration alas as usual. It is extraordinary what a change their Scrimgeour allowance makes to the Westenhanger family, relieved of their financial difficulties. The parents look years younger, and there are all sorts of little extra comforts in the home. It must be very nice for the girls having a dressing allowance etc, although Joko has not appeared in anything new to me. Perhaps she keeps them for the soldiers! Dined with W.S.H. and daddy at Simpson's, then off from Euston by the 8 p.m. express.

Wednesday 6

Arrived Stranraer 5.30 a.m. after a good journey; went across to Lame and rejoined the *Invincible* in Harland and Wolff's yard at Belfast at 9 a.m. Everyone rejoined the ship. All the dockyard work complete, and we are ready to sail. The gun-room has been enlarged and improved during our absence, which is a mercy. Some people went ashore in the afternoon. I spent it rambling round the dockyard, a perfect beehive of shipbuilding industry. Went over the monitor *Earl of Peterborough* and the gigantic monster the *Britannic*; quite interesting. Wrote some letters. During our absence Mr. M. has been promoted to mate; he is a good chap, but hardly the sort for commissioned rank. Proceeded out of dock at 8 a.m., met an escort of two destroyers off Carrickfergus, and proceeded out of Belfast Lough, and shaped a course for Mull of Cantyre and Oversay.

Thursday 7

I kept the morning watch, proceeded past Dubh Artach, Skerryvore, Barra Head, and through the Minch and round Cape Wrath. G.Q.s in the forenoon. Everything pretty efficient in "A" turret. The men hardly seem to have got as much benefit from their leave as I hoped. I think forty-eight hours, considering the time they spend travelling and the long periods elapsing between their leave, is too short, as they have a very monotonous time otherwise. Personally I should try and give seven days on end every nine months to all the ship's company, but I suppose that is impossible. It is my ambition to get into touch with the feelings of my men as far as possible. I am sure all officers should do this. Ran the Pentland Firth at 2 p.m. and joined up with the Second Battle Cruiser Squadron north-east of Duncansby Head, then altered course S.S.E. and made for Rosyth. I kept the first watch.

Friday 8

Arrived in the Forth at 8 a.m., anchored, and the collier (S.S. *Camerata* good derricks, narrow-mouthed holds) came alongside immediately. A terrific "coal ship," 1,400 tons, the biggest we have had, lasting until 4 p.m. Very tedious and hard work. Coaling is an evil no landsman, not even the hardest worked soldier, has experienced. The foc'sle hold swept the board;

I worked the in-board winch fairly satisfactorily, and de Lisle seemed very pleased as he stood me two sherries afterwards. Felt really done up at the end. The Commander does not encourage the men as much as he really should, although, of course, I should not criticise my superiors. Mr. Martin left the ship for the *Whaley*, and Surgeon McEwan for the monitor *Marshal Soult*. I am very sorry both are leaving—Martin as I hoped to learn a lot of gunnery from him, and Mac as he is a damned good fellow. I lost £2 of my pay two minutes after being paid by old Mainprice; most annoying, as finances are rather on the "slump" at present, due to one thing and another. We are moored just astern of the *Canada*, who has just finished her trials. She is a magnificent ship; old Dalglish is Commander, and Stromeyer one of the "snots."

October 8th 1915
H.M.S. INVINCIBLE

Dearest Mammy,

How are you all up at the cottage? I hope the move went off all well. I dined with daddy and Hutchinson before leaving on Tuesday night. The old ship was not quite ready when we rejoined, and I spent the day wandering round the shipyard and exploring the new "freak" monitors they are building, and went over the new monster new White Star liner Britannic, which is also building here.

I hope you have quite recovered from the evil effects of my stay at home.

Give daddy my love when you see him, and say I thoroughly enjoyed my dinner, although not quite so much as the lunch in the City. I shall live for another such as that.

I hear that the Alexander-Sinclair family have left their Edinburgh house and migrated into the wilds of the northern highlands until Xmas, so I shall not see Stroma again for the present.

"Sammy," the Admiral's little boy, is five on the 15th, and I had been commissioned to buy the gun-room birthday present, a silver egg-cup and spoon. Of course, I forgot, so we are now in a panic.

I hope you won't forget all my wants, photos, washing, shoes mending, messages, etc., ad lib. I believe I left the copy of the six-hour concert in the Alsatian in one of my mufti coat pockets, so please don't lose it.

My very best love to all.

Heaps of kisses.
TOBY.

Saturday 9

We have shifted our Naval Instructor from the *Indefatigable* to the *New Zealand*, which is rather a jar. I ran the first picket-boat all day, pretty busy. Arranged Portal's stations after much cagging with old Borrett. Provisioned ship in the afternoon. The Third Battle Squadron went to sea at 4 p.m. The old "wobbly" Third are a damned useful lot, in spite of the universal contempt in which they are held by most Battle Cruiser Fleet officers. Three stripes night in the gun-room; guests, Commander Townsend (G.) Dannreuther, Shore, Eng.-Commander Weekes, Major Colquhoun, Fleet Pay Mainprice, and Fleet Surgeon Bearblock, and the Chaplain. Quite a success; most of the S.O.B.s thoroughly enjoyed themselves. I looked after old Bearblock, an ancient but dear old chap. An excellent dinner, and we filled them all up. Afterwards two bridge fours, and the remainder became young again with "Up Jenkins." Then some songs, "Recky" at the piano, and so at twelve to bed.

Sunday 10

Usual Sunday routine. Went up to Admiralty House in the afternoon with S.O. Fisher, "Flags," and W.S.H. Old Robin and Mrs. Campsie Dalglish there; she is very nice, and they seem very fond of each other; he is Commander of the *Canada*. Commodore and Mrs. Goodenough also looked in. Got in four sets of tennis; I played very well for me. It is rather funny playing tennis up here in the middle of October, but very convenient. The weather is getting cold, but quite dry at present.

Monday 11

"Out nets" evolution all the forenoon; port fore working guy parted, much to Borrett's annoyance. The skipper got very excited and strafed signal officer. In the Gunnery-Commander's section (incidentally mine as well) all went without a hitch, except that I repeatedly forgot to exhibit the "all-well" flag. Went over the *Canada* in the afternoon, examined her turrets, magazines, shell-room, bridge, fire control, and general gunnery arrangements. Had a fearful cag with old Ferrugia the messman. He is trying to do me for several quid with my mess bill. Mr. Hunt, gunner of the ship, promoted to chief gunner.

Tuesday 12

Working for the Naval Instructor of the *New Zealand* in the forenoon. Accompanied Mr. Cameron refitting the director training gear of "P" turret in the afternoon; spent the day on board. I am very keen indeed to get five first-class certificates in my exam for Lieutenant next year, but I am afraid it will be almost impossible, as a whole year was wasted in the *Crescent* and *Alsatian*, and the Gunnery-Commander and the Torpedo-Lieutenant do not take very much interest in our instruction here, although old Dan is a ripper.

Wednesday 13

Third Battle Squadron returned. I ran the second duty steam-boat (our first picket-boat) all day. Mr. Ferrugia, our gun-room messman, developed serious fever and was sent off to hospital, leaving us in the lurch. After much discussion and argument, the question was got down to the basis that either Powell should mess us, or else Logan, the wine steward, should do it. No other officer except Powell volunteered for the job. A silver egg-cup and spoon arrived as the gun-room present for Sammy's fifth birthday on Friday. I was busy with ammunition work most of the day when not away in my boat.

Thursday 14

Robert Ross amused us with a navigation lecture in the forenoon. In the afternoon I had intended to go up to Edinburgh, go to the dentist and to Gieves, and to tea with Stroma. Of course, just to spite me, we had to prepare for sea and all leave cancelled, although we did not go to sea till 10 p.m. I spent another afternoon at ammunition. Had a long chat with de Lisle; he, like me, strongly disapproves of the mate "ranker" scheme, and thinks it will ruin the Service. He has just had a great quarrel with Cory.

Friday 15

Sammy's birthday. The gun-room have given him a silver egg-cup and spoon, chosen by daddy. G.Q.s in the forenoon. Went up north of the Moray Firth mine-field, then ran down the Sutherlandshire coast and into the Cromarty Firth, anchoring between Cromarty and Invergordon at 4 p.m. Commenced to coal at seven and took in 420 tons from the collier *Kilsyth* (single derrick); finished 10.30. Very uncomfortable and tricky work coaling in the dark. The *Indomitable* and *Inflexible* both got good colliers. We don't "trade on our flag" like some flagships do, as we seldom get the best collier and never shirk duty steamboat. Other squadrons in harbour: First Battle Squadron, Second Cruiser Squadron, several minesweepers, and auxiliary.

Saturday 16

Weighed at 8 a.m. and went out to do full charge heavy gunfiring in the Moray Firth. A cinema of the firing taken from the light cruiser *Active*. We fired with the *Indom*, and the *Inflex* fired with the *Vanguard* of the First Battle Squadron. Firing medium only, but all the loading went off swimmingly in "A" turret, much to the delight of de Lisle and myself. All glass in the ship broken by the firing and all small fittings dislodged. A gorgeous day. Left the Firth and proceeded into the North Sea, going over towards the Norwegian coast in the afternoon, and in the evening we ran into a thick fog.

Sunday 17

Joko has not answered my lovely long letter nor has Byron acknowledged my cheque. I wonder if they received the letters. I kept the morning watch. Entered the Firth of Forth and anchored in our usual billet at 9 a.m. Coaled ship from the collier *Slav*, 800 tons in very nearly record time. A beautiful collier, and everything went swimmingly except Campbell got jammed by a hoist of empties and twisted his hip very badly and is going on the sick list. I ran the first picket-boat. A fine day, but the nip of winter returning in the air. Old Harold Begbie paid us a visit from the *Antrim* after dinner.

October 17th 1915
H.M.S. INVINCIBLE

Dearest Mother,

Many thanks for all your letters, which I fully appreciate; Peg's
and Jim's are quite good, especially the former. All the clothes
have arrived safely.

Now as to this matter of Spicer's bill. I have gone into it
thoroughly, and I find from my diary and my accounts that the
following took place:

On June the 8th and 9th I made use of Spicer's motor to go to
Margate and to go to Canterbury.

Re the Margate expedition, it took place on the day that Harry
Baird motored daddy over to Margate to see Henry; I took Nita
and Joko. I directed Spicer to give me his bill, which he did.
Before leaving I gave you the bill and also a £1 note with which
to pay the majority of it. I did not think it necessary to ask you
for a receipt. On the following day I used Spicer's motor to take
me to Canterbury on my way back to Liverpool to join the
Alsatian.

By comparison with your own accounts you should be able to
find out whether the bill has already been paid or not; I expect
you have already paid it. In any case, it seems most
unbusinesslike to send in a bill in October for services rendered
in June. Please let me know the result of your investigations.

Now for more jobs for you, provided you are willing.

On October 6th I sent Byron a cheque for £2 for the golf club,
as he told me they were very short of funds. He has not
acknowledged the receipt of this cheque. Would you mind
asking him whether he got it? If he did not, it would save time

if you wrote to the bank and asked them to stop it for me if it is not too late.

The address is—

London Joint Stock Bank, Ltd.,
Russell Square Branch,
1, Woburn Place,
London, W.C.

The number of the cheque to be stopped was "A 158689," and was made out and endorsed by me (Alexander Scrimgeour is my signature) and payable to E. Byron Kelsey. If he has not already got it, it has probably been stolen in the post.

Item No. 2:

I left all my snapshots of the Alsatian, Crescent, etc., at Westenhanger, with solemn promises of their being sent on. If you are in that direction, please walk boldly into the drawing-room, procure the photos and send them on to me, otherwise I shall never get them.

If I have the time and inclination ever, I may call on Jim in Edinburgh, but I see no opportunity at present.

Winter is beginning to close in, and although the weather is still pretty fair, the cold is noticeable, and I am afraid we are into the thick of it for another six months.

No more now.

Very best love to all at home.
TOBY.

Monday 18

I am afraid all the letters I wrote in Belfast must have been lost, as neither Byron, Joko, nor Mrs. Gedge have answered. Thick fog all day and very cold. "Out nets" evolution in the forenoon. Everything fairly satisfactory. Dear old signal officer is a ripping fellow in every way, but he is a damned bad officer. Sammy's and the Admiral's birthday celebrations. Several of us landed and went up to Admiralty house to a tea-party, which was quite fun, games, etc. Gun-room guest night; unluckily the First Battle Cruiser Squadron and *Lion* sailed at dark, so we only had one guest, the Captain's Clerk from the *Commonwealth*. I would have had Findlay from the *Princess Royal*.

Tuesday 19

A miserable, wet, mucky, cold day. We had the duty steamboat in the first picket-boat, and a most unpleasant job it was too. Big changes made in the routine to cope with the long hours of darkness; they seem most satisfactory. Heard from Byron at last, also Cockerill. Poor Allan Hardy has been killed. Sent a small party of seamen to help run the *Prince Charles*, a tramp commandeered by the Admiralty for the anti-submarine service. She is one of quite a large number of tramps, manned by naval officers and men, dressed as ordinary merchant seamen, and disguised in every way. They have concealed guns, and have proved (and are still doing so) most successful.

Wednesday 20

Went to the *New Zealand* Naval Instructor in the forenoon. Hydraulic work with old Nixon in the afternoon. Feeling very mouldy all day. Pessimistic due to the Service news, and bored with life and generally fed up with things in general. Still, I must fight against these fits of depression and their causes and conquer them. Determination and will-power can do anything. I wish Joko would write, it would cheer me up immensely. I am going to write my impressions of all the officers in the ship, as I did in the *Cornwall* and *Crescent*, but neglected to do in the *Alsatian*.

Thursday 21

Poor young Blacker (who is in the Coldstreams) and John Kipling in the Irish Guards are both missing. Temporary Surgeon Jones joined the ship via old McEwan, who has gone to a monitor. Rugger match, *Invincible* officers v. *Indomitable* officers, at South Queensferry; we were short of A.J.S.R. Unsworth, Franklin, Campbell, and O'Reilly, but we wiped the board with them 35-0; we should have a pretty useful three-quarter line, W.S. Hutchinson, Morse, Portal, and de Lisle. I managed to get two tries, but was very blown at the end, feeling like death. O'Reilly, who runs the ship Rugger, refused to play at the last minute, as he wanted to go up to Edinburgh to meet his fiancée; very slack of him. I am sure she would have been just as pleased to watch him play Rugger. By the way, poor young Campbell has fractured his hip, and he may be permanently incapacitated; now we have only four junior midshipmen, which is most annoying for the senior members of the mess. Young Campbell was a promising young officer, although a bit slow.

Friday 22

The *Lion* and rest of First Battle Cruiser Squadron, except the *Queen Mary*, returned to harbour and commenced to coal at 8 a.m. Third Battle Cruiser Squadron picket-boat manoeuvres all the forenoon. We went to G.Q.s and exercised auxiliary loading for the right gun in "A" turret, then to "Abandon Ship" stations, and finished up with "Out Nets." I went ashore and up to Edinburgh in the afternoon, saw "Keynotes," then went to Nicholson the dentist for an hour. Shopped, and then had tea with Scott, Bowlsby, Annesley, Battersby, and Burghersh. Gun-room guest night; I asked Hall from our ward-room, whence came also Macmullen and Cory.

Saturday 23

A miserable swine of a day, pelting with rain from morn till eve. I ran the first picket-boat and got stopped several times, doing all the routine trips, while "Recky" Portal in the second picket-boat did the odd work and thought he had a soft job, but I drew fires and moored up at seven, and he had all the night work, much to his chagrin. More hydraulics with Mr. Nixon in the forenoon; he has gone through a complete hydraulic course and knows a lot of bookwork, but as far as this ship goes he doesn't know a thing. The ship played *Inflexible* at Soccer and won 3-2. The "Bloke" is in very good spirits just now; his wife and children have now got a house up here; he is devoted to them (very much married) and haunts the beach.

Sunday 24

Joko's birthday present arrived, a waist belt with a naval crown as clasp. I sent it off. All squadrons in the Forth went to one hour's notice; all leave cancelled, etc.; no one knew why, as there were no developments. Bill

Midshipman Alexander Scrimgeour – a photograph taken of the portrait that graced the hall at Thorncombe House in Surrey.

Above: Alexander began
the war in the armed
cruiser HMS *Crescent*,
flagship of the Tenth
Cruiser Squadron under
Admiral de Chair.
(IWM Q 21126)

Left: Admiral Dudley
de Chair (1864–1958),
photographed in 1924 at
Government House just
after he became Governor
of New South Wales,
Australia. According to
Alexander he earned
himself the nickname
'Old Make-a-Signal',
'owing to the large
number of unnecessary
signals he issues'.
(State Library of New
South Wales, Australia)

Opposite: Rear-Admiral Horace Hood (1870–1916), commander of HMS *Invincible*. Alexander had already encountered him at Osborne College before he was transferred to the battle cruiser under Hood's command. (Conway)

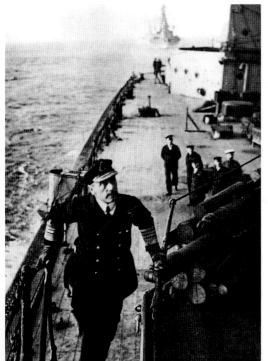

Above: Admiral Sir David Beatty (1871–1936), Commander of the Battle Cruiser Fleet, pictured here on the deck of HMS *Queen Elizabeth* in 1917 with Rear-Admiral Hugh Evan-Thomas (1862–1928), who was in command of the Fifth Battle Squadron at Jutland. (Conway)

Left: Admiral Sir John Jellico (1859–1935), Commander-in-Chief of the Grand Fleet during the First World War. (Conway)

Top: HMS *Invincible* explodes at 6.34 p.m. on 31 May 1916. (Conway)

Bottom: The haunting wreck of *Invincible*, taken about half an hour after the explosion that ripped her apart. The torpedo boat destroyer *Badger* approaches to pick up the few survivors, four of whom are on a raft that can just be seen between *Badger* and *Invincible*'s bow. (Conway)

Adams, the Flag-Lieutenant, went off to London on three days' leave. It is rumoured that he is going to return to his old pre-war job of harbour work in connection with munitions, where he is a very valuable man; but we shall all be frightfully sorry to lose him. I supped with old "Puroj," the Gunnery-Commander, in the ward-room. He is a dear old chap, and we had a long chat in his cabin after. He is a bit too prone to talking shop.

October 24th 1915
H.M.S. INVINCIBLE

Dear Daddy,

I enclose a guinea for the egg-cup and spoon, and have posted the soup-ladle back to Quaives, where I imagined it would be best to send it. Thank you very much indeed for your trouble. The present was an enormous success; the ladle was very sweet, but hardly so appropriate as the egg-cup. The birthday party had to be postponed owing to unforeseen circumstances, but was a great rag when it came off.

Did you send the gun off, as it has not yet arrived at Dalmeny Station? I hope it has not gone astray. I hear from Mother you have had a day at Aldington with the new tenant. Please thank mother for her regular letters, and say I have heard from Byron, but have not yet received my snapshots from Westenhanger.

I have discovered a damnable abscess under the stump of the broken tooth, and am paying periodical visits to a dentist when I get the chance.

Give my love to Jack and Arthur Russell and to G. G. W. when he returns.

Best love from
TOBY.

Monday 25

I ran the first picket-boat. Quite an easy day, but very cold. "Fire Stations" and then "Out Nets" after divisions. More hydraulic work with old Nixon. A.B. Bird is leaving the ship with a draft for depot tomorrow. This notorious bad sheep of the foc'sle division will not be much missed by most people, but I am sorry he is going, as it was my ambition to strike the right note in his character (I am sure it exists somewhere) and try and reform him. Amongst the others leaving are C.P.O. Goldring, a very good man, and A.B. Satchell, an inveterate rotter.

Tuesday 26

Usual routine all day. The aeroplane ship *Engadine* came in, and the seaplanes showed great activity all day. Stewart's brother in the R.A.M.C., on five days' leave from the Front, arrived last night from London and spent the night on board, sleeping in Fisher's cabin; we had a great rag last night before turning in, turning the chest flat into an absolute shambles. Landed in the afternoon, and our gun-room team played the *Indomitable*'s at Rugger, winning 9–3; quite good, but we should have done much better if only the forwards would heel, and the outsides take their passes. I got a try and played pretty well, but my language rather disgusted old Mrs. Weekes who was watching, I am afraid. A very heated argument in the gun-room over respective officers' principles of work; I got very excited.

Wednesday 27

The hydraulics craze with old Nixon, the gay and debonair marine gunner at the head, continued apace, although many metaphysical pin-pricks were required to get "Labbie" and into a state of energy, much less enthusiasm. The "Johnnie" de Lisle affair continues without break and with increasing vigour, in spite of the gibes and causticism of the ward-room three-stripe officers, and the vulgar jeers of the lesser gun-room fry. A Rugger craze has arisen in this ship, and Service Rugger, once it gets a hold on a community of Service people, is quite irresistible. Today we landed for one hour's scrum practice at South Queensferry. O'Reilly came and ran the show; he is a fine player, but not much of a coach. It is a great pity old McEwan has left the ship. The Cory controversy has subsided somewhat, but the general unpopularity of the mate system is still more pronounced. Met Sophie Molyneux in her motor on shore with Battenberg, Burghersh, and Captain

Pelly; being covered with mud and in footer rig, I did not expect to be very impressing, but she was most gracious.

Thursday 28

Terrible "Buff" casualty list. D. Lambert and Birkett, the Harlequin Rugger men, Allan Hardy, and poor dear old Kit Davidson have been killed in France. May the fury of all the eternal devils be called down on the fiendish, unspeakable Huns who have caused all our most gallant and best to lose their valuable lives! Poor old Kit, he was one of the very best. May every British subject arise in righteous wrath and never rest until each British life is avenged tenfold; I wish the glorious example of the heroic Serbians would rouse this befogged and lethargic nation to a realisation of its responsibilities. We chafe at our powerlessness to do more good. Went to the Naval Instructor in the *New Zealand* in the forenoon and did a good morning's work. A miserable wet day. Landed and went up to the dentist in Edinburgh in the afternoon, then went on to call on Jim Robertson's family at 30, Inverleith Place; all of them immensely grown and changed, but still under the iron discipline and rule of Miss Shorediche, who showed such extraordinary appreciation of the senior Service that I believe she must be a German spy. Elspeth and Agnes have their hair up, the latter quite a good sort. Billy is at Edinburgh Academy and very keen on Rugger, and Babs is a good sort. A joy party headed by Percy in the *Queen Mary*. Johnnie Cobb, the Nickersens, Portal and sister, and others went to the Haymarket Ice Rink and pronounced it a great success, the rink being, so they said, even better than Prince's.

Friday 29

By the way, of all the awful snobs I have ever met, Wilton of the *Queen Mary* and Bowlby of the *New Zealand* are about the most supreme. H.M.S. *Argyll*, of the Third Cruiser Squadron, went ashore off Bell Rock; a nasty swell, and there seems little chance of getting her off; a flotilla of destroyers went out and took off her ship's company. I am afraid she will become a total wreck. G.Q.s in the forenoon. I went round all the turrets with Mr. Nixon; "A" and "X," the two Vickers turrets, are infinitely superior to "P" and "Q," the two Armstrong turrets, although the details of Vickers' work is rotten. Landed in the afternoon and played the *Hibernia* at Rugger, full strength match, at South Queensferry. After a strenuous and muddy game we won 30-0. We played very well. A huge tea afterwards at Queensferry

Arms. Gun-room guest night. Humphrey Legge (Flag-Lieutenant of the *Princess Royal*), Tollemache, and Borrett guests; a very good night. We had a terrific gamble, and Tollemache swept the board, winning the hell of a lot, and we all lost very heavily.

Saturday 30

I ran the first picket-boat for the last time, I believe, as I am starting three months' engineering duty on Monday.

Salvage work on the *Argyll* continued all day; pretty hard job. The big crane and pontoon came alongside at 11.30 a.m., and the two 4-inch guns on "P" turret were hoisted out of the ship, as we are getting rid of the 4-inch guns on "P" and "Q" turrets. Fellowes-Gordon came over from the *Indefatigable* in the afternoon with rifle drill party and had some tea with us. Owing to a general misunderstanding between the Commander, Commander (G.), Commander (N.), signal officer, Stewart, Portal, and myself, there was a frightful "straf," and after various vows of vengeance against Portal and myself for misinterpreting the Commander's orders, Portal got watch and watch for three days. Most unjust. Borrett stood up for me like mad, chiefly owing to his violent antagonism to the Commander.

Sunday 31

Bill Adams returned to the ship to get his gear, and left at 6 to return to London. He is leaving us for good, worse luck. His new job is naval adviser to Lloyd George on the Munitions Committee. O'Reilly is now acting as Flag-Lieutenant, but he will be unable to do the job as well as signal officer. There is talk of Stewart getting the post, which would be about the limit in the way of good luck for that extremely lucky young officer. There is also talk of old Begbie coming back. Some of the Wobbly Eight* went to sea, and consequently we all went to short notice. I stood all the first picket-boat's crew a bottle of beer apiece to celebrate the successful conclusion of my three months in charge of the boat. Rae asked me to dine in the *New Zealand*, but I refused. A rotten foggy day. Heard from Joko at last.

---

*The 8 King Edward VIII class pre-dreadnought battleships of the Third Battle Squadron were affectionately known as the 'wobbly eight', due to their difficulty in keeping to a steady course.

NOVEMBER

Monday 1
Started three months' engineering duty. My day on as junior engineer officer of the day; not very strenuous, as I spent most of the time finding my way about below and tracing main steam. It will be nice getting my engineering time over in the winter months, as it would be damned cold in a picket-boat. Heard from Harry Baird. I wish to goodness I had the strength of mind to absolutely dismiss Joko from my thoughts and dreams. I am sure she treats me as a sort of toy. I do not say she is not fond of me, but I don't believe she would dream of marrying me, which is after all very sensible of her and lucky for both of us. Still, I think she might not play with heartstrings so; although of course if I said so to her she would say she had no idea I was really in love with her. I cannot make up my mind whether to give up my affair with her altogether and write to tell her so, or to let things dangle on as they are at present which is not very good for my peace of mind, although I still have a fleeting hope that some day she will marry me. I wish things would come to a head. Even if she was in love with me and would marry me, it would be damned silly of me to marry her so young. Again she is very lazy, indolent and a dreadful flirt, although she does have some very good points.

Tuesday 2
Last night Cobb and I had a long yarn with the padre in his cabin *re* the morals of the gun-room officers. The old boy is very sensible and not a bit of a prude, while the state of the gun-room would certainly rival the lowest haunts of the Stock Exchange. Coaled ship at 5.45 a.m., taking in 375 tons. We had a big deficiency, this leading to a great rag between the Captain, Commander, and Engineer-Commander. De Lisle was blamed for swinging in his hoists and so making the bags light, instead of dropping them plumb. L.E.J.'s day on, he relieving me at 9 a.m. Spent most of the day pipe tracing in the boiler-rooms. Payne asked me to dine in the *Lion*, but I refused. "Out Nets" after quarters.

Wednesday 3
"Pipe tracing" in the forenoon down below. I had a very busy afternoon mapped out, but after our match with the *New Zealand* was scratched

Scott arranged a match with the *Princess Royal*. A frightful rag took place, and eventually we agreed to play, but it rained like hell, and they did not turn up, so the whole afternoon was wasted, which was most annoying. Saw Dora and Kathleen Mackintosh in Queensferry.

Thursday 4

Eleana and Katherine asked Bench and me to go to the skating-rink today, with a party including Stroma. Unluckily I had a previous engagement, and Bench a "day on." Spent the forenoon in the engine-room. Landed in the afternoon and went up to Edinburgh with Scott, had a "spot" at the Waverley, where Payne and Troubridge rolled up; the latter is now in the *Comus*. Also saw old John Tovey and Begbie. We went on and played golf at Milebank with two friends of Scott's, I playing with a Mrs. Hill against Scott and Mrs. Crabbie; we won 3 and 2. Both quite nice and knowing Louis Greig well. Jack Crabbie, her husband, and Phipps-Turnbull, her brother, both played for Scotland with Louis, and Major Hill, Mrs. Hill's husband, captained England for several years; altogether a very "Ruggery" crowd. On our arrival back in the ship a bomb fell. Scott has been appointed away and is to go up to the Admiralty to report. He is being relieved by Campbell-Cooke, late of the *Collingwood* and *Argyll*. We shall be very sorry to lose Scott. He is an exceptionally nice fellow, very tactful and intellectual, though perhaps a trifle weak. I like him very much indeed.

Friday 5

G.Q.s in the forenoon, nothing much doing. De Lisle, Richardson, and I examined the director training clock in "A" space, and then the "A" magazines. My engineering "day on," but managed to get ashore in the afternoon. We played the *Queen Mary*, Portal away (leave stopped) and Cobb (crocked)— we won rather unexpectedly 25-9. Hutchinson crocked when we were down 6-9, so we did jolly well. A fierce game; Stevens, the constructor, playing a very questionable game. I managed to get two tries. Saw Mrs. Richardson and the two young "Shishlets" on shore. The Milebank crowd came over to watch us play. Betty Molyneux and Sibyl rather surprised by the language in the scrum. O'Reilly said I was the worst offender, but all signal officers are alike. Very busy in the evening with the main and auxiliary steam system.

Saturday 6

Turned out at five and went round the engine-rooms. At 5.45 a.m. we got orders to light up all boilers and get ready for sea. Rather a nuisance, as I wanted to go up to Edinburgh and finish off the dentist and also call on Stroma and ring up Aunt Jessie. Sub-Lieutenant Campbell-Cooke, Scott's relief, joined the ship at 10 a.m. from the ill-fated *Argyll*. Rather wet, but seems quite a good sort. We unmoored, weighed, and proceeded to sea at noon in company with the *Lion*, First Battle Cruiser Squadron, and rest of Third Battle Cruiser Squadron. Carried out 1-inch aiming tube firing at splash targets towed by our opposite numbers off May Island. Then parted company with the *Lion* and First Battle Cruiser Squadron and proceeded east for the Skager Rack. The Germans have set a line of armed trawlers across to prevent the ingress of our submarines into the Baltic. Two light cruisers are going over to do a little "strafing" on the aforesaid trawlers, and we are supporting them in case of eventualities. The second division of the Third Battle Squadron (Wobbly Eight), under "my boy Sid," sailed from the Forth with us, and then proceeded south; it is rumoured they are off to the Mediterranean. I kept the first dog-watch below in the engine-room and boiler-rooms with Macmullen. The boilers are in such excellent trim that it is very hard to keep the steam down to the necessary pressure.

Sunday 7

Kept the middle watch down below with old Bull, who was in a very surly mood. Very hot. Turned in at four and slept like a log. At six the light cruisers should have been in position for the "straf." At eight we rejoined the *Lion* and First Battle Cruiser Squadron and still proceeded east until noon, then ran down Danish coast for one hour and altered course for the Scotch coast. The result of the stunt has not been divulged. I kept the afternoon and first watches below with Macmullen and Bull respectively, and was damned glad to finish a very long day at midnight. It is very strenuous being in three engine-room watches, as Hutchinson is *hors de combat* with a dislocated shoulder. A nasty sea in the evening, and we rolled heavily. The starboard torpedo boom-heads got adrift and made enough clanking noise to drive anyone off their head, banging against the ship's side just outside gun-room.

Monday 8

Entered the Forth and anchored at 8.45 a.m. in company with the other ships. Started to coal immediately. My "day on," as Bench is sick; spent most of the forenoon in boiler-rooms superintending dying out, blowing down, and cleaning of boilers. Coming into harbour, one of the light cruisers rammed and sank a collier in the middle of the fairway. Finished coaling at 2 p.m., having taken in 850 tons with a very fair average, although the foc'sle men were not up to scratch. We finished cleaning the tubes, etc., in the boiler-rooms by about 4 p.m., and I then had a most enjoyable bath and felt clean for the first time for some hours. Old Scott went ashore and left us at 5.30 p.m.; off to the Admiralty. It is sickening, his going. Went the rounds of the deckplates, etc., and engine-room rounds with old Fry, and then turned in early.

November 8th 1915
H.M.S. INVINCIBLE

Dearest Mother,

Many thanks for your letters (rather infrequent of late).

I am returning the ones you ask for; you seem to be carrying on a very violent correspondence with Harry Baird; I shall have to send his letters to "papa" if it continues.

Please send me the square-toed pair of boots I left at home to be mended. Also I should like you to have a look for a cheap black tin box of paints and brushes I left at Quaives. Try my room, and the chest of drawers in it, and, if that fails, a very modified search in my writing-desk. It is quite a cheap affair with about twenty squares of paint in two rows, and three or four brushes. I want it for colouring diagrams and charts.

Yours in haste,
TOBY.

Tuesday 9

I took Bench's "day on," as he is still *hors de combat*. Spent most of the day looking after work on the oil fuel supply system. The Engineer-Commander had a frightful "straf" on the last engineering section's notebooks. A very nasty day, blowing like a Dutchman from the south-west. We had to let go our sheet anchor, and set an anchor watch; also raised steam in eight boilers in case of emergency; several ships dragged badly. The picket-boats had an awful time. Hoisting in our second at dark, the steadying-line parted and the stern was dashed against the side of the ship. Old Tom Cobb and the boat's crew looked a bit green, as the slings were only hooked on forward, and she was making water heavily. The First Lieutenant sent for the "Bloke," who in his turn sent for the skipper, whose cap went soaring away in the gale on his arrival on deck. Poor Featherston, ordinary seaman, had a bad fall from the fore superstructure, and his state is critical. The picket-boat at length arrived on the booms, rudder smashed to atoms.

Wednesday 10

Heard that W.R. Kennedy ("Calipers"), who left our term at Osborne owing to defective eyesight, and now of Argyll and Sutherland Highlanders, had been killed. Usual boiler-room work in the forenoon. Gale still blowing like blazes; the officers of the watches kept their watch on the bridge, and five of the boat snotties kept watch to run the routine as additional officers of the watch down on deck. A heavy fall of snow; all the mountains away beyond Alloa towards Stirlingshire in the north-west thickly covered, but it did not last long down by the sea. We kept steam up all day, and shifted billet owing to the wind with the rest of the Fleet at 4 p.m. Old Begbie came on board again and moaned about our inability to finish the fire control communication diagrams he commenced.

Thursday 11

Lieutenant Murray joined the ship to relieve Stewart, the latter commencing his duties as Flag-Lieutenant, lucky young cub. Spent the forenoon making diagrams of the steam connections in the boiler-rooms and engine-room. "Young Yonnie" in the soup—fire mains out of order at 7.30 a.m. Landed at 11 a.m. and went to Edinburgh; saw Mrs. Hood and Sammy, Mrs. Alexander-Sinclair, and Stroma (who have returned from Dunbeath Castle) shopping in Prince's Street. I had a spot with Morse at the Waverley, and then went off to lunch with Aunt Jessie at Merchiston

Park. Quite a nice girl called Sheila McDougall, whom I met at Cannes before the war, there. Then went on to the skating-rink at the Haymarket. It is a fine rink, larger than Prince's. Crowds there, including Mrs. Crabbie, Roxburgh and his people, Percy, etc. A ship's company concert run by the padre in the evening; not a bad show. De Lisle and "Young Yonnie" shot with Lord Linlithgow at Hopetoun.

Friday 12

Heavy snowfall in the forenoon. Usual boiler-room work. In the afternoon our hockey team, about ten of the best away, beat the *Antrim* 10–5. The newly fledged "Flags," O'Reilly, T.H.C., L.E.J., R.S.P., myself, and Birch went to a show at the Y.M.C.A. house at Rosyth dockyard, entertainment by Ellaline Terriss and Seymour Hicks and some others. A jolly good show. She is very nice. One hundred men from each ship, parties from the smaller ships attended, and heaps of officers. Mark II.'s birthday; all the Admirals and their families attended, also the old Duke of Leeds, an R.N.R. Commander, whose patrol yacht was sunk the other day, and he is now living in the *Australia* with Rear-Admiral Pakenham. Sir David Beatty made a fine speech after the show; he speaks very well. We all went up to a birthday party at Northcliffe House afterwards; quite amusing. Stroma was there, and we had a long chat; she is off back to the Highlands again till April on Monday, which is rather sad. Gun-room guest night. I had old Commander "Pwoj," who talked shop twenty-five to the dozen till eleven.

Saturday 13

One of the Scapa light cruiser squadrons, *Calliope*, *Comus*, etc., arrived, making a total of sixteen light cruisers here now. Heard from Joko. My engineer "day on." Worked very hard all the forenoon and afternoon making diagrams of the boiler-room auxiliary exhaust system, etc. Gave young Birch a stiff dozen, as he is getting much too slack and impudent. Lieutenant Murray, Stewart's relief, is a wonderful linguist. He is Macmullen's term— viz., Grenvile. He speaks seven foreign languages—French, German, Italian, Spanish, Portuguese, modern Greek, and Russian, both the latter fluently. He served the first part of the war attached as staff interpreter to the Russian cruiser *Askold* at the Dardanelles ("Packet of Woodbines"), and lately he has been on Vice-Admiral de Robeck's staff. He came home on account of ill-health, but some people think it means we are off to the Dardanelles, which I don't believe.

Sunday 14

Very cold indeed. On board all day and hard at work with Macmullen and the boiler party. Heavy fall of snow in the afternoon.

Monday 15

I am changing over from boiler-room duty to engine-room duty this week. Spent the forenoon in the engine-room. Very cold again and more snow. Went ashore at 2.30 and went for a stiff hour and three-quarters' walk past Hopetoun Castle, and then straight back to the ship. A very hilarious dinner in the evening; old Macmullen came in and swigged cocktails by the dozen before Terence herewith, I believe, is going to leave the G.R. and mess in the W.R. in future.

Tuesday 16

On board all day. Engineering work of various sorts kept me pretty busy. Had a long letter from Mother, with reference to "the chit of a girl", which sent thrills through me, which it should not have done. Try as I will, I can't help thinking about her, and the more I think, the more I love her. The Commander very sour-tempered just at present. Another row with his stern and muscular missus, I suppose.

Wednesday 17

Still colder than ever; all the ponds and lakes, etc., in the vicinity are frozen, and several people went up to Dundas Castle to skate. My "day on." Nothing very strenuous. Worked chiefly in the engine-room, where the distillers are being refitted and circulating crank-heads adjusted. Macmullen ran two stokers in for mutinous behaviour towards a chief stoker. B. was in the row; he is very tactless with the men, and in some ways he has no originality, as he copies my methods assiduously; the best of them, I must say, so I ought to take it as flattery instead of being annoyed.

November 17th 1915
H.M.S. INVINCIBLE

Dearest Daddy and Mother,

I have no time at present to write two letters, so you must rest content with one between you. I am returning mother's letters

which she asked for.

Very sorry to hear she has not been up to the mark, and glad to hear that her inane scheme of secreting this indisposition from the old man has fallen through.

Winter has set in with a will, and it is jolly cold; we have had a lot of snow and hard frost. Luckily there are excellent skating facilities in the vicinity, which is great fun. In addition, we are not dependent entirely on the elements for skating, as there is a very good artificial rink in Edinburgh, said by those who know to be the superior of "Prince's," and it is "the" thing to go there when the occasion offers.

I paid old Aunt Jessie Duguid another visit the other day, and she seems very keen that if ever mother comes North she should pay her a call. She is quite an amusing old "bird."

Young Stewart has got his appointment as Flag-Lieutenant. You might congratulate the parent on having produced a phenomenal son. His watch-keeping successor, also a youngster of twenty-one, one Lieutenant Murray, has had the most extraordinary experiences this war, before coming here the other day. It may almost be worth while giving you an outline, as I think they are probably without an equal for variety. So here goes.

The beginning of the war found this young officer an unknown Sub-Lieutenant in a small cruiser on the Mediterranean Station. On the outbreak of hostilities the ship proceeded to W. Africa, and he took part in the operations against German Togoland, where he was wounded and sent to Cape Town. He there joined a transport as Assistant Navigating Officer, and saw some fighting in E. Africa, and eventually arrived in the Mediterranean again about the time of Vice-Admiral Carden's first attack on the Dardanelles.

I should have told you that Murray's father was Consul-General at Warsaw years ago, he himself being born there.

Also he is a brilliant linguist, speaking seven languages in addition to English—viz., Russian, Turkish, and modern Greek fluently, also German, French, Italian, and Spanish.

Consequently he applied for a job as interpreter, and was appointed to the Russian cruiser Askold, in which ship he saw all the preliminary Dardanelles fighting.

The Russians soon realised the value of such a linguistic gem, and he was sent with despatches to St. Petersburg from the British C.-in-C., travelling via Salonika, Bulgaria (before her entry into the war, of course), and Romania. His adventures on this expedition were too numerous to recite.

He now returned to the Balkans, visiting the British Naval Expedition defending Belgrade, under Rear-Admiral Troubridge, and eventually joined Vice-Admiral de Robeck's staff at the Dardanelles, where he remained until September, when he was invalided home with dysentery. The appointment of such a wonderful interpreter to this ship naturally raises the hopes of the optimists that we shall not spend the rest of our lives in the "Germined" Ocean (please excuse the coined word). Personally, however, I am not so sanguine, and am afraid that as soon as he is quite fit he will leave us. But what a fairy story! It makes my mouth water to compare his experiences of the war with mine, and even mine are better than many other poor unfortunates in the finest battleships in the world, who have never even so much as smelt a German.

Don't forget the above story is not to be spouted wholesale to all your Stock Exchange cronies and wine merchants. "Beg parding, guv'ner."

The Balkan outlook does not seem too bright. Greece is in between the Devil (the Kaiser) and the deep sea (the Allied fleets). What a magnificent fight the wretched heroic Serbians appear to have made, and what disgraceful efforts we have made to help them!

Think of me wallowing in the bowels of the ship, surrounded day and night by roaring furnaces and hissing steam-pipes; and although I am terrified by it all, yet it is just as safe, I fear, as the A.A.C.

Good-bye and best love to both of you dear old things.
TOBY.

Thursday 18

I have conceived a grand strategic scheme, in which by abandoning serious participants in the Balkan struggle, we should land a large expeditionary force at Alexandretta and invade Syria, joining with the Persian Gulf force on the Euphrates above Baghdad and eventually with the Russian Caucasian Army thus effectually blocking the Turco German designs in the East, safeguard Egypt and Persia, and convince the Oriental world of our resource and invincibility. This would for once give us the initiative. Examined the air-pump suctions and discharges and engine-room feed suctions in forenoon. Very cold still and foggy. Landed at eleven and went up to Edinburgh in "Recky" Portal's sidecar. Portal, Hutchinson, Reid, and I had a stupendous mixed grill gorge, which developed into a vile debauch at the Waverley. Then, life having a pleasant aspect, we lurched along to the skating-rink at Haymarket and skated for the rest of the afternoon. Great fun. I am not much good, but thoroughly enjoyed it, and it is a magnificent rink. Lots of naval and military officers and fair young things there, Selby and Farquhar being particularly happy. Murray, who is a fine skater (he was born at Warsaw, where his father was Consul-General), in great demand, with his yarns of his experiences in East and West Africa, Mediterranean, Russia, etc. The two Miss Inverarietys skate damned well. A large party went over with the Admiral to skate with the Beattys at Aberdour; others went to Dundas Castle. Payne, Burghersh, and two wonks shot at Dundas and had good fun with the duck. When we got back to the ship, received signals to say a German cruiser squadron with destroyers have come through the Kattegat heading for the North Sea. Lit up all boilers and went to immediate notice, and the Fourth Light Cruiser Squadron and destroyers went off to investigate and "straf" if necessary at once. Started watch-keeping in three watches again, R.H. being crocked now. A damned nuisance. The Serbian situation looks exceedingly black, and all the pessimists are wallowing in their element.

Friday 19

Thick, dense, and impenetrable fog all day; in the circumstances our going to sea out of the question, but we remained at immediate notice with steam for full speed in case the weather should change and the fog clear. No further news of the Bosches; the elements appear to be with them. Tested both steering engines with all the steering positions and controlling shafting in the ship in the afternoon. Everything satisfactory. I kept the middle and afternoon watches. Gun-room guest night; owing to the situation, no guests from other ships were available, so de Lisle from the ward-room was the only one. Campbell-Cooke on watch, so, as Terence Unsworth has gone to the ward-room, I officiated as President, and everything went well.

Saturday 20

Fog worse if anything; intended to coal ship at 6.45 a.m., but the collier failed to come alongside until noon owing to the fog. We commenced then and took in 600 tons, finishing just before three. I had already kept the forenoon watch down below, and coaling on top of it without any lunch made it pretty strenuous. I tipped with old Fisher in the starboard waist. Kept the first watch as well, and turned into my hammock at midnight with a pleasant thrill. The continuance of the fog forbids any operations, the ships at sea having to remain there, and those in harbour being unable to get out. Apparently several German squadrons are flitting about round the Danish coast, but it is impossible to get any authentic news.

Sunday 21

Fog as per routine. The Deutsches, finding that we are not asleep, decided to return to Kiel, without venturing out, so the "flap" subsided at last, and we relaxed to the usual routine. My "day on." Blew down and cleaned boilers as far as possible.

Monday 22

The *Warspite* arrived after her docking early in the morning. Went to G.Q.s after divisions, and then exercised "Abandon Ship" stations. Afterwards I examined our oil fuel sprayers. Landed at 2.30 with some others and went up to kick about and get some exercise on the Rugger ground; very hard, but greasy on top. Had tea at Queensferry Arms. Payne came to dinner from the *Lion*, and S.P.E.G. Turner came over afterwards, and, as might be expected, a large amount of liquor disappeared. Very cold again, but the fog was not nearly so thick.

Tuesday 23

Warspite left for Scapa at 2 p.m. Spent the forenoon with Chief Stoker Barton going round the pumping, flooding, and draining arrangements. Oil fuel sprayers again in the afternoon. Henderson, breaking from his torpor with a great effort, his first for weeks, succeeded in arousing Macmullen's righteous ire. Our hockey team beaten by the *Indefatigable*'s 2–7, but we had a very weak side out. The new cinema gave a show in the evening on the quarter-deck, but I was too busy to go. Heard from Aunt Jessie of dear old Aunt Do's death. I felt she had been doing too much lately, but didn't realise there was any danger. She was a wonderful old lady, a great patriot, and as kind as could be. I am sure that she got more enjoyment out of her last four years of life than the previous forty in strict retirement. I was awfully fond of her, as were all her relations.

Wednesday 24

Our Rugger match with Loretto arranged for today scratched owing to the frost, fog, etc. Usual routine and work all day. Hutchinson is getting on my nerves terribly, owing to the way in which he continually copies everything I do. His notebook is an absolute crib of mine, and he seems incapable of originality, or, rather, all his original work is very inferior. Wrote to Rankine and Joko. The *Lion* proceeded to sea at dark; she is going to Newcastle to dock. Old Payne's four days' leave will be a perfect holocaust of festive orgies; no rules, regulations, or Provost Marshal will stop him. The Vice-Admiral commanding the Battle Cruiser force is shifting his flag and staff temporarily from *Lion* to the *Queen Mary*.

Thursday 25

The *New Zealand* returned at 4 a.m. and coaled ship. At nine we went on board and spent the forenoon with her Naval Instructor, old Litchfield. This prevented anyone going on shore to lunch, but Hutchinson and Johnstone went up to the skating-rink in the afternoon. Johnstone has got his charmer in Edinburgh; she is a Red Cross nurse, going through a cookery course at the R.A.M.C. depot. I have not met her, but believe she is A1, only just eighteen. Katerina was there with the stolid and sphinx-like Miss Evans in attendance, and also the Milebank crowd, Sibyl, Betty Molyneux, etc. My "day on," so I could not get ashore. Finished a lengthy description and diagram of an oil fuel sprayer. Old Macmullen returned on board very festive and wrote up the engine-room artificers' workbook, singing blithely. E.R.A. Pengelly left the ship, and the E.R.A.'s mess breathed freely again.

Friday 26

G.Q.s in the forenoon and everything as usual. De Lisle very anxious over the personnel of "A" turret, as we are losing so many of our reliable men, being drafted from the ship to barracks to man the new ships. Our guest night in the gun-room; a large number of guests; I meant to ask Self, but I got a nasty touch of 'flu, with a headache and diarrhoea, so I did not put in an appearance, but turned in early at seven. Had a rotten night, could not get to sleep, and had frequent fits of shivering.

Saturday 27

Coaled ship at 7 a.m., taking in 400 tons from the collier *Mostyn*. I felt too bad to turn out till ten, when I lurched out of my hammock and waddled along to the gun-room. I meant to go up to Edinburgh today, but felt much too bad. Slept most of the day and ate nothing but a little soup. Very nasty rheumatism in my right shoulder. I wonder what has affected me. O'Reilly very kindly gave me the use of his cabin to sit in during the day. Heard from Joko.

Sunday 28

Feeling better. Intended to go up with Macmullen to lunch with the Crabbies, but the fates intervened, and at eleven we went to short notice, raised steam, and at five proceeded to sea in company with the rest of the Battle Cruiser Fleet. I kept the first watch below. Campbell-Cooke told some very funny yarns about Captain Judge d'Arcy of the *Africa* after dinner.

Monday 29

I kept the morning and second dog-watches below. We represented the German battle cruisers, and the First and Second Battle Cruiser Squadrons represented our Battle Cruiser Fleet. We approached the Norwegian coast and then tried to slip up north unobserved, and escape to the Atlantic, but they scotched us; rather a dull affair. Full speed all the forenoon without undue forcing; we averaged twenty-five knots and touched twenty-six and a half—much ado down below in the engine- and boiler-rooms. Old Weekes, the Engineer-Commander, the only one not to be flurried. Mogg sent me requesting the old boy to come down to the starboard engine-room at once, as the vacuum was dangerously high or low, or both, I forget which; the dear old chap insisted on my squeezing into the engine-room lift with him; he stopped it half-way down, and suggested that this was an ideal place for kissing the girls, and also recounted how he told this to Sir B. Milne when the latter was inspecting the ship, Sir B. answering: "Go on, go on, Engineer-Commander, I am not a damned girl." He is a fine old boy, old Weekes. G.Q.s and sub-calibre firing at 10 a.m. Everything in a hopeless muddle in "A" turret; de Lisle in a philosophical mood; P.O. Bailey, the director trainer, is a useless ullage. Range-taking exercise in the afternoon. During the "dogs" the sea got up badly, and we began to roll and pitch like old Harry, and the weather got worse all night. The whole Fleet proceeded north-west at eighteen knots between the Shetlands and the Norwegian coast. I dined with Macmullen after the second dog. We were both pretty tired, but some dinner and claret-cup bucked us up, and we listened with interest to some of Murray's Balkan yarns.

Tuesday 30

Passed the *Orcona*, armed merchant cruiser, of the old Tenth Cruiser Squadron on patrol during the middle. I wonder how the old *Alsatian* is getting on! The weather still very bad; all the galley-fires put out, and the atmosphere in the gun-room rotten, as we were battened down. No cooked food going, and things reminded one of the old *Crescent* days last year. I kept the forenoon and first watches below with Findlay and Bull. Steaming steadily at from fourteen to fifteen knots. Going south in company with the rest of the Fleet, as it is too rough to fire at present, and we are supposed to be going to carry out some 4-inch practice firing.

DECEMBER

Wednesday 1

The weather moderated a good bit after daybreak, although a good big swell remained. Carried out 4-inch firing in the forenoon; being off watch, I went up in the foretop to watch the firing. After an hour's PZ exercise we formed line ahead in following order: Third, First, and Second Battle Cruiser Squadrons, *Invincible* leading the Fleet, and carried out the firing. To me our show seemed execrable, and the first B.C.S. very good, but I could not see much of the other squadrons. I kept the afternoon watch below with Self; 12-inch sub-calibre firing in the afternoon, while I was below. The firing finished, we re-formed the Fleet and proceeded back towards the Scotch coast, hoping to make the Forth early tomorrow.

Thursday 2

Turned out at midnight to keep the middle watch below with Findlay, but I regret to say that the attractions of the pages of a small volume called the "Adventures of an Irish R.M." prevented me from taking a very close interest in the phenomenon attending the transference of heat energy to the propulsive energy of the ship by the medium of thirty-one Yarrow boilers and the Parson's reaction turbines of H.M. battle cruiser *Invincible*. I ensconced myself in a nook above the condensers, and was intensely amused by some very clever pictures of Irish life. Turned in at 4 a.m. after a very enjoyable middle. We entered the Forth and anchored at 5.15 a.m. in company with the rest of the Battle Cruiser Fleet except the *Australia*, *Princess Royal*, *Tiger*, and *Indefatigable*, who have gone for more firing to Scapa. Commenced coaling and oiling at 7.30 a.m., and took in 1,400 tons of coal and 200 tons of oil. Finished coaling at 2.30 p.m. after a weary and very dirty coal. I spent most of the day below with Macmullen superintending the cleaning of the boilers. Had a letter from Jessie Gedge. The detachment of marines in this ship is the rottenest impertinent lot of scoundrels I have ever met.

Friday 3

Went to the Naval Instructor in the *New Zealand* all the forenoon. My "day on," working on the oil fuel system in the afternoon. Self said he would not want my valuable services after seven, as it was guest night. I had O'Reilly to dine; he is a very good chap, and took 21s. off us at Van John, rivalling Tollemache with his run of naturals. Other guests were de Lisle, old Fisher (a good old sort), Murray, and S.O. Owing to Campbell-Cooke having the first watch, I took president of the mess. I hear from home those Carabiniers, or anyhow Charlesworth and Fuller, are at home again.

December 3rd 1915
H.M.S. INVINCIBLE

Dearest Mother,

Many thanks for all your letters; I am so glad to hear that you have quite got over your indisposition. (I probably said this in my last letter, but it fills up space.)

I am sending a parcel of collars home to be washed; please return them when finished. I am also thinking of sending some waistcoats, which you might get relined by old "Stick-in-the-Mud" at Littlebourne.

As regards your Xmas arrangements, originally you told me you had decided to visit the Duguid clan in Aberdeenshire, and I suggested that if you did this you should spend a night or two in Edinburgh, either going north or when returning. I should strongly deprecate your coming up to Edinburgh specially to see me, in view of the heavy expense entailed and the fact that the odds are that I should be unable to see anything of you, as we might be away or I might be unable to get ashore. I am afraid Aunt Jessie is going to Cannes for a few months very shortly.

If you intend to give Xmas presents this year, I suggest presents of utility; personally I should like a nice new big sponge.

I was extremely cut up to hear of dear old Aunt Do's death; I should have loved to have seen her once more. She was a wonderful old lady. I am sure that the last four years of her life were worth infinitely more than the previous thirty. Poor old Izzie and the servants will be rather adrift now, I suppose.

With regard to Harry Baird, as you know, I would rather you did not send on my letters or extracts from them to him, for various reasons, the chief one being that I feel they would not really interest him, although he would never be impolite enough to say so. Still, I leave the matter in your hands. If he is very dull and bored, I would try and write him a letter, but I feel it would be very difficult to interest him. Are you absolutely convinced that his enthusiasm over your letters is not rather forced and the result of extreme courtesy and appreciation of your eminently kind intentions?

Daddy seems to be having some good shooting now; tell him to give my love to Kenneth Greig. The latter has been appointed to the King George V., George Baird's ship, and I may possibly see him some day later on.

Please send my best love to Aunts Ethel and Maud; thank them very much for their letters which I love, and explain that I will try and write when I can, but that my time is extremely limited.

I am very sorry for Mrs. Handfield-Jones, but more so for Dr., as it was probably her own fault. I wonder if Dr. will live to usher your grandchildren into the world.

Please repeat the Auntie E. and M. formula to Peg and Jim, and tell them both I am longing to have their company again.

We have just completed a very trying spell of North Sea November weather. All our galley-fires were out for three days, and so no cooked food—quite like old Crescent days. The engine- and boiler-rooms are hell, at sea; one cannot realise the life of the stokers and other "saints who toil below" until one actually experiences it. These men's work can vie with any, trenches and deserts not excluded; their whole life in war-time is a vivid succession of discomforts and hardships, unparalleled in severity and monotony.

Goodnight, "mammy," now.

Very best love to you and daddy.
TOBY.

Saturday 4

Mugged up a few odd jobs in the forenoon and landed by the eleven boat and went up to Edinburgh. Very cold and snowing. Had a lobster with Campbell-Cooke at the Café Royal, and then went on and had a mixed grill at the Waverley. We then went to "Iolanthe" by the D'Oyly Carte Company at the Lyceum. Very good show, old Henry Lytton* being excellent. A big crowd of naval officers there, including "Flags," Fisher, Jones the "Micro-doctor," O'Reilly, Cobb, Portal, and Johnnie, the latter with his latest love, nicknamed "Cookery" by us, a very pretty girl to whom I sat next. Betty Molyneux, described by O'Reilly as a vision of golden hair, appealing blue eyes, and "come-into-the-office-and-shut-the-door" lips, was there in a box with Lords Burghersh and Wilton. She is a damned pretty girl. Bench and Chalmers from the *Lion*, a young man whose experiences this war would fill a volume, accompanied Marks I. and II. to lunch at the Caledonian, and then on to a charity show under Lady Beatty's auspices, Miss Evans in attendance as chaperon.

Sunday 5

A miserable wet day. Portal went to lunch with the Admiral and family. I was invited, but after a rag with "Flags" and No. 1 I decided not to go and spent the day working on board. Hutchinson and I went to dine with Payne in the *Lion*, and we had the usual hilarious evening.

Monday 6

Wet again. Went over to the *New Zealand* Naval Instructor again in the

---

* Henry Lytton was a famous English actor and singer and was the leading exponent of the comic baritone roles in Gilbert and Sullivan operas.

forenoon; we are supposed to go twice a week nowadays. Superintending work on the test tanks in the afternoon and making diagrams. Hutchinson and Johnstone are in the thick of a great burst of energy at present, egged on by Macmullen, Mogg, and the Engineer-Commander. The *New Zealands* were quite hospitable this morning for a change, and we all had cocktails in the gun-room. Bowlby, Poland, and Rae were most affable, and old Annesley and O'Donnell were in great form.

Tuesday 7

A better day; bright sunshine, but a high wind. My "day on." Pretty busy all day on various jobs. The *Commonwealth* and some of the destroyers, who went out for practice firing yesterday, returned in the forenoon as it was too rough. The *Albemarle** also came in; she was supposed to have left for the Mediterranean, but had a frightful "doing" in the Bay, and so returned, lots of damage being done, including the loss of her bridge; five officers (including Commander Nixon) and fifteen men were drowned, and three officers and seventeen men were injured. Mott of the St. Vincents, who was snotty officer of the watch, had a miraculous escape, being swept off the bridge and right aft on to the quarter-deck, where he was brought up with a round turn by a stancheon, with only a broken collar-bone and a few bruises. Some of the Scapa light cruisers came in for shelter; they have been jiggering about round Heligoland.

Wednesday 8

A busy day for me; anniversary of the victory of the Falklands, so the ship's company piped down all day and did no work, and most of the officers landed in the afternoon. I took Johnstone's day on for him, as he wanted to lunch and play golf with the Admiral. We lit up all night owing to the high wind, so as to prepare to shift billet if necessary, and so had to keep watch during the night till 8 a.m. I had the devil of a lot of paper-work all day, drawing, writing, etc. All the Falkland veterans went over to celebrate in the *Inflexible*; on their return we had them in the gun-room and did great execution in the cocktail line, everybody very cheery. A ship's company concert in the afternoon, which, I believe, was very good, but personally I was swimming in work and could not go to it. At about five, after dark, in

---

* HMS *Albemarle* was badly damaged in heavy weather in November 1915 while in the Pentland Firth. Her bridge was swept away in mountainous seas and numerous lives were lost.

the middle of the concert an urgent signal arrived from the Rosyth signal station from Cobb in the first picket-boat, stating that he had been rammed by a mud barge at the entrance to the dockyard and was in a sinking condition and requested instructions. Much commotion caused. Murray, who was officer of the watch and was in the gun-room, rushed out in chase of an elusive boatswain's mate; the Commander bawled orders from the poop, and in record quick time called away the second picket-boat, and sent it in Tottenham's charge to assist the first. The second returned two hours later with the crew of the first and all the details. Cobb appears to have acted in the most excellent manner, and in spite of the sleepy inefficiency of the dockyard authorities, managed to arouse the King's Harbour-Master and get the boat alongside and hoisted by the big crane on the quay just before she sank. The accident occurred owing to the mud barge being very low in the water at the end of a long tow and without lights. The accident did not prevent a rousing evening in the ward-room, where all gun-room officers and warrants were guests of the ward-room, in addition to Captain Beamish, who was the Flag-Captain, and Commander Bingham, another old Invincible. We had a quiet evening in the gun-room.

Thursday 9

Old Bull promoted to chief artificer engineer. Went over to the *New Zealand* Naval Instructor in the forenoon, but he was busy and very kindly gave us a day off, so we returned to the ship, and I did a few odd jobs before going ashore at eleven for a very welcome day off. Hutchinson, Murray, and I motored up to Edinburgh with Payne and young Molyneux of the *Lion*. A whole deputation of Swedish journalists were at Hawes Pier awaiting a visit to the Fleet. They looked a weird lot of ruffians, mostly Hun spies, I expect. Campbell-Cooke got lured to go as our gun-room representative to a preliminary meeting of the Junior Officers' Club Committee, a club which is to be formed at South Queensferry; rather a poor show, I should imagine. Burghersh lured Selby to go from the *Lion*. Old Captain Gartside-Tippinge appears to be fathering the enterprise. Our party went to Gieves after an adventurous drive up under the auspices of "Spica." We then went on and had a terrific ultra-jovial lunch at the Café Royal of crab, lobster, oysters, etc., sandwiches galore, cocktails and stout and liqueurs. Lieutenant Peploe, Captain of Cobbold's T.B. No. 36, a great Rugger man and a friend of Louis, joined us; a very good sort; also an R.N.V.R. motor-boat man from Leith and another friend of Bench's. Then we motored to the rink at Haymarket, stopping to do some "tasting" for the mess at Ballantyne's on the way. A jolly good afternoon, excellent skating and a very good chocolate tea-party at the end, our guests including Mark I., a Miss Mary Scott, a Miss Foley, a Miss Stewart, a wet male creature in plain clothes, and Lady Mar. A thoroughly A1 time. Then we motored back to Hawes Pier, and came off, giving young Molyneux a lift to his ship, with a top-hat of Burghersh's in which he is to do a "Gilbert the Filbert" stunt à la Basil Hallam at Lady Beatty's charity matinée on Saturday. Incidentally I sat on the top-hat. Payne came over to the *Invincible*, and he and I dined with Murray in the ward-room, and I again drank more than was good for me. I think I must go on the water-cart for a bit.

Friday 10

A miserable day. We had a gun-room Rugger match versus the *New Zealand*, but scratched it owing to the damnable weather. G.Q.s in the forenoon; nothing very exciting occurred. De Lisle went on leave owing to family troubles; something pretty serious, I suppose, otherwise they would not have let him go. It leaves me in charge of "A" turret, so let's pray for a scrap while he's away. Franklin, the Naval Instructor from Dartmouth, joined the ship. Inspecting and making diagrams of boiler stop valves and feed check valves all the afternoon and evening.

Saturday 11

Heard from mother of Tootie and Humphrey's decision to secure themselves with a West Country whipping. I was very pleased to hear it and sent Toots a telegram. I am afraid poor old Dunk has gone back to the Front again. My "day on." The Admiral asked me to accompany a party up to lunch and then on to Lady Beatty's charity matinée for her home for lost dogs or sailors or something. Unluckily I could not get anyone to take my "day on," although I always seem to be taking other people's for them. Johnstone's mother is stopping here, and Bench had a previous engagement, but Henderson only refused out of pure "cussedness;" Cobb went instead and thoroughly enjoyed himself. A big lunch party, including Vice-Admiral and Lady Beatty, Rear-Admirals Pakenham and Brock and Johnstone, and his mother. The matinée was a tremendous success, and they made £1,000 or more. Margaret Cooper and Ethel Levey sang, and some damned prima donna and a Russian violinist performed, Corbett from the *Indomitable* sang comic songs, four *Indomitable* snots danced a hornpipe, Burghersh did "Gilbert the Filbert" and "The Constant Lover," and everyone said he was even better than Basil Hallam himself. He and Corbett did a skit on "The Watch on the Rhine," and there were a few other stunts. Burghersh in real life is just the sort of man typified on the stage by Basil Hallam. The whole show was an unqualified success. I had to spend the day mugging on board. Franklin came in after dinner and chatted over Dartmouth and Cornwall days.

Sunday 12

Heavy fall of snow in the night, and it snowed most of the forenoon. The new accelerated war promotions scheme came out. Under this scheme we shall come up for examination in May next year, four months earlier, which, added to the four months earlier due to recommendation, makes a total of eight months. Morse and Reid and all the "highflyers" are to come up this January. It is rather sickening their being promoted over our heads, as we have been six years to their two and a half in the Service, but as they are all well over twenty and none of us are yet nineteen it is excusable. In the afternoon Hutchinson and I landed at Rosyth and walked round to Admiralty House to tea. In the evening I had young Findlay from *Princess Royal* to supper. A most exemplary young gen'l'man, T.T., non-smoker, and doesn't gamble.

Monday 13

Received a very sweet letter from Joko, which I answered with a hurried chit. The Fleet Surgeon told me that de Lisle's leave is due to a bad nervous breakdown. In his absence I am left in charge of "A" turret, which is a big responsibility and entails much work. I can't help wishing we might go to sea and have a scrap while he is away, although it is rather horrid of me. Very busy in the afternoon evolving new schemes of organisation with No. 1. Life seems very much taken up just at present, but I am afraid I take things rather too seriously. Spent the forenoon in the boiler-rooms superintending work in "F" Group which is being opened out. In the evening a superfluity of paper-work. Our engineering time is to be cut down to two months owing to lack of time. Rugger match v. *Lion* arranged for today scratched owing to snow.

Tuesday 14

The burst of energy aroused by the proximity of examinations combined apace, and practically no one went ashore. I had a very busy day again from 6.30 a.m. till midnight, with short intervals for meals. Hutchinson is getting terribly on my nerves. Everything I do he copies, damn him. I shall have a big row with him sooner or later, I can see. Campbell-Cooke gave a very amusing account of his views on marriage, just what one would expect of the slack, blasé individual.

Wednesday 15

Coaled ship, took in 350 tons. Morse, Reid, and myself did not turn out till about 7.10. Old Borrett came along and had a frightful "straf"; he saw me after lunch and talked glibly about getting us dipped six months' seniority, and finally stopped our leave for a fortnight, and told me to report in future every morning at 6.30 when the flat is cleared. I spent the morning in the boiler-rooms with Macmullen. My "day on" with Self. Inspecting armour belts with a view to a report in the afternoon; everyone seems extraordinarily ignorant about our armour. We borrowed the wardroom piano, which "Recky" played to us in the evening. He is a beautiful pianist.

Thursday 16

I am seriously considering the advisability of specialising in engineering. I seem to have a bent in that direction. The pay is excellent, the work interesting, the conditions poor, and future problematic very, but with great possibilities. The question will have to be fully discussed with Daddy, Louis, old Finnis, Broadbent, and possibly Admiral de Chair. It transpires that de Lisle had a scene with the Rear-Admiral and the Captain before he left; his nerves were in a terrible state, and I am afraid he will not be allowed to return to the ship. He will be a great loss, as he was an extraordinarily keen, conscientious, and capable officer, an indefatigable worker, a fine athlete, and a damned nice fellow. I hope he will absolutely recover and live to continue a distinguished career to an illustrious conclusion. Boiler-room work all the forenoon, my last day in the boiler-room, so I was pretty energetic. All the lucky ones gadded up to the skating-rink in the afternoon, and I took Johnnie's afternoon so that he could go. Very busy with old Jennings' papers for the rest of the day. The padre dined in the gun-room in the evening with "Heim," it being the latter's birthday. Murray is taking de Lisle's place in "A" turret; he is a nice chap, but lacks his predecessor's zeal, and it will mean much more for me to do.

Friday 17

Down in the engine-room all the forenoon, mucking round with Self most of the time. Superintending work on the evaporators and distillers in the afternoon. Then came up after four o'clock and did some more swatting. Gun-room guest night; I asked Macmullen, and he refused after an initial acceptance. No less than eight people refused from the ward-room. I wonder why Tollemache and two clerks came. I played *vingt-un* and won a little.

Saturday 18

Ran through the turbine thrust arrangements and radial and facial dummy systems with Self in the morning. Landed at 12.40 to play Rugger against the *Lion*; de Lisle, Cory, and Powell away from our side, and we rather expected to be beaten, as A. L. Harrison*, the England and Navy man, had been coaching his side, while we had not played for six weeks. They started off well, and their scrum was far heavier than ours, but eventually we beat them 18–5, to our great surprise. I managed to get a try. All the popsies arrived from Northcliffe House, and George in khaki. He hasn't wasted much time, as he only left Eton two days ago. Worked all the evening.

Sunday 19

Very cold. All the family came off to church in the forenoon. I did a certain amount of work in the afternoon, but not so much as I should have done. My "day on" with Findlay. Richardson's young brother from Osborne and a friend named Tyrie, a chief cadet captain, both Blakes, three below us, came off to tea. Young "Shishishism" is a nice little chap.

Monday 20

In the port engine-room all the forenoon, overhauling the evaporators and distillers and their pumps, etc. The skipper came down about eleven with the Engineer-Commander and Mogg to examine the new auxiliary steering arrangements, which have been fitted to the port steering engine. Spent the afternoon writing a description and report on condition of the fresh-

---

* A.L. Harrison won two caps for England before the war, and was involved in the Grand Slam winning side of 1914. He was killed in action at Zeebrugge in April 1918, after which he was awarded a posthumous Victoria Cross.

Lieut Fleming James, Midship vice de Hoste.

Gorell-Barnes, the old Exmouth who shewed up so
badly & left the navy from Dartmouth 3 years ago,
has just got the D.S.O. He was in the same battalion
of the Rifle Brigade as poor old Mike, who looked him.

Thursday 23 (357-8) Away in the E.R & B.R of the 2nd P.B
all the forenoon, got to know all about the he
meaning arrangements, ejectors pumping system's etc
O'Reilly invited me to lunch with him at the Edinburgh
Services club & go on to the rink afterwards, but
unluckily it was too late for me to shift so I
took an afternoon off and slept till 3.30 & then
worked for the rest of the evening till 6.30. Cobb & I
dined in the W.R. with the Padre, & he was very
cheery & we had quite an amusing evening considering all. He is quite a broadminded priest anyhow & a good man

Friday 24 (358-7)
Sketching in the forenoon most of the time, although I
paid a few flying visits to the Captains Engine
flat to look after work going on there. Landed
in the afternoon & the G.R Rugger team played the
P.R's ditto. We won 16—5, altho' our forwards had
an off day. Hutchinson & Henderson at the top of their
form. A good supply of letters & cards for Xmas,
includes 2 cheques for "fivers". Spent quite a quiet
Xmas Eve, everyone being too tired after Rugger to enthuse much

Saturday 25 (359-6) Christmas Day. LESSONS.
A very muddy day to start Matins—Isaiah ix. to v. 8; Luke ii. to v. 15
off with. Owing to the Evensong—Isaiah vii. r. 10 to v. 17; Titus iii. r.
                                              4 to v-9
boggy weather we have had of late, we raised steam, in case the Bosches try
any games in the fog, as there was no leave. In the forenoon,
backed by the R.A, we all went round the mess decks, which were wonderfully
well decorated, as was the whole ship. We raised cheers etc. from parties
the day merrily wearily on, at 3.20 in the afternn the W.R challenged us
to a water race, & some minutes accepted, impressed a crew & got madly
beaten by 2 lengths. Mrs Howd presented us with a plum pudding
& a Xmas tree which was very good of her. We dined at
7.30 & about 7.45 things began to look up a bit; eventually we had an
A1 dinner with heaps of everything to drink & we all got most hilarious
& "Xmassy". After the thing we had 2 solemn toasts in "absent friends" & fallen
"comrades" & skin croads pinched & punched & down "Falkland veterans" "Our visitors
from the "Inflexible" "The Invincibles" "Ireland of the Irish" "our allies' enumerated by me,
& Gin No. "Sir D. Beatty" "the Howd family" Scotland, the Scotch" "England holds the fort"
"The Army" (very popular, but "Lott's reform took" (??) & G. quited the effort & caused an uproar), "Sir
I believe she took" "Sir G.R staff" "the President" & lastly the British Empire. Inside 3 speeches,
& we all got very bottled, & sang & shouted till midnight, when we sorked howling on deck & about
12.30 reached the W.B.s who were so joined in another sing-song, & so to bed at 2.30.

water distilling plant and making the necessary diagrams. I have been told in confidence that poor de Lisle has gone clean off his head and is now a raving lunatic. If true, it is very sad, especially to me who saw such a lot of him, for he was such a splendid man and officer in every way.

Tuesday 21

Examined the steering gear, tiller gear, and hand steering arrangements, etc., all the forenoon, and did a lot of paper-work in the afternoon. I have had Borrett's permission to get a table and chairs rigged up in our flat forward during the daytime. It should be a great boon, as the gun-room is so cramped. The *Inflexible* sailed at dark; she is going off to dock. France-Hayhurst and Mercer came over to us, so that they can do their examinations for Acting-Sub-Lieutenants while the *Inflex* is away.

Wednesday 22

Went round the fire main, fresh-water, and compressed-air systems in the forenoon with Chief Stoker Barton, and sketched in the afternoon. A cinema show in the evening on the quarter-deck; they have them every few days now when we are in harbour. The awning which was rigged up for the occasion was unequal to the occasion, and we sat there muffled up in overcoats, etc., with a torrential downpour dripping through on our heads. This was too much of a good thing, so I went below and did some more work. Stroma sent me a pair of gloves she had knitted for a Xmas present, which was very sweet of her.

Thursday 23

Lieutenant Fleming joined the ship vice de Lisle. Gorell-Barnes, the old Exmouth, who showed up so badly and left the Navy from Dartmouth three years ago, has just got the D.S.O. He was in the same battalion of the Rifle Brigade as poor old Mike, who loathed him. Away in the engine-room and boiler-room of the second picket-boat all the forenoon. Got to know all about her manning arrangements, ejectors, pumping systems, etc. O'Reilly invited me to lunch with him at the Edinburgh Services Club and go on to the rink afterwards, but unluckily it was too late for me to shift, so I took an afternoon off and slept till 3.30, and then worked till 6.30. Cobb and I dined in the ward-room with the padre, and he was very cheery, and we had quite an amusing evening, considering our host. He is quite a broad-minded priest, anyhow, and a good man.

Friday 24

Sketching in the forenoon most of the time, although I paid a few flying visits to the capstan engine flat to look after work going on there. Landed in the afternoon, and the gunroom Rugger team played the *Princess Royal* ditto. We won 16–5, although our forwards had an off day. Hutchinson and Henderson at the top of their form. A good supply of letters and cards for Xmas, including two cheques for "flyers." Spent quite a quiet Xmas Eve, everyone being too tired after Rugger to enthuse much.

Saturday 25

A very mouldy day to start off with. Owing to the foggy weather we have had of late, we raised steam, in case the Bosches try any games in the fog, so there was no leave. In the forenoon, headed by the Rear-Admiral, we all went round the mess decks, which were wonderfully well decorated, as was the whole ship. The usual ship's company funny parties. The day dragged wearily on; at 3.30 in the afternoon the ward-room challenged us to a cutter race, and some lunatics accepted, impressed a crew, and got badly beaten by two lengths. Mrs. Hood presented us with a plum pudding and a Xmas tree, which was very good of her. We dined at 7.30, and about 7.45 things began to look up a bit; eventually we had an A1 dinner with heaps of everything to drink, and we all got most hilarious and "Xmassy." After "The King" we had two solemn toasts in "Absent Friends" and "Fallen Comrades," and then crowds more cheery ones, including "Falkland Veterans," "Our visitors from the *Inflexible*," "The Wonks," "Ireland and the Irish," "Our Allies" (enumerated by me and nine in No.), "Sir David Beatty," "The Hood Family," "Scotland and the Scotch," "England, Wales, and the Jews," "The Army" (very popular, but Cobb's reference to the 6th Dragoon Guards spoiled the effect and caused an uproar), "Sir John Jellicoe, the C.-in-C.," "The Gun-Room Staff," "The President," and lastly "The British Empire." I made three speeches, and we all got very biffed and sang and shouted till midnight, when we rushed howling on deck, and about 12.30 reached the warrant officers' mess, where we joined in another sing-song, and so to bed at 2.30.

Sunday 26

Turned out very much the worse for wear after last night's carousal. One or two were fearfully tight, and everyone had the most awful heads this morning. Short notice was washed out at midday, and some people visited the beach. Personally I stopped on board and wrote letters and did some work, beginning to recover during the afternoon. Heard of Louis' engagement to Phyllis. Helped Campbell-Cooke with the mess wine-books in the evening. An R.N.R. A.P. joined the ship.

Monday 27
A miserable day, blowing like sin from the north-east. On board all day, employed on various jobs, but not feeling very energetic, and very cantankerous. Lieutenant Fleming is taking over "A" turret *vice* de Lisle and Murray. He can't be more ignorant than Murray, anyhow. Received short notes from Tootie, Peggy, and Joko. My "day on."

Tuesday 28
Examined air compressors and refrigerators in the forenoon and overhauled the fan engines spare gear. The light cruisers went out at 4 a.m. and returned at 10 p.m. after a short trip to sea for range-finding practices. After a long harangue I managed to induce Macmullen to arrange coaling duties for tomorrow, he being in an obstinate and argumentative mood.

Wednesday 29
Coaled ship at 7.30 a.m. A cold job (note pun). Took in 350 tons from the *Frances Duncan* in just on the hour, this constituting a record for the ship, not only since she first commissioned, but since she was built. Accompanied by Chief Stoker Barton with the usual entourage, I went the rounds of the bunkers and made out the coal estimate. Had a bath, and worked in the gun-room most of the afternoon and evening. Heard from Denniston and Effie Robertson.

Thursday 30
A head schoolmaster has just joined the warrant officers' mess. Chief Artificer-Engineer Bull left the ship to join L.B.35 as engineer officer in charge. Sorry to lose him, as he is an efficient and capable officer. He is relieved by Temporary-Engineer-Lieutenant A. McL. Hine, an elderly, quiet-looking man, who has no previous naval or sea experience. Excitement among the "knuts," as the Germans are reported to be preparing to "sweep" the North Sea again. The light cruisers and destroyers rushed off to sea at 7 a.m., and we went to short notice. Picket-boat manoeuvres all the forenoon, the Battle Cruiser Fleet exercising

"concentration of fire" practice. "Out Nets" together by general signal at nine, followed by G.Q.'s. Old Tipples is very noisy in "A" turret, now that de Lisle has gone. Short notice washed out in the afternoon. I was engaged making a list of all watertight compartments and particulars of them. A few people landed, Tottenham going to call on Mrs. Townsend.

Friday 31

Went to "general night defence" stations for exercise in the forenoon, and then I finished my drawings of a fan engine eccentric rod. Landed in the afternoon, and the gun-room took on the third watch of stokers at Soccer. They beat us 5–0 in a howling gale of wind. We did quite well, notwithstanding the score, considering we have not played Soccer seriously since Osborne days, and we had quite a lot of the game. Heard of the destruction of the *Natal**, which is a bad loss. She was blown up in harbour, apparently, but we have no details at present. Four hundred were saved, but poor old Havers and "Charley" Chaplin were blown up. We had quite a convivial dinner, and then all went down to the warrant officers for a sing-song, and we performed in great style. At midnight Esmonde (the youngest officer in the ship) rang out sixteen bells in the traditional manner, and a huge gathering sang "Auld Lang Syne," in spite of a very high wind, then on down to the ward-room for hot punch. C. C. very "cheery to tight," and only with great difficulty we got him to bed. Finally piped down at about 1.30. The gunnery training expedition for tomorrow in the *Prince Charley* has been postponed owing to the weather.

---

* Shortly after 3.20 p.m. on 30 December 1915, and without warning, a series of violent explosions tore through HMS *Natal* while she was lying in the Cromarty Firth. She capsized five minutes later, killing 390–421 men. The likely explanation was that a fire had broken out, possibly due to faulty cordite which ignited a magazine.

1916

January 22nd 1916
H.M.S. INVINCIBLE

Dear Uncle Jack,

I am writing to answer your letter, and to say that I think you
are wrong when you say that you are not a good correspondent.
Personally I am extremely bad in this line, which fact, coupled
with our uncertain mail system, makes regular correspondence
very difficult.

I agree very largely with your views on the war, although
impeaching sounds much too good. A drumhead court-martial
would be far swifter and more efficacious. Nevertheless, I am
no politician; they are all the same to me, and I have no faith in
anyone in either House.

The country at last appears to be waking up to the necessity of
ruthless warfare. For eighteen months now nearly we have
maintained a strict blockade of Germany, and not a ship has
entered German ports from the North Sea. Yet although we
have starved Germany by holding her neck, the neutral
Scandinavian nations have, metaphorically speaking, fed her
through a stomach-pump.

Month after month the old Tenth Cruiser Squadron maintain
their arduous patrols from Scotland to the Arctic Ocean, and
not a ship reaches Europe from America without first being
examined by Admiral de Chair's ships. Yet owing to the
criminal weakness and vacillating hesitancy of the Foreign
Office they cannot prevent huge quantities of foodstuffs and
raw materials being taken on to Norway, Sweden, and
Denmark for subsequent transhipment to Germany. Even in
cases where munitions are discovered on board, and the ships
are sent into British ports with prize crews, yet the Customs'
regulations are so hopelessly corrupt and futile that the ships
often proceed to their original destinations with their cargoes
still on board.

All the above is in confidence, of course.

The Admiralty are now mad on uniform alterations, and have ordered that committees should be formed in the various fleets and naval bases to consider the question of alterations of officers' uniform. I was very surprised to find myself called to sit on the committee here, in company with a miscellaneous collection of officers of all ranks and all branches of the Service, Rear-Admiral Hood being president, and the remainder consisting of one commodore, one captain, one engineer-captain, one engineer-commander, one lieutenant-commander, one fleet paymaster, one staff paymaster, one surgeon, one sub-lieutenant, one midshipman (myself), and one warrant officer. The "hot air" and "balderdash" produced by this committee were most amusing, and strongly enhanced my views that the modern "democratic" system of ruling by committees, conventions, boards, etc., is hopelessly inferior to a more autocratic type.

The loss of the Natal was peculiarly sad, in view of the fact that she had just come into harbour, after a long spell of arduous work, for a short rest. Several of the officers' wives and children were on board to lunch, and all were lost in the explosion. Both the Captain (a very brilliant officer) and his wife were killed, leaving his mother, herself the widow of another Captain in the Royal Navy killed in action some thirty years ago, in sole charge of three tiny grandchildren under ten. It seems very pathetic.

As I dare say you may have seen in the papers, they have evolved a new system of sending parties from the Grand Fleet on periodical visits to the Front in France and Flanders, ostensibly with the object of proving to the Navy what a far worse time the Army are having, a fact of which they are already very well aware. Anyhow, all the people I have met who have come back to the Fleet from the Front affirm that they would willingly exchange our life of comparative comfort and long months of weary waiting for the extra discomfort of the trenches and the activity, excitement, and chance of distinguishing themselves. A man from the battle cruiser New Zealand was wounded, blown up by a mine, and worked a machine-gun for five hours alone (for which he has been awarded the Distinguished Conduct Medal) before he had been in the trenches a single day. Pretty quick work this, after months and months of waiting for nothing in the North Sea.

I hear that Newcome has been mentioned in despatches and been given the Military Cross. This is excellent news.

Weddings seem to be de rigeur just at present, what with Phyllis and Louis and Humphrey and Toots. What a clannish family we are! There seems to be a perfect horror of marrying anyone except a relation or close connection.

Now I must stop.

Please give my best love to Cousin Sittie. With best wishes.

Your affectionate nephew,
TOBY

January 24th 1916
H.M.S. INVINCIBLE

Darling Mother,

Please thank P., J., and B. for their letters, which I loved getting. I suppose the first two will be off back to school again now, before long. I expect they have thoroughly enjoyed themselves.

How is the invalid? I hope he will soon be fit again. I thoroughly endorse Uncle Jack's point of view about daddy still doing this ridiculous job in the A.A.C. I think it is the supreme height of absurdity, and you may please tell him so from me. If there is nothing for him to do in the City, why does not he employ his time at home, where, with all the men away, there should be plenty of good hard pottering about to do, which would be infinitely better for him. There is no necessity for him to fritter away his health in a perfectly useless job, which anyone could do; in fact, I consider it a crime that a man of his abilities should waste his time star-gazing on London house-tops.

If he feels it incumbent upon him to do something, he should first regain his health, and then use his ingenuity to find a suitable job. Personally I suggest that when the weather is warmer a few months later on a spell of deep-sea fishing in the Cornish smacks would be a good thing. If he liked the job, he might get something to do in a minesweeping trawler.

By the way, it may amuse daddy to know that my latest duty at night when we are at sea is to control the searchlights if they should be used; so we are both on the same sort of job at present.

With regard to Auntie Jessie's request, it really would have been far more suitable for her to have written to daddy instead of me. He, if you can arouse his energies, will be able to give her far more accurate details of the procedure necessary for her to try and get her friend's son into the Navy than I can. Please thank her very much indeed for her letter to me, and ask daddy to do what he can in the way of supplying information (when he has recovered, of course). By the way, if Jimmy intends still to enter the Navy, which in wartime (in spite of whatever old Roderick may say) he will have no difficulty in doing, I should think it is about time daddy did something about it.

I had a fine letter from Burberry the other day, and shall address an answer to Quaives, which I request may be forwarded to him. He says that Bob has disgraced himself and is not an ornament to the Army by any means.

How is George getting on? I suppose he will be on active service again soon.

The Admiralty have got a frightful craze on about alterations of naval uniform. The R.N.V.R. officers have been given a much thicker stripe, which is almost indistinguishable from that of the Royal Navy. This is probably at the instigation of a few influential and singularly useless old "Ullages" who have been given temporary commissions as Captains and Commanders in the R.N.V.R., and who wish to appear as much like real N.O.s as possible. There is no objection from our point of view to these old buffers wearing anything from fur coats to pyjamas, but the disadvantage lies in the fact that the change affects the whole of the R.N.V.R., and to put those young temporary officers and gentlemen, who evidently do not know how to behave themselves, in uniform closely resembling that of the regular Service, will tend to lower the dignity of the R.N. even more than the behaviour of many officers of the R.N.A.S. has done at present.

The Natal disaster was very sad, as she had just come into harbour for a rest after a long and weary job. A large number of the officers' wives and children were on board to lunch, and all were lost. I can't help repeating the story of the Captain (an extremely brilliant officer), which is very pathetic. His mother was the wife of a naval officer, who was killed in action about twenty-five years ago, and she was left with three small children to bring up entirely on her meagre pension. Two of these have since died, I believe, but the late Captain of the Natal she managed to put into the Navy, and he was the apple of her eye, and a most successful man. He was married, with three children under ten, and when the ship blew up his wife was on board and went too. So now his mother is left in exactly the same position as she was twenty-five years ago, alone with three small grandchildren to bring up. This is quite true, and makes you wonder how some people can have the face to grumble.

Please thank Auntie Ethel very much indeed for her most interesting letter. I might almost send it to you as an example.

I hope that you have carried out all my instructions about my clothes. Next time I come home I want all my dress-clothes to be ready for me in London.

Now I must stop.

My very best love to all.
TOBY.

February 20th 1916
H.M.S. INVINCIBLE

Dearest Mother,

Many thanks for all your letters; I am afraid I have not written
for some time, but we have been on detached service and have
had fewer opportunities than usual of sending mails, and this
may be some time in getting home.

I am afraid I was very remiss in not thinking of a wish when I
sent you the bead, so I will do it now, if not too late.

May you live to enjoy the appreciation of your children and
grandchildren, and may that appreciation develop into a more
apparent and vital state (as at present, in some cases, it may be
in danger of passing unrecognised).

Pride of ancestry and hope of posterity are both very large
factors in my views of life, although both are somewhat
subordinated to a firm belief in the all-importance of self (not
selfishness). Do your own job and go your own way, and let the
others go to damnation by their own roads. Consequently the
present generation should not be overwhelmed by thoughts of
the past or glimpses of the future.

Enough hot air; I don't know what led me on to produce all this
bilgy vapouring of a diseased brain.

Next time I come home I shall want two pairs of trousers
(uniform) patched in the seat. I shall want two suits of mufti
in London (one of them the one that used to be daddy's),

including my two mufti caps, overcoat, cape, etc. I have a large
number of socks that want darning, and innumerable buttons
missing, and holes in my pants. My servant is willing but
unskilled, and, being a marine bandsman, wields the piccolo
with more skill than the needle. Where are all my stiff collars?
I sent them home to be washed and they have not returned—
you only sent soft collars, many of them size 14; my minimum
size round the neck is 15; I wear 15 and upwards indefinitely.

Please send me an old pair of black uniform shoes which I left
at Quaives, and have my black brogues brought to London
(also one pair of grey flannel trousers).

As a final word to all these impending domestic movements in
my clothing department: "It is quite unnecessary to even
spread rumours of the journeys or intended journeys of any of
my clothes." If your common sense does not tell you at what I
am hinting, dear mother, try your conscience.

Are you in London permanently now?

If you have nothing better to do one afternoon, should you
happen to visit one of those accursed cinema shows at the
"Empire" music-hall, you may, I am told, have the privilege for
a few seconds of seeing your first-born flash past on the film.
A scene entitled "Battle Cruisers at Work" depicts the
Invincible steaming at full speed (the leading ship of a
squadron of three), and on the foremost turret your first
"trouble and worry" is standing. One of our staff who has been
in London saw the thing a few weeks ago, otherwise I should
never have believed that my versatility would have led me to
appear on a leading London music-hall stage, even on the film.

They must have taken the beastly thing from a hospital ship or
something, I suppose.

March 5th 1916
H.M.S. INVINCIBLE

Darling Mama,

I am so glad to hear that you are better again. You two silly old
things are always getting ill, first one, then the other, like a
Jack-in-the-box.

During your indisposition daddy wrote me a splendid letter—
extremely interesting and amusing—and this honour, one I
seldom enjoy, was highly appreciated. Thank him very much
indeed for his birthday present.

Tell him he is not so old as he thinks, and anyway fifty is the
prime of life.

I don't agree with his modesty saying that he hopes I shall have
a better life to look back on, when I am his age. If I have a
family of sons and daughters like his, I shall be quite satisfied.

Apparently he thinks that having begotten us is nothing to be
proud of; just show the old devil the error of his ways.

Many thanks for looking after my clothes. They sent the wrong
shoes from Quaives—viz., patent leather, when I said uniform.
But don't bother. Another item: please have plenty of white kid
gloves at the flat for me. I have got dozens of pairs somewhere
at home.

I expect to get some leave any time within the next two months.
It is getting on for six since I was home now, and I am quite
ready for another drop.

I shall be in London, if you can put me up, until I am cleaned
out, and then shall proceed as the spirit moves me.

I promised over a year ago to stop with some people named

Culme-Seymour in Hampshire, so I might go there for a night or two, although the shooting season would he a better time.

I hope you and daddy won't mind tying my ties, etc., when I am in London, otherwise I shall be helpless without a valet. I really must learn to tie my own, although it is a little eccentricity that I am secretly rather proud of.

Have you seen that Sir Dudley de Chair has been appointed naval adviser to the new Blockade Ministry. He always struck me as being too polished for a sailor, and would have been an ideal diplomat.

We have returned to our usual haunts again, and everything is inches deep in snow at present, although except for the cold the weather would be very fine for this month, which is usually one of the worst.

We spend most of our spare time now when in harbour, and not able to get ashore, making munitions. And the output of the Battle Cruiser Fleet is very considerable, I believe.

Who is Nander engaged to? I thought he was the last person to have been fooled by a woman.

There have been several little "flaps" in the air lately, which are kept very secret up here. Although I expect the Stock Exchange and City are alive with fantastic inventions almost before the C.-in-C. himself knows that anything of interest has occurred.

Good-bye now.

Best love and kisses to you both, my revered parents.

Your dutiful (?) son,
TOBY.

_____

March 19th 1916
H.M.S. INVINCIBLE

Darling Mother,

Many thanks for your letter, which arrived very quickly after
being posted, much more so than usual. I am so glad to hear that
you both are better. Is daddy still going to persist with his old
searchlights? I must confess to being rather disappointed that
you are having to give up the flat, as I should have thoroughly
enjoyed the use of it once more. I expect to be on leave either the
first or second week in April, although one can never make
absolutely certain, of course. I suppose it would be quite impossible for you to keep on the flat for a fortnight or three weeks
longer, although it does not matter very much, as I can easily
stop at my club. But I should have enjoyed being in a "home"
more. It would be very convenient if you could leave all my
things, which you now have at the flat, in a box or trunk or bag
in London, as it would be such a nuisance having to drag them
up again. Possibly daddy could keep them with his things, wherever he takes them, as I shall probably be home quite soon now.

Please forgive all this, which is very selfish of me, trying to add
to your worries. But "leave" comes rather rarely nowadays,
and I had made lots of plans for this time, and have been
looking forward to giving the Invincible a short rest like
anything.

How very funny your seeing Stewart's photo in the Blunts'
house.

I told him that my parents were very much struck by his
likeness.

When are Peg and Jim starting their Easter holidays? I
suppose I shall just miss them again. Is Auntie Maud still with
the Gedges at Strawberry Hill? As I shall go down and look her
up if she is.

No news for you at all, I am afraid. We are all very sorry to lose old Tirpitz; he seems such a familiar landmark.

How frightfully sad poor Harry Baird losing his leg. You never told me yourself; I only gleaned it from Grade's letter which you enclosed.

Best love now to all the family, and heaps of kisses.

From
TOBY.

April 12th 1916
H.M.S. INVINCIBLE

Darling Mother,

Just a line in haste to thank you and daddy frightfully for being so long-suffering with me last week. I enjoyed every minute of my leave to the full, and am quite sorry to be back again. I enclose a letter to Cousin Alex Thomson, and I should be pleased if you would ask daddy to put it in another envelope and post it on.

I find that I have left a book in the shelves near the fireplace in the sitting-room of flat 69, and it is called "The Admiralty Manual of Seamanship, Vol. II." (a blue book). I should be pleased if you would send it on.

Also I have left the yellow clothes-brush that Jimmy gave me behind (the one you said was a nail-brush). I am not sure whether it is at the flat or whether I left it in Jerram's room at Westenhanger.

I hope you and Peggy enjoyed your dinner with the Handfield-Jones, and that you are glad to be home again. I envy you in the glorious sunshine of the South; it is very cold and windy up here, and the snow is not all melted yet.

Very best love to you all.
From
TOBY.

May 28th 1916
H.M.S. INVINCIBLE

Darling Mother,

Many thanks for the usual supply of letters. Did you address
my clothes to the Indomitable or the Invincible? I have made
inquiries and cannot trace them to either ship at present.

I enclose the card of a weird old Canadian soldier I ran across a
short time ago. He does not know a soul in this country, and in
view of the unvarying kindness and courtesy that is always
extended to naval officers in the colonies, I thought it would do
no harm to offer him a meal or a bed if ever he happens to be
in our part of the world. Funnily enough, he knows Francis
Alexander Carron Scrimger, the Canadian Captain, who,
perhaps you remember, got the V.C. last year.

We have been away from our usual haunts of late, and I have
been ashore at Swanbister several times, and managed to get
some fishing at Kirbister in the loch.

For the first time for many months I have found time to enjoy
the luxury of a book, and have just finished "Bleak House."
Have you read it lately? If so, does not "Mr. Skimpole" remind
you vividly of a mutual acquaintance of ours. Some of this
gentleman's characteristics are absurdly similar to the person
of whom I speak.

No more now.

Very best love to all.

TOBY.

P.S.—Please jog daddy's memory regularly until he keeps his promise about the wedding presents.

June 5th 1916
R.N.C. Dartmouth

Dear Scrimgeour,

You will all be grieving at Alexander Scrimgeour's death, and I hasten to send a word of sympathy. You know already how highly we thought of him here—but we should like his parents to know. He was a most unusually strong, reliable character—and able; he is a real loss to the country. But such an occasion for death is enviable—here we doubt if the Germans will ever show themselves outside again—and in any case the battle was a complete vindication of all we believed the Navy to be. That the battle involved great self-sacrifice is to the everlasting fame of those who died. Such comfort there is, but I know it is inadequate to those who feel the loss most nearly; one can only state this point of view, and, please God, the comfort will come.

Yours most sincerely,

E. H. ARKWRIGHT.

June 7th 1916
5 Clements Inn
Strand, W.C.

Dear old Jim,

Mother and I are sending you two books for your birthday. I have not been able to look in to them to see if they are good reading so you must take them for what they are. If you know

one or the other or both, and have read them already, post them
back to the booksellers they came from or to me—that is why I
did not write your name in them. If you like them and keep
them I will write your name in during the holidays.

Mother and I have just had a call from Lieutenant Sandford
who was saved from Toby's ship. He was simply splendid. He
saw a lot of the battle before they were scuttled and then a lot
more from a raft to which he and Commander Dannreuther
were clinging and later on again from a Torpedo Boat that
picked them up. He told us that Commander Onslow on the
Torpedo Boat Onslaught steamed right up close to a great
German battleship and sank her putting six torpedoes right into
her as the Germans' last shell swept the bridge of the
Onslaught and killed Onslow and everyone on the bridge—but
little Onslaught got home eventually. I will tell you more when
we meet. I had a fine letter from Commander Dannreuther
which I will show you someday. He says, "Your dear son died as
I am sure he would have chosen, full of fight and giving the
Derrflinger a good hammering with the 12-inch guns of A
Turret." Commander Dannreuther is coming to see me when
he returns to town.

Heaps of love from us both.

Yours,
Daddy

_____

June 16th 1916
Woodside Cottage,
East Cowes
Isle of Wight

Dear Mrs. Scrimgeour,

I must write you a line to offer you both our deepest and most
sincere sympathy.

The country has paid a heavy price in officers and men, but she has lost no more promising officer than your son.

He had many fine qualities, and one of his greatest assets was his power of concentration on whatever he was doing. Mr. Culme-Seymour, who went new to Dartmouth when the Drakes did, knew them very well, and he was saying to me yesterday that he thought the best thing Scrimgeour ever did was to go in for a special History prize from 4-6.30 (and win it), knowing that he was fighting the final of the heavy-weight boxing at seven. Very few could have done it. I assure you it is very hard to do one's work here just at the moment.

Everything reminds one of many we shall see no more.

Please don't answer this just now, but later on I hope you will write and say that I shall have his brother here. He will have a fine example before him.

Believe me,

Yours very sincerely,
F.M. BROADBENT.

Friday, August 11th 1916
Aldro School,
Eastbourne (Tel 205)

Dear Mrs. Scrimgeour,

It was only last evening that I heard from Mr. Fox that Alex was in the Invincible when she went down in the Jutland Battle. I have some slight glimmering of what this loss must be to you, and I wish much that it were in my power to do anything to lighten your sorrow. May it be some little comfort to you to know that I have always considered him one of the best specimens of what a British boy really should be. We have the very happiest recollections of him at Aldro. I have never had a straighter boy, or one whom I would more entirely trust in every way; he had the essence of the true sporting spirit and always "played the game." I have never had a boy who was more universally popular with old and young alike. May the recollection of his straight life and noble death help us all for the future.

My very kindest remembrances to you all.

Yours very sincerely,
HAROLD R. BROWNE.

Wednesday
East Sheen Lodge
Sheen

Dear Mrs. Scrimgeour,

My mother, Mrs. Hood, asked me to send you a letter which she received the other day, and which she is sure you and yours would like to see. She was so comforted by it.

The letter was written to her by the mother of an officer who also went down with the Invincible, and does make one feel how happy they were up to the very second of their most glorious death.

I hope it will help you as it did us.

Yours sincerely,

(Signed) ELEANA NICKERSON.

I saw Commander Dannreuther, who was saved. You will love to hear all that he has to tell us. I am writing fully because I gather that you have not seen him yet, and don't want you to lose a minute of the comfort that I got from his story. He speaks of the glorious excitement and happiness of the rush from Scapa to the scene of action. They were so pleased that the moment had really come. In the Invincible they did not know that the Queen Mary and Indefatigable had gone down. He distinctly told me that he only heard it after he was saved. So they had nothing to damp them. Of course, also, they knew that the Grand Fleet was near behind them.

I think they first became engaged with a light cruiser at about 5.15 and sank it, then a pause, then they took on the Derflinger. More than one of our ships fired at her - she sank. Your husband telephoned up to Com. Dannreuther: 'The firing is excellent. Keep it up as fast as you can; every shell is telling.' He passed the message on to the gun-turrets, and so my darling in turret 'X' knew that they were giving satisfaction with their gun.

Then the crash came, and Com. Dannreuther thinks the shock of the explosion killed them. Anyhow, there was no struggle, no minute to think, because the ship sank (so he says) in ten to fifteen seconds. He was in some high-up position with Leo, and was thrown into the water some way off. He went down thirty feet and came up again at once, and when he reached the surface there was no one to be seen except the other five who were saved.

I am so thankful that they had no minute to grieve or think of us. They were translated. I am writing all this fully because I want you to have with me the comfort of knowing that they were all so happy and satisfied up to the moment when they passed without feeling the passage into the next world. There is no separation in spirit, and I know we shall feel that more and more as the almost physical shock wears off us.

APPENDICES

INTRODUCING THE APPENDICES

The sudden end of Alexander Scrimgeour's young life demands rather more in the way of context than his diary entries. For example, how did he get on with his fellow officers, his contemporaries and his seniors? Fortunately he left a series of acute pen portraits of those he served with on the *Crescent*. It had long been common practice for Royal Navy officers to compile confidential character sketches of fellow officers, both their contemporaries and their seniors. The exercise developed the ability to assess character, a vital command tool, and provided considerable entertainment value from the increasingly fractious relationships that inevitably developed on extended cruises. Scrimgeour was no exception; his sketches retain a remarkable freshness, the men who emerge are instantly recognisable. In the case of Admiral de Chair the portrait is strikingly similar to those provided by admirals, statesmen and the officer directing his pre-1914 War Course. Having read Scrimgeour's assessment it will come as no surprise to discover that de Chair spent the second half of the war working ashore liaising between the Admiralty and the Foreign Office on blockade questions.

The next four appendices present Scrimgeour's war from the perspective of journalists, boat crew, British naval officers and a German gunnery officer.

The British Government enlisted every tool to make the blockade effective. *The Times* leader columns reprinted here are part of the war effort, and were intended to be read by American politicians, and fellow newspaper men, for whom the London *Times* carried real weight. The main problem was to keep the Americans neutral, while violating pre-war norms. Fortunately the Germans handed the British a massive propaganda coup by sinking the Cunard liner *Lusitania* without warning, killing over 100 Americans in the process. The legal niceties of using neutral flags to disguise British ships, under debate in February 1915, was quickly overtaken by the German decision to sink all shipping in the war zone. The March leader took a robust line when the Americans protested at British 'reprisals' and the food blockade. It stressed the far more heinous crime of the Germans – common piracy. Potent parallels with the Napoleonic wars reflected growing acceptance that this was a total war of national survival, while the citing of Germans and American Civil War practice – a fruitful source of precedents for a common law legal system, was topped off by a scarcely veiled hint that the Americans should mind their own business. We might assume Scrimgeour's father would have been an avid reader of *The Times*.

While it might not carry the same international significance as a food blockade the basic tool of the Tenth Cruiser Squadron was the stopping and searching of neutral ships on the high seas. The relevant passage of the Admiralty *Manual of Seamanship* would have been Scrimgeour's constant companion throughout his training at Dartmouth.

The explosive events of Jutland bring the book to a sudden close, and Appendix IV reproduces the official reports of the senior surviving officer of the Third Battle Cruiser Squadron, the captain of the *Inflexible* and Commander Dannreuther, the senior officer of *Invincible*'s six survivors. These first-hand reports describe the last battle of the *Invincible*, as seen from the two ships astern, and her own gunnery control top, in great detail. The accompanying track chart provides visual reference to the myriad twists and turns of the action, but does not reflect the limited visibility that bedevilled both sides at various times.

While the view from the other side of battle is equally important it is vital to remember that German times were two hours ahead of the British throughout the battle. Among the handful of German accounts of Jutland that appeared in English, Georg von Hase's narrative is the most significant for this book. As gunnery officer of the battle cruiser SMS *Derfflinger* he directed the guns that sank the *Invincible*. The *Derfflinger*, a new ship of 28,000 tons, was the exact antithesis of her victim, the extra 10,000 tons bought her the protection of a battleship, a powerful 5.9-inch secondary battery and two or three knots more speed. The best balanced, fast capital ship design of the era, *Derfflinger* was a very dangerous opponent for a decade-old ship with limited armour. *Invincible* had just crippled *Derfflinger*'s sister-ship, Admiral Hipper's *Lützow*, when the smoke cleared from von Hase's sights.

Professor Andrew Lambert

APPENDIX I

NOTES ON OFFICERS FROM THE END OF THE 1914 DIARY

R.A. Dudley ft. Stratford de Chair, in command of the Tenth C.S. flagship H.M.S. *Crescent.* I consider him as an officer to be rather a nervy, restless sort of man, and hardly the sort of fellow to inspire great confidence as a dashing commander. He almost gives the impression of weakness. He is nicknamed "Old Make-a-Signal" owing to the large number of unnecessary signals he issues. He is very hard on Captain Hyde Parker of the *Endymion,* who, although a most eccentric man, appears at least to be a very thorough officer, laughed at as he is by other officers of the squadron. R.A. de Chair depends largely on the initiative of his Flag-Captain and Flag-Lieutenant for the orders he issues. As a man he is charming, a thorough gentleman, with perfect manners, and very kind-hearted. He is extremely solicitous for the personal comfort of all those under his command as far as is compatible with war routine, in direct contrast to the Spartan rigours of R.A. Pakenham of the Third C.S. He is a tall, big man, but clumsy and unwieldy in appearance, and not very athletic. He is rather overcome by the responsibilities of his job, and, I should imagine, is better as a theoriser at the Admiralty than as a man of action.

Captain G. Trewby, a capable officer, who has the knack of instilling the greatest confidence in his officers and men. He exercises great influence over the R.A. He is a calm, self-possessed man, the direct antithesis of the Admiral. Very reasonable. Is, perhaps, not quite so thorough as he might be, but this may be as he suffers terribly from lumbago. As a clean-shaven man he is good looking, but the beard he has grown has aged him considerably.

Fleet Paymaster Lawford, R.A. de Chair's secretary. An awfully nice little man. Very high spirited, always keen for a rag, and an excellent sort in every way, with a keen sense of humour. He must be quite forty, yet he always joins in the rags, games, and exercises on the Q.D. with the greatest energy. He reminds me both in looks and manner of A.G. Denniston, the Osborne master. His one *bête-noire* is whistling, as tuneless whistling sets his teeth on edge, and puts him into a furious rage always. Very popular with everybody in all the officers' messes.

A.P. Gallichan, R.N.R. (I mention him next as he is leaving the ship today.) Quite a good sort, he joined the Reserve about nine months ago, and is a Jersey bank clerk in ordinary life, with a wife and child. He is, perhaps, a bit conceited now, as, being twenty-six years old, he is allowed in the ward-room, although as a one-stripe A.P. he should be in the gun-room. He is also rather an ass, and is probably too old to get it knocked out of him. Quite all right at heart all the same. A keen photographer, and has taken some excellent snaps lately.

Lieut.-Commander H.B. Robinson, Flag-Lieutenant. An excellent fellow. Very entertaining, tells jolly good stories, and sings well. He is rather short-tempered with the signal staff, but a Flag-Lieutenant's job in war is a very trying one. He is a married man and is always talking about his wife. Has visited every corner of the earth. Was No. 1 of the Signal School, and a bit of a martinet before he came here.

Lieutenant G.A. Wilson. Appointed to battleship *King Edward VII*. He is a weird man, fearfully wet, and very eccentric in every way, hopelessly incapable, and on the whole a thorough ass with his whims and stupid ways. Still, he is very harmless and kind-hearted. I don't think he is by any means fitted for his new position, or, indeed, for any other position of any responsibility. Spent many years in a West African gunboat. He is the Captain's *bête-noire*.

Captain Gillespie, R.M.L.I., for W.T. and Intelligence duties, a dark, middle-sized man. Very quiet and unassuming. See little of him.

Commander T.F. Wardle. In peace-time is Acting Captain of the ship. Not bad as commanders go, and reputed to be very clever, but has given no indications of this so far. At daggers drawn with the G.L., as he was a G.L. before his promotion. A narrow-minded, fussy, stubby little man, always has a whine and no sense of humour at all. Not as popular or unpopular as he might conceivably be either way.

Lieut.-Commander A.L. Popham, First Lieutenant. A tall, fair-haired man, with a big bit of seniority in. He hardly looks his age, which must be at least thirty-seven. A good-natured, kind-hearted chap, although he gets very snappish at times. Very fond of his bunk, and difficult to rouse once he gets to sleep. Gets quite merry sometimes in the evenings. Very out of date and much at sea with modern appliances and inventions such as fire control, etc. Clever with his hands, and loves muddling about with some useless old V.P. and a hammer and chisel, knocking and filing. A keen sportsman with more zeal than skill. Married, with one child; has a penchant for nocturnal cocoa.

Lieut.-Commander F. A. Beasley. A very sound, steady, capable officer, not over-brilliant, but thoroughly reliable in every way. He is rather pious, and the more rowdy members of the W.R. think him a hypocrite, but I don't think he is. Keen on the fair sex; sings and plays well. He took the Prince of Wales' term, the old Exmouths, at Dartmouth, May '09–May '11. Has had interesting experiences in the *Drake* on the Australian station.

Lieut.-Commander J. Kiddle, R.N. (Ret.). A thoroughly cantankerous, snappish, bad-tempered old idiot of a dug-out. He retired four or five years ago, and was then a very senior man. He is over forty now. Was considered a promising officer in his youth, but he had a row with the Fisher clique and was promptly shelved. He is now interested in several Stock Exchange concerns, and lives a gay life in Paris. Has had many interesting experiences, not all drawing-room ones, in the Pacific and Australia, when in the mood to recount them, which is seldom. He is quite ignorant of all the modern requirements of a good N.O., and, to add insult to injury, refuses to be told by his more efficient juniors, and his obstinate stupidity is a bugbear to the ship. A bad-tempered messmate, always grumbling and criticising the conditions in the W.R. Nevertheless, at the bottom of his heart he is a kind-hearted old duffer.

Lieutenant G. V. Kenyon (G.). Very keen and clever at his job. In my opinion the most capable officer in the ship, and shall expect to see him go far in the Service. Had the pleasure of serving as his assistant for three months. He is a jolly good chap. Not at all frivolous, but quite good company. Has weird Socialistic ideas. Violent antipathy to the Commander (who was a Lieut-G., and tries to interfere). His only fault is criticising his superior officers before their juniors.

Lieut. Marshal L. Clarke (N.). A quiet, nice chap. Very steady (T.T.) and reliable at his job. Gets a bit short-tempered at sea, but his work is full of responsibility and very nervy. Knows the Sandhills people and A. and L. Greig well. I am his assistant now, and he is very nice to me.

Lieutenant F. N. Attwood (T.). Reputed to be clever, and seems quite keen and good at his job. But is very objectionable at times. A tall, cadaverous, dirty-looking man. A fine bridge player. Not very well off, and is usually on the rocks and envious of other people's good fortune.

Lieut.-Commander C.H. Oxlade, R.N.R. One of the very best chaps I have ever met. An awful good sort in every way. He is aged about thirty-nine, but does not look it, and is very comfortably off, only doing this job as a hobby. He has knocked about in every corner of the globe, shot grizzlies in the Rockies, duck on the Yangtse, elephants and lions in Africa, and tigers in India. He was in the South African War, has been Chief Officer of a C.P.R. liner on Japanese-'Frisco service, also Captain of a cross-Channel boat. As a naval officer he is not much catch, as he is totally ignorant of any of the modern contrivances of gunnery, torpedo, etc., and is very deaf. Is rather liable to moods, and, I think, is a little bit balmy. Lives near Bexhill; is a great sportsman, of course. He is a tall, lanky devil.

Lieut.-Commander S. K. Bacon, R.N.R. Another awfully nice man of whom I am very fond. If all R.N.R. officers were as nice as Oxlade and Bacon, what a damned good lot they would be! Bacon is a little bit unsophisticated. Aged about forty, is youngest son of a Hants J.P., and lives near Hindhead. Desperately keen on hunting, fishing, and shooting. Has been in the P.O. line all his life until three years ago, since when he has been Captain of an Egyptian coastguard ship in the Red Sea. Knows Egypt, India, China, Japan, and the East Indies very well. He is a short, stout, stumpy man. Excellent company, and has a bevy of most excellent stories, risque, worse, and otherwise. Some of his reminiscences of early days in the P.O. Co. are excellent. Has a mania for hot cocoa in night watches and for cheap cigarettes, of which he smokes from fifty to sixty a day.

Eng.-Lieut.-Commander Fletcher. A big, well-proportioned, red-faced, jovial-looking chap, but thoroughly morbid and morose, especially in his ideas about the war. Very old womanish, although he is by repute a good engineer. A terrible pessimist. Nearly due for promotion to Engineer-Commander.

Eng.-Lieutenant Sims. A little meek, thin man. He used to be in the *Cornwall* years ago, and knows Meggs quite well. I should not think he is any earthly use at his job, as he spends most of his time fooling about with Cockrem on deck.

Staff Surgeon W. P. Walker. A tall, pleasant-looking man, but very unpopular, as he is an awful bore and gas-bag and no good at his job. Always spouting his opinions about the war and laying down the law. Loves buttonholing the Admiral about it and worrying him to death. Has just married a very pretty girl.

Chaplain, the Rev Alfred Shell. In my opinion a mealy mouthed bugger. Extremely unpopular with everybody. He is a terrible hypocrite and very mean and miserly. He swizzles everybody. We all feel sure he appropriates the men's funds to his own ends.

Surgeon Joseph A. Maxwell. A very nice man, quite young, as he has only just left Dublin University, where he earned a valuable reputation on the Rugger field, but did very little doctoring, I am afraid. Inclined to be quiet and is reticent on occasions, but still waters run deep, and Joe Maxwell never misses a real opportunity for a good rag.

Temporary Surgeon Roger Buddle. A New Zealander, a jolly good sort. Knows as little of doctoring as Maxwell, with whom he is great pals. Gets very tight every now and again, and is jolly good company. A very good bridge player when sober, they tell me. He has met daddy's friend Acland at Christchurch in New Zealand.

Staff Paymaster Weston. A nasty little man, very objectionable and bad-tempered. A close friend of the padre and of S. S. Walker. Nothing really wrong with him except that he is one of those alternately surly and over-pleasant people who always grate up the wrong way.

Assistant-Paymaster Cockrem. A two-striper of about twenty-nine years of age, although he looks seventeen. Is senior clerk to Secretary on the

Admiral's staff. A quiet, unassuming chap, although he has "nights" occasionally. He made a ridiculous attempt to grow a beard.

Assistant-Clerk Glanvile. A young officer of seven months' seniority, junior clerk to Secretary on the Admiral's staff, and junior G.R. officer. On the whole quite a good little chap; we all like him. He was in the *Lion* before the war started, and is full of Beatty-isms and the tour to Russia. There is not much of him, but he has got a will of his own.

Assistant-Paymaster Egleton, R.N.R. Captain's clerk. A terrible fool who knows nothing, and does nothing - right, and rubs everyone up the wrong way, and withal so meek and innocent a countenance that I am constrained to pity him, though most folks ignore and despise him. An ugly man, who looks almost as big a fool as he is.

Assistant-Paymaster G.T.E. Cockerill, R.N.R. A tall, spectacled, fair-haired youth of about nineteen. Took on his present job in August, as owing to his defective eyesight he could not get into any military force. Quite a nice chap; a bit green at first, but he will soon settle down into the Service way of things.

Ch. Sig. Bos'n Mr. Champion. A jolly, red-faced old chap of about fifty. A thoroughly good sort, Senior W.O. in the squadron. Has always got some moan, but this is only a sort of hobby. Very respectful to his superiors, in antithesis to some of the younger W.O.s of more modern date.

Gunner Mr. F.E. Lowman. Not a bad chap, although a bit short-tempered. He suffers badly from gout, and spends most of his time in his bunk, otherwise quite a good officer. Loves relating dull yarns about his family.

Bos'n Mr. G. Ford. A typical old bos'n of the Mr. Gearing class; wears the most extraordinary, antique, picturesque old uniforms. He is not so loquacious as Mr. Gearing, or so energetic, and he does very little work, and I really believe knows but little of his job. A queer old cuss altogether.

Bos'n Mr. McLachlan. A small, insignificant young man, quite a nonentity; very seldom seen, and does nothing, except very occasionally when he has fits of cantankerousness. Tries to ape the "knut" when on shore.

Acting-Gunner Mr. Croughan. A young chap, not at all bad at heart. Very talkative. Most abominably familiar, which is a great drawback, I am afraid. Quite a capable man if he was not so full of gas, and even might be quite interesting if he would only stop talking a minute to let you digest what he says.

Torpedo-Gunner Mr. King. A very nice man, quiet, and good at his job. Prematurely white hair makes him look twenty years older than he is. Very interested in the development of Canada, especially British Columbia, as he did three commissions in the *Rainbow* based on Esquimalt.

Carpenter Mr. Lane. A thorough old tartar, with a red bearded face, and hot stuff in every way. Always very busy, but you can never get his staff to do anything; they are always so fully occupied tinkering about doing nothing. Mr. Lane is a tremendous character, a good supply of language, and plenty of tall yarns, he would bamboozle Lord Fisher, if you gave him half a chance.

Artificer-Engineer Botling. A dark-eyed, morose man of forbidding aspect. Looks on life with a dark eye.

Warrant-Engineer French, R.N.R. Quite a good, stout old chap. From the Union Castle Line. Lives at Cowes. Very anxious to rise into higher society, and is always pleased and eager for a chat.

With regard to the eight midshipmen of the ship, I shall not indite separate notes on my seven colleagues and myself. We have all come through the training together in the same term, and have known each other intimately for nearly five years. In this ship, for various reasons, such as the partial inefficiency and ignorance of a large number of the officers of the ship, or rather the lack of very efficient officers, for with one exception none are really hopeless idiots; and as the war entails far heavier work being thrown on the willing back of the N.O. in consequence, the midshipmen of this ship have been entrusted with far greater responsibilities than we should have in most ships. I think I can say without exaggeration or conceit that the midshipmen have acquitted themselves well, and, without thinking that they absolutely run the ship, they certainly have a good share in it. I will not discriminate between my colleagues except to say that Tottenham is far less efficient than the others; this is as he is so terribly eccentric and mad (as I believe he has plenty of latent ability somewhere). Unluckily he doesn't realise his shortcomings.

APPENDIX II

THE TIMES EDITORIALS ON
THE BLOCKADE, 1915

"Blockade" and the Neutral Flag. 12 February 1915, p.9.

Yesterday the State Department of Washington forwarded dispatches to London and to Berlin, dealing with the Lusitania incident and with the German proclamation of a "war area" round the United Kingdom. We feel confident that the conversation which MR PAGE is instructed to have with SIR EDWARD GREY will be as friendly and satisfactory as our Washington Correspondent has foretold. He has assured us that nothing approaching a protest was to be expected, but that informal representations would probably be made as to the dangers to American shipping which an habitual use of the American flag by British vessels within the war area would involve. Any representations of the kind will, of course, be received in the spirit in which they are addressed to us. The fair and reasonable attitude which America has observed in all the problems raised by the war has strengthened our customary desire to respect, not only her rights, but her wishes and her susceptibilities. Both nations recognize the same general principles of international law, and both are anxious not to strain claims which are merely technical. As regards this particular question, which we consider the use of the neutral flag to avoid an enemy as an undoubted right, it is a right which we are most unlikely to exercise so as to expose the shipping of neutral States to serious peril or inconvenience. In these circumstances, and in view of the hearty good will which happily exists between both Governments and both peoples, a satisfactory accommodation should be promptly and easily reached. No doubt is felt in England, or amongst those conversant with maritime law and history in the United States, that the action of the Lusitania in coming into Liverpool under the American flag was perfectly lawful and in strict accordance with precedent. It continues, our Washington Correspondent tells us, to be much discussed in America, but both in Washington and in the Eastern Press the discussion is temperate and friendly to this country. The exceptional severity with which the censors deem it judicious to treat American news makes it difficult to learn American opinion so fully as we could desire, but the

New York Tribune is, perhaps, right when it affirms that the interest of the flag incident would be academic, were it not for Germany's extraordinary version of the rules of warfare.

That version, it is understood, is the subject of the American communication to Berlin. This document is also perfectly friendly, but it makes clear, we are told, that any German attack upon ships flying the American flag, without examination and proof that its use is for purposes of disguise, would be deemed to be a very grave event and might cause serious complications. It is clear that that whole incident of the Lusitania arose from the fact that the Admiralty had information of Germany's real intentions before these were proclaimed in the Memorandum of February 4. They knew that she intended to sink enemy merchant ships without examination and without warning to the crews. She had so sunk the Tokomaru; she had attacked the Icaria, and she had even attacked the hospital ship Asturias. With these instances of her contempt for law and humanity before them, they recommended our merchant shipping to use the neutral flag in order to avoid the wholesale sacrifice of non-combatant lives. The step was so regular as to be almost a matter of course, without necessity, gave the Germans a dialectical advantage.

The advantage lay in the fact that just when American indignation at the German menace was very vehement the statement of the Foreign Office and the arrival of the Cunard liner under the American flag suddenly revealed that the Admiralty had, in fact, advised British merchantmen to resort to the familiar device of flying the neutral flag. There has not been any "misuse" of that flag, as the Germans falsely asserted, but resort was had to the old custom of the sea at a time when the step was particularly likely to cause discussion, and to afford the Germans in the United States a fresh opening for misrepresentation. The cool sense of the American people and their respect for the recognized rules of international law have apparently prevented them from being misled. They are not pleased at the incident. But they are obliged to acknowledge that—unlike the German "blockade"— it has a sound legal basis. The Foreign Office Statement establishes that beyond dispute. The practice is sanctioned alike by international law and by British municipal law. Ships of war of all nations have habitually sailed under all sorts of disguises in order to surprise enemy ships, whether armed or unarmed. The raid of the German cruiser Emden at Penang is a recent instance in point. Why, it may pertinently be asked of German critics, is it illegitimate and unfair for British merchantmen to sail under the neutral flag in order to avoid destruction, if it was legitimate and fair for the Emden to use false colours in order to destroy? We do no claim to make any use of the flag of neutral States which we do not allow belligerents, when we are neutral, to make of our own. The chief object of the ruse, in the case of merchantmen, is to compel enemy ships to comply with the recognized obligations of international law. It forces them to search the suspected vessel and her cargo before capture. That is just what the Germans have declared that they will not do within the "war area." They propose to sink all British ships at sight, and to take their chance of sinking neutrals. This, as the Foreign Office declare, is sheer piracy upon the high seas.

But even "friendly communications" with American might have been avoided, as it seems to us, had the Admiralty and the Foreign Office worked in this matter more closely together. We have no evidence that the use of the neutral flag, when the Admiralty advised it, had suddenly become so urgent as to override all other considerations. The Foreign Office are better judges of some amongst these considerations than the Admiralty possibly can be. It is the business of the Admiralty to look upon matters from one point of view, and the business of the Foreign Office to look at them from another. But the constant and intimate cooperation of both is essential in many matters if serious blunders are to be avoided. Nothing very serious has happened, or is likely to happen, this time, but the incident is an object-lesson in the disadvantages to which the independent action of separate Departments of the Administration exposes us. We hope that the less will be taken to heart.

Neutrals and British Reprisals, 4 March 1915, p.9

We regret the general condemnation in the American Press of the policy of reprisals against Germany announced by the PRIME MINISTER. That policy was certain to provoke criticism, but the objections urged against it in the United States and in other countries whose trade interests it affects are largely founded, we fancy, upon misapprehension. Americans have been described as "Pro-German" in England, and denounced as "Pro-British" in Germany. It seems to us that their attitude on the reprisals question, like their attitude upon all previous questions, is intended to be quite impartial. Their sympathies, as we learn by a thousand signs, are very heartily with us, so far as the overwhelming majority are concerned. But they have not allowed their sympathies to deflect them from the "real neutrality" at which they have aimed from the first. They have shown all along a natural and legitimate anxiety that their rights as neutrals should meet with due regard. That feeling was very manifest in the substance and in the tone of their Reply to the German proclamation of piracy. It obviously underlies and inspires a good deal of the newspaper comment upon the British counter-stroke. It is a feeling which Englishmen, with their long tradition in favour of the rights of trade, cannot but respect. We have been extremely careful, as SIR EDWARD GREY has pointed out in his Replies to the American Note of December 28, to safeguard those rights so far as the manifest necessities of our own military position have allowed. We do not intend to depart from the usage. But, while we are confident that the measure we shall adopt may be reconciled with the fundamental principles of international law, as applied to the wholly new state of circumstances which have arisen in the present struggle, and which have culminated, for the present, in the German claim to sink all vessels in the war area without examination, we admit, in the words of SIR EDWARD'S last dispatch, that we may have to take belligerent action "in various ways which may, at first sight, by regarded as a departure from old practice." Americans have studied the common law, which is part of their and our joint inheritance, too long and too well not to know that the adjustment of old principles to new conditions is of the essence of legal progress.

That the conditions of the present contest are latterly different from those of the past wars, in which international law has mainly developed to the stage now laid down in the text-books, cannot be denied. A very large part of it was evolved before, or during, the conflict with NAPOLEON. Great armies were engaged on both sides, but it was only towards the very end of the struggle that SCHARNHORST'S idea of an armed nation was realized. In this war all the Continental armies are conscript armies raised in accordance with that idea. This single circumstance goes a long way to destroy the old distinction between the armed forces of a nation and the civil population. If the army is the "people in arms," food for the people is necessarily, to a great extent, food for the army. Foods may be imported for the use of civilians, but it is quite certain that if the army wants them it will take them. The German decree of January 25, placing all imported grain and flour under Government control, introduces another element into the question for which there is no precedent. The subsequent modification of February 6 does not appear to be material. The decree in effect makes the German Government the ultimate consignee of all imported foodstuffs. How can any precedent, or any rule based upon precedent, for permitting consignments to civilians and for civilian use, be wrested to defend consignments which the enemy Government have announced that they will seize? Several Continental Powers have always maintained that foodstuffs are liable to seizure. When the present German Government denounces such seizure as "murderous" and "inhuman," neutrals should remember that two German Chancellors in succession, BISMARCK and CAPRIVI, defended it in the strongest and most comprehensive terms, that Germany, so far as is known, has never disavowed the practice, that she resorted to it ruthlessly in the siege of Paris, and that BISMARCK indulged his humour by talking of the starving Parisians "eating babies" while he was at Versailles. The doctrine of "continuous voyage," which the American courts did so much to elaborate in the Civil War, and against which England raised no protest, was just such an application of old principles to novel facts as is implied in our answer to German piracy. It might be extended, our Washington Correspondent suggests, to imports into Germany through neutral States.

The German answer to the "suggestion" in the American Note of February 22 cannot lessen our difficulties in assenting to that project. Germany tells Washington, in substance, that she may suspend her piratical operations and refrain from endangering American ships and lives, if England will allow her to import all the food she needs, through agencies whose names are communicated to the United States, and who will hand it over to licensed dealers for consumption by the civil population only. We have already explained that a surrender by us to any proposal of the kind would be, in the circumstances, a surrender to blackmail. It would be an admission that German piracy had intimidated us, and a direct invitation to our enemies to resume the process at their convenience—say, when they had imported food enough to carry them on to the next harvest. But there are other objections to the project which should appeal to a practical nation like the Americans. What security should we have under such a scheme that the food would go to the civil population alone? Germany's word? The Americans know its worth, as well as we do. Are they going to guarantee it, and if so how, and how do they propose, in case of need, to enforce the guarantee? Are they to send, and is Germany to admit and to pay, a host of American officials who will supervise the German agencies in the ports, and the German licensed dealers in every town and village of the Empire? If disputes should arise between the German agents and dealers on the one hand, and the American inspectors on the other, who would decide them? Germany has pleaded "necessity" as a sufficient reason for all her violations of treaties and of law. Why should we suppose she would refrain from urging it as a reason for breaking any new engagements she might make? We are satisfied that, on reflection, the utterly impracticable nature of this project will be perceived across the Atlantic, and that the plan will be seen to be a mere diplomatic trick. American opinion for the moment seems to have forgotten that in all great wars belligerents take action against which neutrals who chose to stand on the bare letter of the law might plausibly protest. Our Washington Correspondent reminds us that this was very markedly the case during their own Civil War. The victory of the Union was in great part due to the ruthless blockade of the Southern States, which it was one of LINCOLN'S first acts to proclaim. The blockade was certainly irregular, under the Declaration of Paris, for many months after it began. The Washington Government knew and confessed that it was irregular. All America knew the terrible loss and hardship which it inflicted on the whole population engaged in one of the chief of English industries. But LINCOLN'S Government appealed for toleration and for indulgence, and the appeal was not in vain. Under the guidance of men like BRIGHT and W.E. FORSTER, who understood the greatness and the value to mankind of the ideals for which the North was fighting, the British democracy did not scrutinize too closely the acts of a kindred people struggling for its life. Therein they showed the large wisdom and the large generosity of their race. May they not hope to-day, when they have been plunged against their will into a conflict yet more deadly, for aims which are not less high, that America will do unto them as, in the day of her visitation and of her trial, they did unto her?

APPENDIX III

EXTRACTS FROM CHAPTER VI BOATWORK IN MANUAL OF SEAMANSHIP VOL. I, 1905 (REVISED AND REPRINTED 1915)

Lowering a Sea Boat.—On a sea boat's crew being away they man their boat instantly and put on their life-belts. The life-lines are crossed to prevent the boat surging in a fore and aft direction, and the crew on the inside stand by with stretchers ready to bear the boat off from the ship's side. No one is to be abaft the after fall or before the foremost fall.

The lee boat is always the one to lower, and in a rough sea a good lee should be made and, if necessary, oil used before lowering the boat.

Sea boat lowerers, consisting of a leading hand and two others, are told off to each fall; the leading hand slipping the gripes (with a hammer specially supplied for the purpose and secured to the davit with a lanyard) before starting the falls.

The officer lowering the boat as she nears the water gives the order "Out pins," and then, watching his opportunity so as to drop the boat near the water, orders "Slip," the coxswain slips (the inertia given the boat by the ship and the helm being over, she will sheer away from the ship), the crew at once get their oars out and give way.

Hoisting a Sea Boat.—A lee is formed, and as the boat approaches, the boat rope should be passed into her as soon as possible by means of a heaving line, and manned inboard, and when secured, the boat hauled under the davits; a stern line is also passed into the boat if necessary and secured.

The foremost fall should be hooked on first, and then the after one, life-lines crossed, and stretchers used as in lowering. All the crew are hoisted in the boat, the falls being strongly manned.

When the boat is up and the falls secured, the crew get her weight off the pins by setting up the fore and after and griping her to, life-lines left clear and life-belts in place, tiller stopped over towards the ship, and boat-rope secured.

The coxswain reports to the officer of the watch that his boat is off the pins and ready for lowering. The falls are also reported "clear for running."

Boarding a Wreck, or a Vessel, under Sail or at Anchor, in a Heavy Sea.
The circumstances under which boats have to board vessels, whether stranded or at anchor, or under way, are so various that it would be impossible to draw up any general rule for guidance. Nearly everything must depend on the skill, judgment, and presence of mind of the coxswain or officer in charge of the boat, who will often have those qualities taxed to the utmost, as undoubtedly the operation of boarding a vessel in a heavy sea or surf is frequently one of extreme danger.

It will be scarcely necessary to state that, whenever practicable, a vessel, whether stranded or afloat, should be boarded to leeward, as the principal dangers to be guarded against must be the violent collision of the boat against the vessel or her swamping or upsetting by the rebound of the sea, or by its irregular direction on coming in contact with the vessel's side; and the greater violence of the sea on the windward side is much more likely to cause such accidents. The danger must, of course, also be still further increased when the vessel on the lee side, if broadside to the sea, is the falling of the masts or if they have been previously carried away, the damage or destruction of the boat amongst the floating spars and gear alongside. It may, therefore, under such circumstances, be often necessary to take a wrecked crew from the bow or stern; otherwise a rowing-boat, proceeding from a lee shore to a wreck, by keeping under the vessel's lee, may use her as a breakwater, and thus go off in comparatively smooth water, or be at least shielded from the worst of the sea. If unable to approach a wreck in the manner above described, anchor to windward of the stranded vessel, and then veer down to 100 or 150 fathoms of cable, until near enough to throw a line on board. The greatest care, under these circumstances, has, of course, to be taken to prevent actual contact between the boat and the ship; and the crew of the latter has sometimes to jump overboard, and be hauled to the boat by ropes.

In every case of boarding a wreck or a vessel at sea, it is important that the lines by which a boat is made fast to the vessel should be of sufficient length to allow of her rising or falling freely with the sea; and every rope should be kept in hand ready to cut or slip it in a moment if necessary. On wrecked persons or other passengers being taken into a boat in a seaway, they should be placed on the thwarts in equal numbers on either side, and be made to sit down. All crowding or rushing headlong into the boat should be prevented, as far as possible; and the captain of the ship, if a wreck, should be called on to remain on board to preserve order until every other person has left her.

APPENDIX IV

REPORTS OF SENIOR OFFICERS OF THE THIRD BATTLE CRUISER SQUADRON, BATTLE OF JUTLAND OFFICIAL DESPATCHES, 1916

Report of Senior Officer 3rd Battle Cruiser Squadron
Enclosure No. 8 to Battle Cruiser Fleet Letter No. B.C.F. 01 of 12/6/16.

No. 363/16.

H.M.S. "Indomitable,"
2nd June 1916.

SIR,

I HAVE the honour to report that H.M. Battle Cruisers "Invincible," "Indomitable," and "Inflexible," H.M. Light Cruisers "Chester," and "Canterbury" and H.M. Destroyers "Christopher," "Ophelia," "Shark," and "Acasta" left the Pentland Firth at 9.35 p.m. on 30th May 1916, just ahead of the Grand Fleet, with which visual touch was kept by the late Rear-Admiral Commanding Third Battle Cruiser Squadron, The Honourable Horace Lambert Alexander Hood, C.B., M.V.O., D.S.O., through "Chester" till we were in Latitude 57.49 N., Longitude 4.42 E. at 2.23 p.m. on 31st May.

2. At 2.23 p.m. we received from "Galatea" our first intimation that the enemy were actually at sea; we were then steering 115°, speed of advance 14 knots; the speed of advance during the night had been 16.8 knots. Telefunken signals of strength 10 had just previously been heard. From then onwards many signals giving various positions of the enemy were received.

At 3.13 p.m. the Rear-Admiral Commanding 3rd Battle Cruiser Squadron increased speed to 22 knots; at 3.18 p.m. he ordered ships to "Action Stations"; 3.45 p.m. he altered course to 137°, the squadron was then in single line ahead with "Canterbury" ahead distant 5 miles, "Chester" on starboard side bearing 256° to 212° distant 5 miles and the four destroyers ahead of the Battle Cruisers as a submarine screen. By 4.12 p.m. we were steaming at full speed.

3. As usual, the positions of the enemy received in the W/T signals did not agree, but they all pointed to the enemy steering 345° or 298°, and it is evident that the late Rear-Admiral acted on this; at 3.57 p.m. we received signals from the Senior Officer, Battle Cruiser Fleet: "Am engaging enemy

1500." At 5.30 p.m. the sound of gunfire was plainly heard. At this time the visibility greatly decreased owing to the mist, the density of which was various degrees; for, on some bearings, one could see 16,000 yards, whilst on others only 2,000 yards. From then till dark the visibility ranged from 14,000 to 5,000 yards, which was, in my opinion, a great handicap to us, the attacking force; in fact much more of a handicap to the attacker then the defenders.

At 5.40 p.m. flashes of gunfire were seen on a bearing about 215°, but I could not distinguish any ships. The Rear-Admiral, "Invincible," altered course to starboard without signal, turning about 9 points, thus bringing the engaged vessels and "Chester" on the port bow of the 3rd Battle Cruiser Squadron, and leaving our destroyers off our port quarter; after a short time we made out the engagement to be between the enemy's light cruisers and "Chester." The Rear-Admiral led the squadron between "Chester" and the enemy's light cruisers whom we engaged; at 5.55 p.m. we opened fire on the enemy with our port guns. Shortly afterwards some more of the enemy's cruisers were seen following at some distance astern of the light cruisers which we were engaging, and I observed our destroyers developing an attack on them. At the same time these enemy vessels opened a heavy fire on our destroyers, and I am afraid that "Acasta" and another destroyer were either sunk or damaged for I only saw two of them afterwards, nor did I again see either "Chester" or "Canterbury." I desire to record the fact that, when I saw them, they were heading to make a determined attack. At this moment my attention was called to the enemy's light cruisers turning 16 points; they were at that time under a heavy gunfire from the 3rd Battle Cruiser Squadron, and a few minutes later one was seen to be heavily on fire and apparently she blew up. There was also observed amongst them a four-funnelled cruiser, apparently of the "Roon" class. She was observed to lose two funnels, to be steaming and firing very slowly and heavily on fire amidships.

4. The First Battle Cruiser Squadron was then sighted on our port bow, heavily engaged with some enemy whom I could not see owing to the mist. At 6.13 p.m. "Invincible" turned to starboard, apparently stopped, and large quantities of steam were observed to be escaping from her escape pipes. At the same moment "Inflexible" turned to port and tracks of torpedoes were observed by "Indomitable" coming from the enemy's light cruisers with whom we had been engaged. The range at which I engaged them was about 12,000 yards. I turned away from the torpedoes and increased to full speed. One torpedo actually ran alongside this ship at a distance of about 20 yards, which we managed to outrun. As we turned, two torpedoes passed close to

the stern of the ship, but they had run their distance, for I managed to turn ahead of them and resume my place in the Squadron as did "Inflexible" astern of "Invincible," which ship was then again going ahead, having turned to about 153°. In all about 5 torpedoes' tracks were seen coming from the enemy's light cruisers.

At 6.14 p.m. "Invincible," while steam was escaping, hoisted the "Disregard," but hauled it down at once and followed it by hoisting 1 flag and the squadron got into proper order again. About 6.20 p.m. at a range of 8,600 yards the leading ship of the enemy's battle cruisers was seen firing at the 3rd Battle Cruiser Squadron. They were promptly engaged, and I realised that "Invincible" could have sustained little or no damage from a torpedo, as I had thought she had when she stopped at 6.13 p.m., for I had to go 20 knots to regain station in the line; 6.32 p.m. shells were falling about "Indomitable" from the enemy's battle cruisers, which were distant about 8,000 yards.

At 6.33 p.m. "Invincible" was straddled by a salvo and was hit in the after part; 6.34 p.m. a salvo or one shot appeared to hit her about "Q" turret, and she immediately blew up. Wreckage, &c. was thrown about 400 feet in the air. She appears to have broken in half immediately, for, when the smoke cleared and we had got to the position, the bows were standing upright about 70 feet out of the water and 50 yards away the stern was standing out of the water to a similar height, while in a circle round was wreckage and some few survivors. The visibility, which I have before said was sometimes up to 14,000 yards, was now generally much less than that.

5. The positions of affairs, when I took charge of the 3rd Battle Cruiser Squadron on the lamentable death of Rear-Admiral Hood, appeared to me to be as follows:—

We were steering 153°, as shown on attached chart [not included]. The enemy's battle cruisers were disappearing out of sight, but were still firing on "Indomitable" and "Inflexible." The Director Gunner, Mr. James H. Moore, reported that about this time one of the "Derfflinger" class fell out of enemy's line and he saw her sink. The Lieutenant-Commander (G) in the Control top at same period remarked that she was very low in the water. The 1st and 2nd Battle Cruiser Squadrons were coming up astern of "Indomitable"; "Inflexible" being about 3 cables ahead of latter. When "Invincible" blew up, "Inflexible" turned sharply to port, and I did the same and eased the speed as I wanted to continue the action in the same direction as previously and wished, if "Inflexible" turned 8 or more points to port, to turn possibly under her stern, or, at all events, to get the 3rd Battle Cruiser Squadron to resume their original course and then alter it further to starboard in order to continue the action. However, "Inflexible" quickly turned to starboard and continued to turn towards the enemy. By being compelled to ease my speed I had dropped astern of "Inflexible." I made no signal to her as she was turning as I desired. You then ordered the 3rd Battle Cruiser Squadron to prolong your line, which we did. Shortly after this I saw the Grand Fleet astern of us bearing about 340°.

6. Until 7.20 p.m. none of the enemy could be distinguished owing to the mist; but at that time it commenced to lift, and at 7.26 p.m. "Indomitable" reopened fire on the enemy's rear ship, the range being about 14,000 yards and decreasing. Towards the head of the enemy's line dense quantities of grey smoke could be seen and out of this came a destroyer attack, which was beaten off but caused our battlefleet astern to turn away from the enemy. At 7.40 p.m. our fire was checked owing to lack of visibility. At 8.26 p.m. ranges could again be got on the enemy, and "Indomitable" engaged the 2nd ship from the enemy's rear, which, as the range decreased, appeared to be "Seydlitz." The enemy very quickly straddled us and continued to do so, even after we ceased firing. I believe that "New Zealand" was also firing on this ship; at all events, "Seydlitz" turned away heavily damaged, and her fire lessened. At 8.42 p.m. we ceased fire the enemy bearing 307°, but we could not see to spot.

7. The only damage sustained by "Indomitable" was a small hole in her middle funnel, though many splinters from shells fell on the deck, but no one was injured. At 8.44 p.m. "Indomitable" received so severe a shock that I was knocked off the compass platform. I thought that the ship had been mined or hit by a torpedo, but no damage has so far been discovered. I assume that we either hit some wreckage or a submarine.

8. From then onwards I conformed to your orders and nothing further of importance occurred with the exception that at 3.12 a.m. on 1st June a Zeppelin was sighted on the starboard quarter coming up from the Southward. At 3.17 a.m. fire was opened by "A" and "X" turrets, the Zeppelin then turned 101°, but had not been damaged in any way. At 3.21 a.m. she turned to 10° and continued her course astern of us, but at too great a range to justify a further expenditure of ammunition. Several light cruisers stationed on our port quarter engaged the Zeppelin, but apparently without causing her any damage.

*   *   *   *   *   *

[1] Part omitted here, referring solely to personnel, recommendations &c., in no way bearing on the course of the action.

11. The following is amount of ammunition expended by this ship during the action:—

98 rounds of A.P. Lyddite, 12-in.

66 rounds of Common Lyddite, 12-in.

10 rounds of Powder Common, 12-in.

12. I desire to emphasize the fact that, when "Invincible" blew up and sank, the Captain of "Inflexible"—Captain Edward Henry Fitzhardinge Heaton-Ellis, M.V.O.—without warning such as he would have had in the case of a wounded ship, found himself leading the squadron, and he at once followed the highest traditions of our Service by closing the enemy.

13. As the Officer left as Senior Officer of the 3rd Battle Cruiser Squadron, I desire to record the sincere sorrow of all the Officers and men of the 3rd Battle Cruiser Squadron in the loss that the Nation has sustained in the death of Rear-Admiral The Hon. Horace L. A. Hood, C.B., M.V.O., D.S.O., Captain Arthur Lindesay Cay, Royal Navy, and the Officers and men of H.M.S. "Invincible," many of whom were personally known to me and friends of mine.

Of Rear-Admiral Hood's attainments it is not for me to speak, but he drew from all of us our love and respect. The Officers and men of "Invincible" had previously been our chums in the Mediterranean.

13. Since compiling the above report, I have seen Commander Hubert E. Dannreuther, who was the Gunnery Commander of H.M.S. "Invincible" on 31st May. He states that the cause of "Invincible" stopping at 6.30 p.m. was that her helm jammed when put "hard-a-port."

I have the honour to be,

Sir,

Your obedient Servant,

F. W. KENNEDY,

Captain and Senior Officer,

3rd B.C. Squadron.

The Vice-Admiral Commanding,

Battle Cruiser Fleet.

THE BATTLE OFF JUTLAND

MAY 31ST 1916

3.55 2nd & 3rd L.C.S.

3rd L.C.S.
2.58

Galatea 2.0
3.50

3.25 Sighted Enemy Battle Cruisers

2.35

2.52

3.12

LION 2.0 P.M.
2.17

3.01

2.0
3rd L.C.S.

2.35
2nd L.C.S.

9.24

Enclosure No. 9 to Battle Cruiser Fleet Letter No. B.C.F. 01 of 12/6/16.

Reports of the 3rd Battle Cruiser Squadron on the Action of 31st May 1916.

No. 20 S.

Submitted.

2. I concur in the attached reports as far as was seen and known in "Indomitable."

3. I know that the late Rear-Admiral Commanding, 3rd Battle Cruiser Squadron, had a high opinion of Commander Dannreuther's abilities and zeal.

F. W. KENNEDY,

Captain and Senior Officer of

3rd Battle Cruiser Squadron.

The Vice-Admiral Commanding,

Battle Cruiser Fleet.

Report of Senior Surviving Officer, H.M.S. "Invincible."

H.M.S. "Crescent,"

2nd June 1916.

SIR,

I DEEPLY regret to report that H.M.S. "Invincible," commanded by Captain A. L. Cay, R.N., and flying the flag of Rear-Admiral the Hon. Horace L. Hood, Rear-Admiral Commanding the Third Battle Cruiser Squadron, was blown up and completely destroyed when in action with the enemy at 6.34 p.m. on Wednesday the 31st May.

The total number of officers and men on board at the time was 1,031. Of these only six survived. The names of the survivors are as follows:—

Commander H. E. Dannreuther, R.N.

Lieutenant C. S. Sanford, R.N.

Chief P.O. (P.T.I.) Thompson.

Yeo. Signals Pratt (Walter Maclean), 216963.

Able Seaman Dandridge (Ernest George), 239478.

Gunner Gasson, R.M.A.

Of the above, all are free from injury with the exception of Gunner Gasson, who was severely burnt about the head and arms. They are now accommodated in this ship except Gunner Gasson, who is in the Hospital Ship "Plassy."

The circumstances of the destruction of the ship are briefly as follows:—

The "Invincible" was leading the 3rd B.C.S. and at about 5.45 p.m. first came into action with an enemy light cruiser on the port bow. Several torpedoes were seen coming towards the ship, but were avoided by turning away from them. "Invincible's" fire was effective on the light cruiser engaged, and a heavy explosion was observed. A dense cloud of smoke and steam from this explosion appeared to be in the same position some minutes later.

"Invincible" then turned and came into action at about 6.15 p.m. with the leading enemy battle cruiser, which was thought to be the "Derfflinger." Fire was opened at the enemy at about 8,000 yards, and several hits were observed.

A few moments before the "Invincible" blew up Admiral Hood hailed the Control Officer in the Control Top from the fore bridge: "Your firing is very good, keep at it as quickly as you can, every shot is telling." This was the last order heard from the Admiral or Captain who were both on the bridge at the end.

The Ship had been hit several times by heavy shell, but no appreciable damage had been done when at 6.34 p.m. a heavy shell struck "Q" turret and, bursting inside, blew the roof off. This was observed from the control top. Almost immediately following there was a tremendous explosion amidships indicating that "Q" magazine had blown up. The ship broke in half and sank in 10 or 15 seconds.

The survivors on coming to the surface saw the bow and stern of the ship only, both of which were vertical and about 50 feet clear of the water.

The survivors were stationed as follows prior to the sinking of the ship:—

Commander Dannreuther (Gun
    Control Officer)
C.P.O. Thompson   } Fore Control Top.
A.B. Danbridge

Yeo. Signals Pratt   Director Tower platform.
Lieutenant (T) Sandford   Fore Conning Tower,
                               hatch of which was
                               open.

Gunner Gasson   "Q" turret, at the range-
                                        finder.

There was very little wreckage, the six survivors were supported by a target raft and floating timber till picked up by H.M.S. "Badger" shortly after 7 p.m.

Only one man besides those rescued was seen to come to the surface after the explosion, and he sank before he could reach the target raft.

The "Badger" was brought alongside the raft in a most expeditious and seamanlike manner, and the survivors were treated with the utmost kindness and consideration by the officers and men.

I have the honour to be,

Sir,

Your obedient Servant,

H. E. DANNREUTHER.

Captain Francis W. Kennedy, R.N.,   Commander.
H.M.S. "Indomitable."

Captain's Report.—H.M.S. "Inflexible."
Engagement on 31st May 1916.

No. 199 W.

"Inflexible,"

2nd June 1916.

SIR,

I HAVE the honour to inform you that "Inflexible" left Scapa Flow at 9 p.m. on Tuesday, 30th May 1916, in company with "Invincible" (flying the Flag of Rear-Admiral the Hon. Horace L. A. Hood, C.B., M.V.O., D.S.O.), "Indomitable" (Captain Francis W. Kennedy), "Chester," "Canterbury," and the four destroyers "Ophelia," "Christopher," "Shark," and "Acasta." This Squadron, which left in advance of the main fleet, which sailed shortly after, under the command of the Commander-in-Chief, was stationed 10 miles ahead of the armoured cruiser screen; speed of advance of fleet was 17 knots.

2. At noon on Wednesday, 31st May, the position of the Third Battle Cruiser Squadron was 58° 7' North, 3° 55' East. At 2.20 p.m., the first reports of the enemy were intercepted by W/T.

3. At 3.15 p.m. speed of Squadron was increased to 22 knots and at 4.0

p.m. to 24 knots, gradually working up to full speed, course being altered as necessary by "Invincible," presumably with the idea of joining up with the Battle Cruiser Fleet, reports having been intercepted that "Lion" was engaging the enemy.

At about 5.30 p.m. firing was heard ahead, and at 5.40, four hostile light cruisers were sighted on the port bow, apparently engaging the "Chester." On seeing the battle-cruisers, these ships turned away; fire was opened on the second light cruiser from the right at a range of 8,000 yards, but was checked at 6 o'clock as the ship fired at was enveloped in a high column of smoke and was not seen again; it is presumed that she blew up. Fire was re-opened on the next cruiser, but after one salvo was fired she disappeared in the mist. Meanwhile the four destroyers in company had left the Squadron in order to attack the enemy and were last seen hotly engaged.

4. At 6.15 p.m., two tracks of torpedoes were observed; course was altered to avoid one which was seen to pass down the port side at a distance of about 20 ft. (the torpedo was going very slowly—apparently near the end of its run); the other torpedo passed astern.

At about this time another torpedo was observed to pass underneath the ship, and emerge the other side.

5. At 6.20 p.m., enemy's heavy ships were observed ahead, course was altered about 8 points to port and fire was opened at a range of about 8,000 to 9,000 yards. Owing to the haze and smoke only one ship was visible, apparently a battleship of the "Kaiser" or "König" class, and some direct hits were considered to have been obtained on this vessel. At 6.30 p.m., the "Invincible" blew up, apparently owing to being hit amidships abreast "Q" turret by a salvo. About 6.35 p.m., enemy disappeared in the mist and firing ceased.

During this engagement, "Inflexible" was continuously fired at, and was straddled repeatedly, but the enemy ship fired at could not be determined owing to the mist. "Inflexible" was now leading the line and having passed the wreck of "Invincible," altered course two points to starboard, fire having ceased, in order to close the enemy. At 6.45 p.m., "Inflexible" altered a further four points to starboard, when orders were received from "Lion" for "Indomitable" and "Inflexible" to prolong the line by taking station astern.

6. At 7.25 p.m., enemy's torpedo craft approached to attack, but were driven back by gunfire; the track of a torpedo passed 150 yards astern of the ship.

7. At 8.20 p.m., action was resumed at 6,000 yards range with the enemy's armoured ships—believed to be of the "Kaiser" Class. At 8.30, fire was checked, the enemy's ships disappearing in the mist.

At 8.35 p.m., the track of a torpedo was observed across the bows of "Inflexible."

At 8.40, a violent shock was felt underneath the ship and a large swirl of oil was observed about 100 yards on the starboard beam: this violent shock was presumably caused by the ship coming into collision with wreckage.

8. "Inflexible" remained in company with the Vice-Admiral Commanding until arrival in the Forth A.M. the 2nd June.

At 2.24 p.m., 1st June, "Inflexible" passed a whaler of German pattern marked "V. 29," and later, in about latitude 57° 2' N., Longitude 6° 13' E., passed large numbers of German bodies in lifebelts and a lifebuoy marked "S.M.S.——" (the name of the ship being covered by a body lying over it).

9. Except for the collision mentioned in paragraph 7, which must have caused an indentation of the outer skin, no damage has been sustained, and no casualties have occurred on board "Inflexible" during the recent engagement, but the right gun of "Q" turret, which was cracked for a length of 30 ft. during calibration, was used and this appears to have enlarged the crack.

¹ *   *   *   *   *   *

I have the honour to be,
Sir,
Your obedient Servant,
EDW. HEATON ELLIS.
Captain.

Captain Francis William Kennedy, Royal Navy,
    Senior Officer, Third Battle Cruiser Squadron.

---

[1] Part omitted here, referring solely to personnel, recommendations, &c., in no way bearing on the course of the action.

APPENDIX V

ACCOUNT FROM THE FIRST GUNNERY OFFICER OF THE DERFFLINGER, FROM CHAPTER VIII, KIEL AND JUTLAND

Third phase of the Skagerrak Battle (7.50 to 9.5 p.m.). Heavy fighting against ships of the line, cruisers and destroyers. Destruction of the "Invincible." "Derfflinger" forced to stop to clear her torpedo-net.

By Commander Georg von Hase,
First Gunnery Officer of the Derfflinger

At 7.40 p.m. enemy light cruisers and destroyers launched a torpedo attack against us. We therefore altered course to N.N.E., i.e., about six points to starboard.

The visibility was now so bad that it was difficult for us to distinguish the enemy ships. We were engaging light cruisers and destroyers. At 7.55 p.m. we turned on an easterly course, and at 8 p.m. the whole Battle Cruiser Squadron formed a line of bearing on a southerly course as the destroyers pressed home the attack. This brought us very effectively out of the line of the torpedoes that had been fired against us. At 8.12 p.m. we again altered course towards the enemy. During this time we had only fired intermittently with our heavy and secondary armament. At 8.15 p.m. we came under heavy fire. It flashed out on all sides. We could only make out the ships' hulls indistinctly, but as far as I was able to see the horizon, enemy ships were all round us. As I could not distinguish either the end or the beginning of the enemy line, I was unable to engage the "second ship from the right," but selected the one I could see best.

And now a terrific struggle began. Within a short time the din of the battle reached a climax. It was now perfectly clear to us that we were faced with the whole English Fleet. I could see from her gigantic hull that I had engaged a giant battleship. Between the two lines light cruiser and destroyer actions were still raging. All at once I saw through my periscope a German light cruiser passing us in flames. I recognized the *Wiesbaden*. She was almost hidden in smoke, with only the quarter-deck clear, and her after-gun firing incessantly at an English cruiser. Gallant *Wiesbaden!* Gallant crew! The only survivor was Chief Stoker Zenne, who was picked up by a Norwegian fishing boat after drifting about for three days on a raft; all the rest, including the poet, Gorch Fock, who loved the sea above all else, sealed their loyalty to their Kaiser and Empire by a sailor's death. The *Wiesbaden* was subjected to a heavy fire by an English light cruiser. Again and again her shells struck the poor *Wiesbaden*. Seized with fury, I abandoned my former target, had the English cruiser's range measured, gave the range and deflection, and "crash!"—a salvo roared out at the *Wiesbaden*'s tormentor. One more salvo and I had him. A column of smoke rose high in the air. Apparently a magazine had exploded. The cruiser turned away and hauled out at top speed, while I peppered her with two or three more salvoes.

At this moment Lieut.-Commander Hausser, who had been engaging destroyers with his secondary armament, asked me: "Is this cruiser with four funnels German or English, sir?" I examined the ship through the periscope. In the misty grey light the colours of the German and English ships were difficult to distinguish. The cruiser was not very far away from us. She had four funnels and two masts, like our *Rostock*. "She is certainly English," Lieutenant-Commander Hausser shouted. "May I fire?" "Yes, fire away." I was now certain she was a big English ship. The secondary armament was trained on the new target. Lieutenant-Commander Hausser gave the order: "6,000!" Then, just as he was about to give the order: "Fire!" something terrific happened: the English ship, which I had meanwhile identified as an old English armoured cruiser, broke in half with a tremendous explosion. Black smoke and débris shot into the air, a flame enveloped the whole ship, and then she sank before our eyes. There was nothing but a gigantic smoke cloud to mark the place where just before a proud ship had been fighting. I think she was destroyed by the fire of our next ahead, Admiral Hipper's flagship, the *Lützow*.

This all happened in a much shorter time than I have taken to tell it. The whole thing was over in a few seconds, and then we had already engaged new targets. The destroyed ship was the *Defence*, an old armoured cruiser of the same class as the *Black Prince*, which was sunk on the following night by the *Thüringen* and other ships of the line. She was a ship of 14,800 tons, armed with six 23.4-cm. and ten 15.2-cm. guns, and carrying a crew of 700 men. Not one of the whole ship's company was saved. She was blown to atoms and all the men were killed by the explosion. As we saw the ship at a comparatively short distance in good visibility, magnified fifteen times by the periscopes, we could see exactly what happened. The whole horror of this event is indelibly fixed on my mind.

I went on to engage other big ships, without any idea what kind of ships they were. At 8.22 p.m. we turned on a south-easterly course, but in the general confusion of the battle that was now raging I had lost all grasp of the tactical situation. Once the thought flashed across my mind: "Can we be firing at German ships?" At that moment, however, the visibility, which changed from one minute to the next, but which on the whole was gradually growing worse, improved and revealed distinctly the typical English silhouette and dark grey colour. It is my opinion that our light grey colour was more favourable than the dark grey of the English ships. Our ships were much more quickly concealed by the thin films of mist which were now driving across the sea from east to west.

At 8.25 p.m. Lieutenant von der Decken, in the after-control, recorded: "*Lützow* heavily hit forward. Ship on fire. Much smoke." At 8.30 p.m. he wrote: "Three heavy hits on the *Derfflinger*." Of these one hit the 15-cm. battery on the port side, went clean through the centre gun and burst, killing or wounding the whole of the casemate crew. The explosion also knocked the first 15-cm. gun off its mounting and killed or wounded several men. The other hits were aft.

I now selected my target as far ahead as possible, the leading ship of the enemy line, for I saw that the *Lützow*'s fire was now weak. At times the smoke from her burning forepart made fire-control on the *Lützow* impossible.

At 8.24 p.m. I began to engage large enemy battleships to the north-east. Even though the ranges were short, from 6,000 to 7,000 m., the ships often became invisible in the slowly advancing mists, mixed with the smoke from the guns and funnels. It was almost impossible to observe the splashes. All splashes that fell over could not be seen at all, and only those that fell very short could be distinguished clearly, which was not much help, for as soon as we got nearer the target again it became impossible to see where the shots fell. I was shooting by the measurements of the Bg. man in the fore-control, Leading Seaman Hänel, who had been my loyal servant for five years. In view of the misty weather these measurements were very irregular and inexact, but as no observation was possible I had no alternative. Meanwhile we were being subjected to a heavy, accurate and rapid fire from several ships at the same time. It was clear that the enemy could now see us much better than we could see them. This will be difficult to understand for anyone who does not know the sea, but it is a fact that in this sort of weather the differences in visibility are very great in different directions. A ship clear of the mist is much more clearly visible from a ship actually in the mist than vice versa. In determining visibility an important part is played by the position of the sun. In misty weather the ships with their shady side towards the enemy are much easier to see than those lit by the sun.

In this way a severe, unequal struggle developed. Several heavy shells pierced our ship with terrific force and exploded with a tremendous roar, which shook every seam and rivet. The Captain had again frequently to steer the ship out of the line in order to get out of the hail of fire. It was pretty heavy shooting.

This went on until 8.29 p.m.

At this moment the veil of mist in front of us split across like the curtain at a theatre. Clear and sharply silhouetted against the uncovered part of the horizon we saw a powerful battleship with two funnels between the masts and a third close against the forward tripod mast. She was steering an almost parallel course with ours at top speed. Her guns were trained on us and immediately another salvo crashed out, straddling us completely. "Range 9,000!" roared Leading Seaman Hänel. "9,000—Salvoes-fire!" I ordered, and with feverish anxiety I waited for our splashes. "Over. Two hits!" called out Lieutenant-Commander von Stosch. I gave the order: "100 down. Good, Rapid!" and thirty seconds after the first salvo the second left the guns. I observed two short splashes and two hits. Lieutenant-Commander von Stosch called: "Hits!" Every twenty seconds came the roar of another salvo. At 8.31 p.m. the *Derfflinger* fired her last salvo at this ship, and then for the third time we witnessed the dreadful spectacle that we had already seen in the case of the *Queen Mary* and the *Defence*.

As with the other ships there occurred a rapid succession of heavy explosions, masts collapsed, débris was hurled into the air, a gigantic column of black smoke rose towards the sky, and from the parting sections of the ship, coal dust spurted in all directions. Flames enveloped the ship, fresh explosions followed, and behind this murky shroud our enemy vanished from our sight. I shouted into the telephone: "Our enemy has blown up!" and above the din of the battle a great cheer thundered through the ship and was transmitted to the fore-control by all the gunnery telephones and flashed from one gun-position to another. I sent up a short, fervent prayer of thanks to the Almighty, shouted to my servant: "Bravo, Hänel, jolly well measured!" and then my order rang out: "Change target to the left. On the second battle-cruiser from the right!" The battle continued.

Who was this enemy? I had not examined her carefully nor given much thought to her identity, but I had taken her to be an English battle-cruiser. I described her as such in giving the target, as my gunnery log-keeper recorded. There had been no time to discuss her class while we were engaging her, for there had only been a few minutes in which to recognize her with any certainty. Only the gunnery officers and gun-layers and the torpedo-officers had seen her blow up, the attention of the Captain and his assistants, the navigating and signal officers being entirely taken up with keeping the ship in her station. It was difficult work navigating astern of the *Lützow*, which was hardly in a condition to keep her place in the line.

When, after the battle, the reports came to be drawn up, most of the officers were convinced that she was a ship of the *Queen Elizabeth* class. I was of the opinion that she belonged to the *Invincible* class, but I admitted that I was not at all sure. If you take a naval pocket-book and compare the silhouettes of the *Queen Elizabeth* and *Invincible* classes, there is at first sight a perplexing similarity. We therefore entered in our report that at 8.30 p.m. we had destroyed by gun-fire a battleship of the *Queen Elizabeth* class. Our report ran: "The ship blew up in a similar way to the *Queen Mary* at 6.26 p.m. Clearly observed by the First and Third Gunnery Officers, and the First Torpedo Officer in the fore-control, the Second and Fourth Gunnery Officers in the after control and the Gunnery Observation Officer in the fore-top. Ship of the *Queen Elizabeth* class.'

After the battle, the following statement was made by English prisoners at Wilhelmshaven: "One of the *Queen Elizabeth* ships, the *Warspite*, left the line, listing heavily, and hauled away to the north-west. At 8 p.m. the English destroyer *Turbulent* received a wireless report that the *Warspite* had sunk."

On the strength of our battle report and the statements of the prisoners, our Admiralty authorities were obliged to assume that the ship destroyed by the *Derfflinger* was the *Warspite*, and, accordingly, the *Warspite* instead of the *Invincible* was reported as an enemy loss. That the *Invincible* was sunk we learned from the report of the English Admiralty, and naturally her loss was added afterwards to the previous report. As a matter of fact, it was the *Invincible* we had engaged and blown up and not the *Warspite*. The English reports soon made this quite clear.

On the 3rd June, the *Manchester Guardian* said that the German Admiralty report of the 1st June contained a detailed and frankly exact report of the English losses, except that it gave the name of the battleship *Warspite* instead of the battle-cruiser *Invincible*.

The Times of 6th June, 1916, reports on the evidence of combatants: "The *Invincible*, flying the flag of Admiral Hood, Sir David Beatty's second in command, singled out the *Hindenburg*, and after a hot fight, in which some of our men claim that the *Hindenburg* received mortal injury, the *Invincible* went down."

At this time the *Hindenburg* was still being built. The *Derfflinger* was her sister-ship and the English account is correct but for the names: it was the *Derfflinger* and not the still uncompleted *Hindenburg* that engaged the *Invincible*.

The account of the engagement between the *Derfflinger* and the *Invincible* given by one of the two officers saved from the *Invincible* is perfectly correct with the exception of the time. *The Times* of the 12th June, 1916, reports that the father of a lieutenant who went down with the *Invincible* received from the two surviving officers a letter, in which they say: "Your son was with the Admiral and we were engaged with the *Derfflinger*. There was a tremendous explosion aboard at 6.34 p.m. The ship broke in half and sank in ten or fifteen seconds."

On the 13th June, 1916, *The Times*, quoting a letter from the brother of the late Lieutenant Charles Fisher says: "We learn from Commander Dannreuther, the sole surviving officer of H.M.S. *Invincible*, that a shell fell into the powder-magazine. There was a great explosion, and when Dannreuther recovered consciousness he found himself in the water. Ship and crew had disappeared."

That they were the ships of Hood's battle-cruiser squadron that we had been engaging from 8.24 p.m. onwards, at ranges varying between 6,000 m. and 7,000 m., is confirmed by Admiral Beatty's official dispatch. This reports as follows on the part played by the *Invincible*, *Indomitable* and *Inflexible* of the 3rd Battle Cruiser Squadron:

"At 6.20 p.m. the 3rd Battle Cruiser Squadron appeared ahead, steaming south towards the enemy's van. I ordered them to take station ahead, which was carried out magnificently, Rear-Admiral Hood bringing his squadron into action in a most inspiring manner, worthy of his great naval ancestors. At 6.25 p.m. I altered course to the E.S.E. in support of the 3rd Battle Cruiser Squadron, who were at this time only 8,000 yards from the enemy's leading ship. They were pouring a hot fire into her and caused her to turn to the westward of south."

A Reuter telegram of the 5th June, 1916, states that when the action had been in progress some hours the *Indomitable*, *Invincible* and *Inflexible* appeared on the scene; that this phase was chiefly a duel of heavy guns and that the *Invincible*, after fighting bravely and inflicting heavy punishment on the enemy, met her doom and sank.

My reason for supporting my own description of this event from the English accounts of the battle is that, hitherto, the German reports have left it open as to whether the sinking of the *Invincible* was due to gun-fire or a torpedo. On historical grounds I consider it necessary to make clear that the *Invincible*, like all the other English ships lost in this battle, was destroyed by gun-fire.

The Officer Commanding the 3rd Battle Cruiser Squadron, Rear-Admiral Hood, who went down in the *Invincible*, was a descendant of the famous English Admiral Hood, who distinguished himself brilliantly as a strategist and tactician in the North American War of Independence under Graves and Rodney, and later as Commander-in-Chief at the Battle of St. Christopher (1782). During the Anglo-French War of 1793-1802 he was Commander-in-Chief (1793-1794) of the Mediterranean Fleet and bombarded Toulon.

According to the record of my log-keeper the heavy guns fired until 8.33 p.m. At 8.38 p.m. I gave the order: "Heavy guns stand by!" There was no longer any enemy to be seen. At 8.35 p.m. we had altered course sharply to the west. After the loss of their leader the remaining ships of the 3rd Battle Squadron did not immediately venture into the zone of our death-dealing fire. At 8.50 p.m. the whole ship was ordered to cease fire. Then feverish efforts were made to put out the fires that had broken out in various parts of the ship.

At this time we noticed a destroyer slowly going alongside the *Lützow*. The flagship had a list, that is to say, she was leaning over to one side, and her bows were very deep in the water. Great clouds of smoke were rising from her forepart. Admiral Hipper boarded the destroyer, which then cast off and steered for the *Seydlitz*. While passing the *Derfflinger* the Admiral signalled: "Captain of the *Derfflinger* will take command until I board." Our Captain was therefore in command of the battle-cruisers until nearly 11 p.m., for, owing to the headlong speed of the battle-cruisers, which were almost continuously under enemy fire, it was not until then that the Admiral succeeded in boarding another ship.

The *Derfflinger*, too, was now a pretty sorry sight. The masts and rigging had been badly damaged by countless shells, and the wireless aerials hung down in an inextricable tangle so that we could only use our wireless for receiving; we could not transmit messages. A heavy shell had torn away two armour plates in the bows, leaving a huge gap quite 6 by 5 m., just above the water-line. With the pitching of the ship water streamed continually through this hole.

While we were steering west the Commander came on to the bridge and reported to the Captain: "The ship must stop at once. The after torpedo-net has been shot away and is hanging over the port screw. It must be cleared." The Captain gave the order: "All engines stop!"

I surveyed the horizon through the periscope. There was nothing of the enemy to be seen at this moment. The *Seydlitz*, *Moltke* and *Von der Tann* were not in very close touch with us, but they now came up quickly and took their prescribed stations in the line. It was a very serious matter that we should have to stop like this in the immediate neighbourhood of the enemy, but if the torpedo-net were to foul the screw all would be up with us. How many times we had cursed in the ship at not having rid ourselves of these heavy steel torpedo-nets, weighing several hundred tons. As we hardly ever anchored at sea they were useless and, in any case, they only protected part of the ship against torpedo fire. On the other hand, they were a serious source of danger, as they reduced the ship's speed considerably and were bound sooner or later to foul the screws, which meant the loss of the ship. For these reasons the English had scrapped their torpedo-nets shortly before the war— we did not do so until immediately after the battle of Skagerrak and as a result of our present experience.

The boatswain and the turret-crews of the "Dora" and "Caesar" turrets, under Lieutenant-Commander Boltenstern, worked like furies to lift the net, make it fast with chains and cut with axes the wire-hawsers and chains that were hanging loose. It was only a few minutes before the report came: "Engines can be started." We got under weigh at once.

The *Lützow* had now hauled out of the line and was steering a southerly course at low speed. The Captain wanted to signal to the other ships to follow the leader, but all the signal apparatus was out of action. The semaphores and heliographs had all been shot away and the flags all destroyed by fire. However, our stout ships followed without signal when the Captain turned on a northerly course and led the battle-cruisers to a position ahead of the main fleet.

The lull in the battle lasted until 9.5 p.m. and then suddenly fresh gun-fire flashed out and once more the cry, "Clear for action!" rang through the ship.

INDEX

EXPRESS DELIVERY OF LETTERS AND PARCELS.

etters and Parcels are now accepted at Post Offices in London, to be forwarded diately by Messenger direct to any part of the London Postal area, at the ing rate:—For every mile or part of a mile, 3d. Special conveyances will be f specially paid for, but not otherwise. All charges must be prepaid in postage s, to be affixed to a Post Office form provided for the purpose.

the Provinces such Letters, &c., are accepted at all Post Offices from which is a delivery of telegrams, and they are delivered in any part of the town or district.

TELEGRAPH RATE (INLAND).

xpence for first 12 words, and one halfpenny for every additional word. Postage s are used as payment, but must be affixed to the message forms.

INLAND MONEY ORDERS.

he commission on the issue of Inland Money Orders is as follows:—

nts not exceeding £1	...	2d.	Amounts not exceeding £20	...	6d.
" £3	...	3d.	" " £30	...	8d.
" £10	...	4d.	" " £40	...	10d.

o order can be issued which contains a fractional part of a penny.

orms of application for Money Orders are supplied at all Money Order offices

lthough a Money Order, if still unpaid at the end of twelve months, becomes y void, nevertheless when a good reason can be given for the delay in presenting application for payment, subject to a deduction of 6d., is entertained.

fter once paying a Money Order, by whomsoever presented, the office is not to any further claim.

TELEGRAPH MONEY ORDERS (INLAND).

Ioney may be transmitted by Telegraph Money Order between all Offices in the d Kingdom authorised to transact Telegraph and Money Order business. The iission is at the same rate as for ordinary Inland Money Orders, plus a ementary fee of 2d. and cost of official Telegram of advice. No order issued £40.

POSTAL ORDERS

re issued at all Money Order Offices for any sum from 6d. to 21/-, increasing by The Commission chargeable is:—For orders up to 2/6 inclusive, ½d.; from 3/- inclusive, 1d.; from 15/6 to 21/- inclusive, 1½d. By the use of not more than stamps to the total value of 5d. affixed to the face of the order any broken amount e made up.

SAVINGS BANK.

ccounts can be opened and money paid in and withdrawn at any Money Order in the United Kingdom.

Io less sum than 1s. is received as deposit, but forms can be obtained on which e penny stamps can be placed, and when filled, paid into the Savings Bank as a it. No person may deposit more than £50 in any one year ending 31st nber, or more than £200 in all inclusive of interest, which is allowed at the rate per cent. per annum. When principal and interest together exceed £200, st is allowed on £200 only.

HOME SAFES.

Home Safe for accumulating money for deposit in the Post Office Savings Bank e obtained for 3/- at any Post Office transacting Savings Bank business, and of im 2/- is repaid when the Safe is no longer required, and is given up in good ion.

DESPATCH OF LETTERS BY TELEPHONE.

elephone Subscribers can in many cases telephone messages to a Post Office to t either (1) as an express letter, at the usual express delivery fee for each 30 , or part thereof; or (2) as an ordinary letter, at the ordinary letter rate for each rds, or part thereof. In each case the usual charge for a telephone call is made lition.

Telephone Subscriber can also obtain the services of an express messeng ephoning to the nearest Post Office connected with his Exchange.

POSTAL INFORMATION.

INLAND LETTERS.

When prepaid, not above 4 oz. 1d., and for every additional 2 oz. or part of
No letter, except to or from a Government office, may exceed 24 in. by 12 in.
Letters not prepaid are charged double postage on delivery, if insufficientl
double the deficiency.

CERTIFICATES OF POSTING.

A Certificate of Posting of any Unregistered Letter, Postcard, Half-penn
or Newspaper handed in at any Post Office can be obtained for a fee of ½d.

LETTER CARDS.

Bearing a Penny Stamp are sold at 1d. each; 1/- a packet of 1
packet of 120.

POST CARDS.

STOUT SINGLE CARDS:—One, ¾d.; two, 1¼d.; three, 1¾d.; four,
2¾d.; six, 3¼d.; seven, 4d.; eight, 4½d.; nine, 5d.; ten, 5½d.; eleven, 6d.
THIN SINGLE CARDS:—½d. each; packet of twelve Cards, 6d.;
stamp, 1d. each.
STOUT REPLY CARDS:—One, 1¼d.; two, 2¼d.; three, 3½d.; four,
5½d.; six, 6¾d.; seven, 7¾d.; eight, 8¾d.; nine, 10d.; ten, 11d.; eleven,
THIN REPLY CARDS:—1d. each; packet of twelve Cards, 1/-;
stamp on each half, 2d. each.
Nothing may be attached, except adhesive stamps in payment o
postage, and a gummed label (not to exceed two inches long and three-qu
wide), bearing the address at which the card is to be delivered.

NEWSPAPERS.

For every single Newspaper, duly registered at the General Pos
postage is ½d. If several are sent together, the packet is not liable to
than would be chargeable on a book packet or letter of the same we
parcel must exceed 2ft. by 1 ft. by 1 ft., or weigh above 5 lbs.

BOOK POST.

Packets not exceeding 2 oz. in weight (if open at the ends, or in
envelope) may be sent for ½d. If exceeding 2 oz. they pass uncondit
same rate as letters.

PARCEL POST.

The postage must be prepaid and by stamps affixed to the parcel, w
be put in a letter box, but handed over the office counter. Rates:—

Not exceeding 1 lb.	...	...	3d.	Exceeding 7 lbs. & not exce
Exceeding 1 lb. & not exceeding 2 lbs. 4d.				" 8 " "
" 2 "	"	3 "	5d.	" 9 " "
" 3 "	"	5 "	6d.	" 10 " "
" 5 "	"	7 "	7d.	Limit of weight allow

Compensation for damage or loss of parcels to the amount of £2 with
Parcels must not exceed 3 ft. 6 in. in length, or 6 ft. in length and

REGISTERED LETTERS, PARCELS, ETC.

The fees payable on Registered Inland Letters, Parcels and other
and the respective limits of compensation, are as follows:—
For a Fee of 2d., £5; 3d., £20; 4d., £40; 5d., £6
7d., £100; 8d., £120; 9d., £140; 10d., £160; 11d., £180; 1/-, £
1/2, £240; 1/3, £260; 1/4, £280; 1/5, £300; 1/6, £320; 1/7, £
1/9, £380; 1/10, £400.

POSTAL INFORMATION.

INLAND LETTERS.

When prepaid, not above 4 oz. 1d., and for every additional 2 oz. or part of 2 oz. ½d.

No letter, except to or from a Government office, may exceed 24 in. by 12 in. by 12 in.

Letters not prepaid are charged double postage on delivery, if insufficiently prepaid double the deficiency.

CERTIFICATES OF POSTING.

A Certificate of Posting of any Unregistered Letter, Postcard, Half-penny Packet, or Newspaper handed in at any Post Office can be obtained for a fee of ½d.

LETTER CARDS.

Bearing a Penny Stamp are sold at 1d. each; 1/- a packet of 12; 10/- a packet of 120.

POST CARDS.

STOUT SINGLE CARDS:—One, ¾d.; two, 1¼d.; three, 1¾d.; four, 2¼d.; five, 2¾d.; six, 3¼d.; seven, 4d.; eight, 4½d.; nine, 5d.; ten, 5½d.; eleven, 6d.

THIN SINGLE CARDS:—½d. each; packet of twelve Cards, 6d.; bearing 1d. stamp, 1d. each.

STOUT REPLY CARDS:—One, 1¼d.; two, 2¼d.; three, 3½d.; four, 4½d.; five, 5½d.; six, 6¾d.; seven, 7¾d.; eight, 8¾d.; nine, 10d.; ten, 11d.; eleven, 1/-.

THIN REPLY CARDS:—1d. each; packet of twelve Cards, 1/-; bearing 1d. stamp on each half, 2d. each.

Nothing may be attached, except adhesive stamps in payment of additional postage, and a gummed label (not to exceed two inches long and three-quarter inches wide), bearing the address at which the card is to be delivered.

NEWSPAPERS.

For every single Newspaper, duly registered at the General Post Office, the postage is ½d. If several are sent together, the packet is not liable to a higher rate than would be chargeable on a book packet or letter of the same weight, but no parcel must exceed 2 ft. by 1 ft. by 1 ft., or weigh above 5 lbs.

BOOK POST.

Packets not exceeding 2 oz. in weight (if open at the ends, or in an unfastened envelope) may be sent for ½d. If exceeding 2 oz. they pass unconditionally at the same rate as letters.

PARCEL POST.

The postage must be prepaid and by stamps affixed to the parcel, which must not be put in a letter box, but handed over the office counter. Rates:—

Not exceeding 1 lb.	...	...	3d.	Exceeding 7 lbs. & not exceeding 8 lbs. 8d.
Exceeding 1 lb. & not exceeding 2 lbs. 4d.				„ 8 „ „ 9 „ 9d.
„ 2 „	„	3 „ 5d.		„ 9 „ „ 10 „ 10d.
„ 3 „	„	5 „ 6d.		„ 10 „ „ 11 „ 11d.
„ 5 „	„	7 „ 7d.		Limit of weight allowed, 11 lbs.

Compensation for damage or loss of parcels to the amount of £2 without extra charge.

Parcels must not exceed 3 ft. 6 in. in length, or 6 ft. in length and girth combined.

REGISTERED LETTERS, PARCELS, ETC.

The fees payable on Registered Inland Letters, Parcels and other Postal Packets, and the respective limits of compensation, are as follows:—

For a Fee of 2d., £5; 3d., £20; 4d., £40; 5d., £60; 6d., £80; 7d., £100; 8d., £120; 9d., £140; 10d., £160; 11d., £180; 1/-, £200; 1/1, £220; 1/2, £240; 1/3, £260; 1/4, £280; 1/5, £300; 1/6, £320; 1/7, £340; 1/8, £360; 1/9, £380; 1/10, £400.

EXPRESS DELIVERY OF LETTERS AND PARCELS.

Letters and Parcels are now accepted at Post Offices in London, to be forwarded immediately by Messenger direct to any part of the London Postal area, at the following rate:—For every mile or part of a mile, 3d. Special conveyances will be used if specially paid for, but not otherwise. All charges must be prepaid in postage stamps, to be affixed to a Post Office form provided for the purpose.

In the Provinces such Letters, &c., are accepted at all Post Offices from which there is a delivery of telegrams, and they are delivered in any part of the town or rural district.

TELEGRAPH RATE (INLAND).

Sixpence for first 12 words, and one halfpenny for every additional word. Postage stamps are used as payment, but must be affixed to the message forms.

INLAND MONEY ORDERS.

The commission on the issue of Inland Money Orders is as follows:—

Amounts not exceeding £1	...	2d.	Amounts not exceeding £20	...	6d.
„ „ £3	...	3d.	„ „ £30	...	8d.
„ „ £10	...	4d.	„ „ £40	...	10d.

No order can be issued which contains a fractional part of a penny.

Forms of application for Money Orders are supplied at all Money Order offices gratis.

Although a Money Order, if still unpaid at the end of twelve months, becomes legally void, nevertheless when a good reason can be given for the delay in presenting it, an application for payment, subject to a deduction of 6d., is entertained.

After once paying a Money Order, by whomsoever presented, the office is not liable to any further claim.

TELEGRAPH MONEY ORDERS (INLAND).

Money may be transmitted by Telegraph Money Order between all Offices in the United Kingdom authorised to transact Telegraph and Money Order business. The Commission is at the same rate as for ordinary Inland Money Orders, plus a supplementary fee of 2d. and cost of official Telegram of advice. No order issued above £40.

POSTAL ORDERS

Are issued at all Money Order Offices for any sum from 6d. to 21/-, increasing by 6d. The Commission chargeable is:—For orders up to 2/6 inclusive, ½d.; from 3/- to 15/- inclusive, 1d.; from 15/6 to 21/- inclusive, 1½d. By the use of not more than three stamps to the total value of 5d. affixed to the face of the order any broken amount may be made up.

SAVINGS BANK.

Accounts can be opened and money paid in and withdrawn at any Money Order Office in the United Kingdom.

No less sum than 1s. is received as deposit, but forms can be obtained on which twelve penny stamps can be placed, and when filled, paid into the Savings Bank as a deposit. No person may deposit more than £50 in any one year ending 31st December, or more than £200 in all inclusive of interest, which is allowed at the rate of 2½ per cent. per annum. When principal and interest together exceed £200, interest is allowed on £200 only.

HOME SAFES.

A Home Safe for accumulating money for deposit in the Post Office Savings Bank can be obtained for 3/- at any Post Office transacting Savings Bank business, and of this sum 2/- is repaid when the Safe is no longer required, and is given up in good condition.

DESPATCH OF LETTERS BY TELEPHONE.

Telephone Subscribers can in many cases telephone messages to a Post Office to be sent either (1) as an express letter, at the usual express delivery fee for each 30 words, or part thereof; or (2) as an ordinary letter, at the ordinary letter rate for each 30 words, or part thereof. In each case the usual charge for a telephone call is made in addition.

A Telephone Subscriber can also obtain the services of an express messenger by telephoning to the nearest Post Office connected with his Exchange.